A Concise History of South Sudan
New and Revised Edition

Anders Breidlid (editor)

Avelino Androga Said and Astrid Kristine Breidlid (co-editors)

Anne Farren and Yosa Wawa (additional co-editors of the new and revised edition)

FOUNTAIN PUBLISHERS
www.fountainpublishers.co.ug

Fountain Publishers
P.O. Box 488
Kampala, Uganda
E-mail: sales@fountainpublishers.co.ug
         publishing@fountainpublishers.co.ug
Website: www.fountainpublishers.co.ug

Distributed in Europe and Commonwealth countries outside Africa by:
African Books Collective Ltd,
P.O. Box 721,
Oxford OX1 9EN, UK.
Tel/Fax: +44(0) 1869 349110
E-mail: orders@africanbookscollective.com
Website: www.africanbookscollective.com

© Ministry of Education, Science and Technology, Government of South Sudan and the editors 2014
First published 2010
New and Revised Edition 2014

All rights reserved. No part of this publication may be reproduced, stored in a retrieval system, or transmitted in any form or by any means, electronic, mechanical, photocopying, recording or otherwise, without prior written permission from the publishers.

ISBN: 978-9970-25-337-1

Cover design by GoeunBae
Preparation of photographs by Carlos Galdames Fuentes

Contents

Sources of Photos/Figures .... *xi*
Preface to the New and Revised Edition .... *xiii*
    Postscript .... *xv*
Acknowledgements .... *xvi*

1. What Historians Do 1
    Why do we study history? Why is it important? 1
    Sources of information on history 2

2. The Early History of Sudan 17
    Introduction 17
    New social and political organisation 19
    The Kush Kingdom in Nubia 20
    Kush in the Christian Bible 22
    Confusion over Kush in the Greek translation of the Hebrew Bible 22
    The foundation and growth of the Kush Kingdom 23
    The kings of Kush at Napata: c.750 BC – c.270 BC 23
    The Kush Kingdom at Meroë: 350 B.C-350 A.D. 27
    Economic life 28
    Gods of the Meroites, Amun and Apedemak 31
    Political organisation at Meroë 32
    The three Kingdoms of Christian Nubia 33
    The coming of Christianity to Nubia 35
    Architecture, art and learning in Christian Nubia 36
    Why did Christianity disappear in Nubia around 1500 AD? 39
    The coming of the Arabs to Sudan 41
    The reasons for the migration of Arabs into Sudan in the 7th century 41
    The migration of the Arabs into Nubia in 641-651 AD 42
    Course of migration and settlement of the Arabs 42

Some effects of the Arab migration on the people of Sudan 44
The Kingdom of the Funj: 1504 AD–1821 AD 46
Foundation and expansion of the Funj Kingdom 47
Social life of the Funj 48
Economic life of the Funj.. 49
Political organisation of the Funj.. 51
The decline of the Funj Kingdom... 52
The main languages of South Sudan... 53
The migration of Sudanic peoples to the present day South Sudan ..56
The central Sudanic peoples 57
The Ma'di... 57
Migration history... 58
Political organisation 59
Religious beliefs 59
Economic and social life.. 60
The migration of Eastern Nilotics 61
The civilisation of the Nilotes 61
The Bari of South Sudan 62
Migration history... 63
Economic life... 63
Social and political organisation 63
The migration of Western Nilotics (or River Lake Nilotes) 64
The Luo groups among the Nilotes 65
Beliefs of Nilotes.. 65
Political organization of Nilotes 66
Economic life of Nilotes... 66
The Shilluk (Chollo) Kingdom of the White Nile 67
Origins and migration of the Shilluk (Chollo) 68
Language and formation of the Shilluk (Chollo) 68
Settlement of the Shilluk (Chollo).. 69
Social life of the Shilluk (Chollo) 70
Customs of the Shilluk (Chollo) 70
Beliefs of the Shilluk (Chollo) 71
Economic life of the Shilluk (Chollo)....................................... 71

Political organisation ... 73
The Anywaa ... 74
Origin and migration history ... 74
Social organisation ... 75
Political system of the Anywaa ... 76
Economic life ... 76
The Nuer ... 77
Migration history ... 77
Political organization ... 78
Economic life of the Nuer ... 78
The Dinka ... 78
Migration history ... 79
Religious beliefs of the Dinka ... 80
Political life and values ... 80
Economic life ... 82
The Kingdom of the Azande ... 83
Social organization ... 85
Traditional beliefs ... 85
Customs around birth and married life ... 86
Political organisation of the Azande ... 86
Economic life ... 87

3. **Nineteenth-Century Turning Point** ... 90
Introduction ... 90
Economic and social development in Southern Sudan by 1850 .. 90
Political groups in the South in the 19th century ... 92
Political organization of Sudanic and Nilotic societies in the 19th century ... 93
Economic organization in Southern Sudan around 1850 ... 95
Social organization and women's role ... 96
The Turko-Egyptian conquest ... 98
The conquest of Sudan ... 100
The search for gold and ivory ... 102
Slavery ... 104

The coming of the Christian missionaries to the South 108
The White Nile trade after 1841 110
Elephant hunters become wealthy 111
The *zaribas* 112
The spread of violence 112
The impact of the slave trade on Sudanese during the Turkiyya ...114
The suppression of the slave trade and the annexation of
Southern Sudan 117
Bahr el-Ghazal 120
Political impact of the Turkiyya on Sudan 121
The Mahdist revolution... 122
Why did the Mahdist revolution succeed? 124

4. **Southern Sudan under the Rule of the Anglo-Egyptian
   Condominium (1899-1945)** **129**
   Introduction 129
   The Anglo-Egyptian conquest of Sudan 129
   The Fashoda incident 131
   Condominium: A 'hybrid' form of government 135
   The British begin to rule Southern Sudan 138
   Resistance to the Anglo-Egyptian rule in the various regions.... 138
   Challenges from the pastoralists in Upper Nile and Bahr- el-
   Ghazal.. 139
   Challenges among the Nuer 142
   Cotton growing in Southern Sudan... 143
   Condominium policy... 144
   Phase one 1899-1920.. 144
   Missionaries 146
   Phase two: 1920-1945... 148
   Education under the British 154
   The consequences of British rule for the North-South and
   South-South relations in Sudan... 159
   The beginning of independence.. 163

5. The Independence Struggle 1942 – 1958 167
    Introduction 167
    The Juba Conference 1947 170
    Unrest in the South 173
    The Legislative Assembly 175
    Self-government 176
    Economic and social developments in the South 1942 – 1956 184
    Education 187
    The Torit mutiny, August 1955 191
    The massacre in Abyei 194
    Independence: The transfer of power.............................. 194
    Post – Independent Sudan.. 197
    Southern political parties and the federation controversy.......... 200

6. From Military Rule and Armed Resistance to the Addis Ababa Agreement of 1972 205
    Introduction 205
    Abboud comes to power 1958 206
    Southern response to Abboud's policy 208
    Abboud and the Christian missionary societies.............. 211
    The beginning of the Southern Sudanese armed struggle 212
    The overthrow of Abboud's regime 215
    Social and economic development................................. 223
    National policy 1965-1969 226
    The draft Islamic constitution 230
    Southern factionalism 231
    Support from abroad 234
    Nimeiri takes over in Khartoum 235

7. The Addis Ababa Agreement and the Southern Regional Governments 1972-1983 242
    Introduction 242
    Background of the Addis Ababa Agreement 242
    The Addis Ababa Agreement 246
    Reactions to the agreement 250

The politics of the Southern regional governments 252
The first regional governments 1972 – 1978 254
The second regional government 1978 – 1980 260
The third regional government 1980 – 1981 and the abrogation of the Addis Ababa Agreement in 1983 261
Conflicting issues from the Addis Ababa Agreement to the second civil war 264
Economic development 270
Shari'a law 274

8. **The Second Civil War, 1983-2005** 279
Introduction 279
The founding of the SPLA/M and its aims 280
The formation of the SPLM /SPLA and the leadership question 280
The liberation war 285
Nimeiri's reactions to the mounting insurgency 286
The overthrow of Nimeiri 288
The Koka Dam Declaration 289
The Koka Dam Declaration was not implemented by the new coalition government 290
The Sudanese People's Liberation Army acquires a wider base .. 291
The Sudanese Peace Initiative 292
The NIF military coup 294
Conflicts among Southern Sudanese 297
The impact of Mengistu's departure from Ethiopia on the SPLA 299
The Bor Massacre 302
Southerners help Bashir to fight the SPLA 303
The consequences of war 307
A Southern identity 308
Displaced persons in and around Khartoum during the war 311
The construction of a Southern identity in and around the capital 313
Education in the SPLM/A-controlled areas: Reinforcing Southern resistance 316

9. **The Meaning of the CPA** 321
   Introduction 321
   Peace negotiations: International attempts to bring peace
   between the South and the North 322
   The signing of the Comprehensive Peace Agreement(CPA) 326
   The CPA was not comprehensive 335
   Preparation for the referendum 2011 336

10. **The Referendum, Independence and its Aftermath** 340
    The referendum in January 2011 in Southern Sudan 340
    The independence of South Sudan 341
    Challenges after independence 344
    Corruption in South Sudan... 346
    South Sudan in internal conflict.. 347

Appendix 1: The Addis Ababa Agreement *351*
Appendix 2: The Machakos Protocol... *354*
Further reading *364*
Index *369*

Sources of Photos/Figures

Chapter 2
Fig. 3.   Dillon 21
Fig. 4.   National Geographic Magazine 24
Fig. 7.   Thames and Hudson 27
Fig. 8.   Thames and Hudson 28
Fig. 9.   Dillon 29
Fig. 10. Dillon 30
Fig. 11. Dillon 31
Fig. 12. Dillon 32
Fig. 13. Paulines Publications 34
Fig. 14. Paulines Publications 35
Fig. 15. Paulines Publications 37
Fig. 17. Paulines Publications 38
Fig. 18. Publishers EMI 39
Fig. 19. University of Rochester Press 46
Fig. 23. www.webspace.ship.edu/cgboer/languagefamilies.html 55
Fig. 27. Rochester Press 65

Chapter 3
Fig. 1.   Universitetsforlaget 91
Fig. 2.   DuMont Buchverlag 94
Fig. 3.   Universitetsforlaget 97
Fig. 5.   Cambridge University Press 101
Fig. 6.   Weidenfeld and Nicolson: London 103
Fig. 8.   Weidenfeld and Nicolson: London 106
Fig. 15. Cambridge University Press 124

Chapter 4
Fig. 3.   Paulines Publications Africa 135
Fig. 5.   Cambridge University Press 140
Fig. 8.   Cambridge University Press 147

xii A Concise History of South Sudan

    Fig. 9.   Cambridge University Press 150
    Fig. 11. Cambridge University Press 153

Chapter 5
    Fig. 3.   The Book Guild Ltd 178
    Fig. 4.   Cambridge University Press 181
    Fig. 6.   Cambridge University Press 186
    Fig. 9.   Weidenfeld and Nicolson: London 198

Chapter 6
    Fig. 1.   www.sudan.net 207
    Fig. 6.   Ithaca Press 220
    Fig. 7.   The Macmillan Press Ltd 225
    Fig. 12. Ithaca Press 236
    Fig. 13. Ithaca Press 239

Chapter 7
    Fig. 3.   Indiana University Press 247
    Fig. 4.   Indiana University Press 249
    Fig. 6.   Ithaca Press 256
    Fig. 7.   Ithaca Press 258
    Fig. 8.   Ithaca Press 265
    Fig. 10. www.theodora.com/maps 269

Chapter 8
    Fig. 2.   University of Pennsylvania Press 288
    Fig. 3.   University of Pennsylvania Press 291
    Fig. 6.   Ithaca Press 300
    Fig. 7.   Cambridge University Press 306
    Fig. 8.   Routledge 310

Chapter 9
    Fig. 3.   Cambridge University Press 328

Preface to the New and Revised Edition

This first edition of this textbook in history was primarily intended for secondary schools in South Sudan, but the book proved to arouse great interest to many other South Sudanese both inside South Sudan as well as in the diaspora. Also non-Sudanese with an interest in the country have been keen to read the book. This was not surprising since it was the first history book on South Sudan to cover, albeit not in detail, the whole history from the origin of humankind till the present. For secondary school students in South Sudan the book certainly fills a gap since the students have either studied the history of Kenya and Uganda, or the history of North Sudan with little information about the present day South Sudan. Even though the focus is on South Sudan its history cannot be interpreted in a vacuum, and particularly North-South relations are discussed to some extent in the book.

The first edition of the book was produced as a result of extensive team work, including two workshops which were conducted in Juba in 2010. In the first workshop the chapters were distributed among various authors, most of them with a Sudanese background.

The following authors were involved in writing drafts to the various chapters:

Sister Anne Farren (chapter 1 and chapter 2), Abannik Hino (chapter 3), Patrick Lagu (part of chapter 4), FadwaTaha (chapter 5), Yosa Wawa and Clement Janda (chapter 6), Daniel Thabo (part of chapter 7), Avelino Androga Said (part of chapter 7 and chapter 8), and Inyani Raymond (part of chapter 9). Professor Anders Breidlid wrote part of chapter 8 and part of chapter 9, and Astrid Kristine Breidlid wrote part of chapter 4. Dr Kjell Hødnebø commented extensively on many of the draft chapters and suggested major revisions of chapters 1-5, thereby giving the book a more South Sudan focus. Dr Douglas

Johnson suggested the titles of the various chapters at an early stage of the project.

Anders Breidlid, the main editor of the book, amended and rewrote many of the chapters. Avelino Androga Said served in various capacities as co-editor, and suggested amendments to various chapters. Moreover Androga Said was the contact person with the various authors inside Sudan throughout the writing process. Astrid Kristine Breidlid, an anthropologist with field work experience from Sudan, was hired to help with the editing of the chapters and also to rewrite chapters.

On the basis of the draft chapters historians outside the group of authors were asked to comment on the chapters. In the second workshop the revised chapters were scrutinized in detail where the various authors were asked to critically read the chapters which they had not authored. In addition to focusing on the contents of the various chapters the workshop spent much time on increasing the readability of the book with students in mind. On the basis of the revisions at the workshop and later suggestions by others, the first edition of the history book was distributed to many secondary schools and civil society groups. The teachers of many schools as well as academicians, politicians and aid workers offered valuable suggestions for amendments of the second edition of the book.

The second edition was revised by Avelino Androga Said, Yosa Wawa, Anne Farren and Anders Breidlid during a workshop in Juba in December 2012. All chapters were revised and a new chapter has been written by Anders Breidlid on the period from the referendum in 2011 to the period after independence.

A special thanks to Anne Farren who has worked extensively on improving chapters 1,2 and 3 in particular. Her long experience of teaching history to secondary school students in Rumbek has proven very valuable.

The book is intended to sensitize learners and readers to pose questions not only about what happened, but why it happened. It is hoped that also the new edition of the book will serve to enlighten and critically engage students, teachers as well as others on the history of South Sudan. The book is being published in co-operation with the Ministry of Education, Science and Technology, Government of South Sudan, Juba, South Sudan.

Finally a note on the use of terminology: Southern Sudan and South Sudan. South Sudan was named South Sudan when it became an independent nation on 9 July 2011. In the book Southern Sudan is thus used to refer to the territory in the South of Sudan prior to independence in 2011. Sometimes the term "in the South" is used to refer to Southern Sudan before independence.

Postscript

The manuscript of this new and revised edition was initially sent to the publisher in late October 2013, and was due to be published in December 2013. Unfortunately fighting broke out on 15 December 2013 between the forces of the government and forces loyal to the former Vice President Riek Machar. It was therefore decided to postpone the publishing of the book until the situation was stabilized. On 22 January 2014 the government and the rebels signed a cessation of hostilities agreement in Addis Ababa, and shortly thereafter the manuscript was sent to the publisher. A short section briefly outlining the new development in South Sudan as of January 2014 was added.

January 2014
Anders Breidlid
Oslo University College, Norway

Acknowledgements

We are grateful to the Norwegian Foreign Ministry for generously funding this book project.

Many illustrations are now in the public domain, but those copyright holders that we have not reached are invited to contact the main editor anders.breidlid@hioa.no

1
What Historians Do

History is the study of events that took place in the past. Historians look at the evidence left behind by people who lived long ago. They use this evidence to find out what happened and to explain why it happened. Apart from written sources they can use unwritten sources to complement their research and conclusions.

Why do we study history? Why is it important?

1. The study of history helps us to understand people and societies of the past.
2. History helps us understand how societies have changed and why the society that we live in is as it is. For example, it is important that South Sudanese learn from history about the struggle for freedom. This helps us to understand the present and may help us to plan for the future.
3. History helps us to understand our cultures as well as the cultures of other people.
4. Historians always ask: why, how and when. The students of history learn how to gather information and to analyse it.
5. In history we learn the results of scientific and technological changes in the lives of people.
6. History may help to establish a national identity and a sense of belonging.

Sources of information on history

In the 21st century, the sources of history are many. They can be oral or written. They also include archaeological, anthropological, linguistic and electronic sources. Some of these sources are not easily classified as oral or written as they overlap. For example, archaeological sources include visual and written material and anthropological sources involve observation and written reports.

We will now look at some of these sources in turn.

Oral sources

Oral sources refer to information that is passed on by word of mouth from one generation to another. Oral tradition has been used to rebuild the history of pre-literate societies by giving information on:

a) Origin, migration and settlement

b) Customs, beliefs and traditions, songs, stories and myths, proverbs and riddles

c) Natural disasters, e.g. drought, floods, diseases

d) Type of leadership and administration

e) Successes and failures of the people at war with their neighbours

Oral sources include interviews with knowledgeable people or people who took part in important events. In South Sudan, there are various traditional methods of remembering important events. For instance, among the Kakwa a record of dowry paid is represented by sticks which are kept in the house. The accuracy of oral history is debated among historians. One problem with oral sources is that they must be remembered and retold many times. Much of the history of what is now South Sudan is preserved through songs, stories and myths and has been passed down for many generations. Therefore, they may not be 100% reliable or accurate. They can be exaggerated and stories can be forgotten or changed for various reasons. In addition, oral sources do not always provide dates or an accurate sequence of events.

However, although most historians are aware that they do not record past events accurately, the Sudanese scholar, Francis Mading Deng, contends that oral traditions often give an understanding of the culture of a pre-literate society not found in any other source. In South Sudan, oral data can be crosschecked against the accounts of anthropologists, foreign travellers and Arab/Nubian geographers as well as against studies in linguistics and archaeology.

Archaeological sources

Another group of people who provide unwritten sources of information about the past are archaeologists. Archaeologists work with artefacts. An **artefact** is an object that people made or used in the past (see fig. 1). They include bones, pottery, seeds, weapons, coins, beads, clothes, rock painting and the remains of dwellings. The archaeologist locates a historical site, digs carefully for artefacts and scientifically analyses them. Using these items the archaeologist is able to describe the activities of the people who once lived there and when they lived there. Artefacts are usually stored in **museums.** Currently there is no museum in Juba or South Sudan. The Ministry of Culture is in the process of constructing a museum in Juba, South Sudan. However, some artifacts are being stored in a big tent by the Ministry of Culture in Juba. (November 2012)

Archaeology has many advantages. It gives detailed information on the objects of a culture. It complements other sources of information on the past. It is useful as archaeological methods are scientific and so artefacts can be dated e.g. through the carbon 14 dating method. It makes history real as we can see and touch the objects.

On the other hand, the dates given by archaeologists are not accurate as they are only estimates. It is also sometimes hard to identify who exactly the people were and what language they spoke. Sometimes archaeological excavations lead to destruction of the environment.

4   *A Concise History of South Sudan*

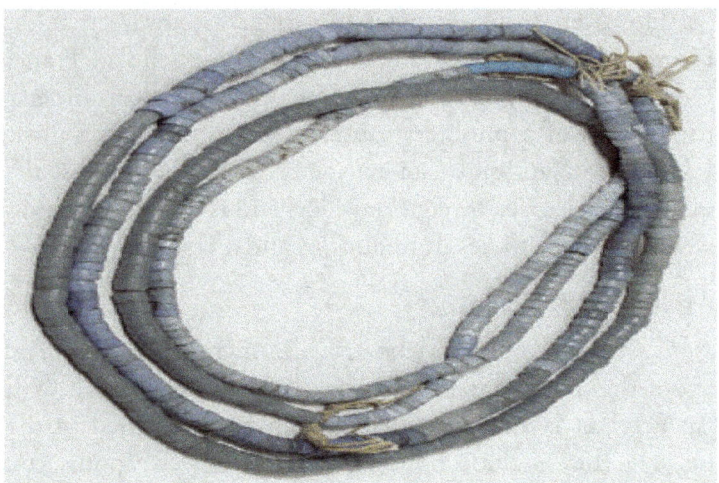

Fig. (1)   Jewellery of the Anywaa (Anyuak). These beads are an example of an artefact.

This artefact is made of glass and cotton yarn plant string before 1935. The beads in this necklace are called dimui. They are used as a form of bride wealth and as compensation for injuries. A string of such beads is made up of about a hundred beads which a man may have taken some years to collect. These strings are very rare, very old and the beads can never be replaced. The Anywaa say that their ancestors brought them from their homeland.

Questions

1. What do historians do? What do archaeologists do?
2. Where do historians get their information about the past?
3. What is an artefact? Give examples of artefacts. List four artefacts in your house that would help a future archaeologist to understand your lifestyle.
4. What would you find in (i) a library; (ii) an archive (iii) a museum? If you have access to internet, enter http://www.dur.ac.uk/library/asc/sudan/ at Durham University in England and see what is contained in their collection on Sudan.
5. Discuss in groups the usefulness of history.

Anthropological sources

Anthropology is a scientific study that attempts to give a deeper understanding of the culture of a people and is often useful to the historian. The anthropologist gathers information through observing people. He/she usually lives among the people being studied for a long period of time. For example, the British anthropologist Evans Pritchard lived among the Azande and wrote about their way of life. Francis Mading Deng wrote similarly about the Dinka. Anthropology is often useful to the historian because it gathers information and gives a deeper understanding of the social organization of a people.

Linguistic sources

Linguistics and word borrowing: Another way of getting information on the past is to study languages as spoken today in the region, and especially to study word-borrowing. Word-borrowing can only take place when there is direct contact between speakers of two languages. This contact indicates migration, trade and intermarriage. Linguistics can also help in dating the migration of peoples. However the reliability of linguistics is debated among historians. In the South of Sudan languages have been studied far more than the archaeology.

Written sources

Some historical sources are written. Books, archives, biographies, newspapers and magazines, diaries, journals and periodicals are all written sources. Also included are official documents like the constitution of a country, government reports, land documents, school reports, birth certificates. The Southern Sudan Population Census Report of 2008 is an example of a valuable written source.

Many written sources are in **libraries** or **archives**.

- **Libraries** store books. One of the greatest libraries in the Republic of South Sudan is in the University of Juba. It has an extensive collection of books on every subject and every many more are added annually to its collection.

- **Archives** are a collection of historical documents or records, especially those which contain classified information of government or organisations. After a period of time these are opened to the public. Archives also refer to places for keeping public, government and other historical records. Archives are therefore resource centres for information. On Independence Day, 9 July 2011, Norway gave the gift of an archive to the people of South Sudan.

Written sources of Southern Sudanese history

There are hardly any sources or records for the pre-1821 period but there are records for the period after 1821. The main written sources of Southern Sudanese history are administrative documents found in the district and province headquarters of present day South Sudan. The most valuable of these documents are those of the last 25 years of Anglo-Egyptian rule. During the 1930-1955 period, the colonial administrators began to assess the policies and activities of earlier colonial administrators. We find their observations and comments in the **district and province archives.** The focus of these documents is on the history of the administration itself. It should however be noted that written documents and sources are also interpretations of events, and these interpretations reflect the position and the interests of those who wrote the documents. There are no neutral historical documents.

Visual sources

Some printed sources are visual. They include photographs, drawings or paintings. Visual sources help us to find out what people looked like and how they dressed. The photo below (fig. 2) is an example of a visual source. It was taken of a potter among the Azande.

Fig. (2) An Azande Potter at Work

The anthropologist E. E. Evans-Pritchard noted that Azande men were expert potters, for he attempted, without much success, to master the art under their guidance. The above is said to be an art of the Ambomu, who made different types of pottery used for carrying water, washing, brewing beer, boiling oil, roasting and boiling meat. On the whole, it was said that small-mouthed pots were made by the Mbomu and that pots with larger mouths came from the South, and mainly made by the Mangbetu.

The advantages of written sources are many.

a) The information in the written source cannot be altered so it is more permanent than the spoken word.

b) Written historical information can be recorded and used by future generations. It can be read and re-read.

c) The written history has the advantage of presenting ideas as they were understood by the author at the time of writing. Likewise, visual sources depict a situation as it was or is.

d) The dates in written sources are more accurate than in unwritten sources.

There are also problems with written sources.

a) No narration of the past tells the whole truth of an event. There are different perspectives and biases on an event or person. Authors can write from a particular point of view and have a certain bias.

b) Authors may also choose to omit significant information thus rendering the document unreliable.

Electronic sources

Electronic sources include the following: (i) micro films, (ii) radio, (iii) television, (iv) CD's and DVD's and (v) computer stored data. Micro-films are films on which very small photographs of documents and printed material are stored. They save storage space and when magnified they can be clearly read.

One advantage of these sources is that they capture events as they happen. For example, on 9 July 2011, the Declaration of Independence and the raising of the flag of the Republic of South Sudan were transmitted live around the world on many radio and television channels. Documentaries are valuable because they give facts about events. Films and DVD's give a deeper understanding of the social life and culture of a people or place with regard to music, dress and leisure activities.

In recent decades, the internet and email have become very important sources of information. In addition, electronic data banks and data bases are stored in a computer so information can be found easily and quickly. For example, the Ministry of Education may have statistical records of students in primary school in each county in the state for a particular year. In a database they may be classified according to age, gender and class. This type of information is very useful to the historian.

The disadvantage of using electronic sources is that the radio or television crew may only use what will appeal to the public and so they may be omit important information. Electronic sources, like any historical source, only give fragments of an event, and the fragments are chosen on the basis of what the photographer and the reporter think is important. The point of view of the television crew and the social context will affect what parts of the event will be recorded and how it will be presented to the viewers. Electronic gadgets are expensive and many South Sudanese may not afford them.

Questions
1. What is history?
2. Why is it important to study history?
3. What is of value to the historian in oral tradition? Discuss the merits and demerits of using oral traditions as historical sources.
4. List sources of written information. Apart from your school report, name one source that future historians could use to find out about you.
5. "Archives are the only source for studying history". Discuss.
6. Assess the validity of using archaeological and linguistic historical sources.
7. What are the advantages and disadvantages of using written and anthropological historical sources?

Two kinds of written sources

Historians and archaeologists divide sources into two kinds: primary sources and secondary sources. A primary source is something that comes directly from people of the past. A letter, a diary, a newspaper, an old tool, a photograph, your school report are all examples of primary sources. Historians do most work with primary sources. An article about artefacts by an archaeologist is a secondary source.

This history book is based on both primary and secondary sources. It contains information about many periods in history and many people who lived in the past. However, the information in it comes to you second-hand. It was written by a group of historians, not by the people of the past themselves.

Exercise
Which of these historical sources are primary sources?
- The Six Protocols of the Comprehensive Peace Agreement.
- A school report card
- History revision notes
- President Kiir's speech on Independence Day, 9 July 2011.
- An 21st century essay on the Azande based on the writings of E.E. Evans Pritchard
- A land document
- A driving license
- A television documentary
- The Transitional Constitution for South Sudan

As you can see from the example below (fig. 3), primary sources are not easy to understand. We need to closely examine their meaning and the views of the writer. James Bruce visited Sennar in Sudan in 1772 on his journey from Ethiopia to Egypt, and wrote about the decline of the Funj Sultanate in *Travels to the Source of the Nile*. In this extract, he describes the Shangalla who were archers from their young days. It shows how an outsider interprets events.

THE SOURCE OF THE NILE. 43

guments above mentioned, stated in greater detail and with more freedom, that they immediately ordered their bookseller to strike out from the subsequent editions of their works all that had been advanced against the negroes on this head, which they had before drawn from the herd of prejudiced and ignorant compilers, strangers to the manners and language of the people they were dishonouring by their descriptions, after having before abused them by their tyranny.

The Shangalla have no bread: no grain or pulse will grow in the country. Some of the Arabs, settled at Ras el Feel, have attempted to make bread of the seed of the Guinea grass; but it is very tasteless and bad, of the colour of cow-dung, and quickly producing worms.

They are all archers from their infancy. Their bows are all made of wild fennel, thicker than the common proportion, and about seven feet long, and very elastic. The children use the same bow in their infancy that they do when grown up; and are, by reason of its length, for the first years, obliged to hold it parallel, instead of perpendicular, to the horizon. Their arrows are full a yard and a half long, with large heads of very bad iron rudely shaped. They are, indeed, the only savages I ever knew that take no pains in the make or ornament of this weapon. A branch of a palm, stript from the tree and made straight, becomes an arrow; and none of them have wings to them. They have this remarkable custom, which is a religious one, that they fix upon their bows a ring, or thong, of the skin of every beast slain by it, while it is yet raw, from the lizard and serpent up to the elephant. This gradually stiffens the bow, till, being all covered over, it can be no longer bent even by its master. That bow is then hung upon a tree,

Fig 3. Extract from the *Sources of the Nile*

> **Questions on the extract**
> - How long were the bows of the archers according to the author?
> - Describe the arrowheads used by the Shangalla archers.
> - Bruce was amazed at one of the customs of the Shangalla. What was that custom?
> - Do you think Bruce respected the archers? Support your answer by reference to the extract.

Is this source reliable? Is the author telling the truth?

All narratives about the past have levels of bias. Historians try to recognise bias by comparing historical sources. They try to find as many sources as possible and compare them.

When was a source written or made?

To answer this question, historians and archaeologists have to work with dates. Dates allow historians to put events in the order in which they happened so that they can tell their story more clearly.

> **Individual task:** Dates matter to you too. You are often asked: When were you born? What year did you start school? Make a timeline showing the important dates in your life. Then push it further back by putting in the ancestral line of your clan and any significant events during their lifetimes in the community e.g. times of famine, flood, massacre, marriage, invasion of the Turks, inter-clan fighting. Add the Declaration of Independence of the Republic of South Sudan. You may have to look up some of these dates.

Using the Christian calendar

In all these cases you used dates that began with 18-, 19- or 20-. These dates come from the Christian calendar. According to some sources, the Roman abbot Dionysus Exiguus devised the Christian calendar in 533 A.D. He started with an event that is important to all Christians

– the birth of Jesus Christ. He called that 'Year One'. He used the letters AD to describe years after Year One. That stands for the Latin words, Anno Domini, meaning 'the year of the Lord'.

The English abbreviation "BC" came much later.

Timeline

1080 BC	Eleventh century (second millennium) BC
250 BC	Third century (first millennium) BC
80 AD	First century AD
150 AD	Second century AD
901 AD	Tenth century AD
1504 AD	Sixteenth century AD
1821 AD	Nineteenth century AD
1956 AD	Twentieth century AD

As you can see from the timeline, the years from 1 to 100 were the first century AD. Then the years from 101 to 200 were the second century. This is why the century just past (from 1901 to 2000) is called the 20th century, even though the dates were known as 19-. And this century is the 21st century, even though it is written as 20-.

Historians also divide time into groups of years. The main ones are millennium (1000 years) centuries (100 years) and decades (10 years). In which decade and century were you born?

Historians also group centuries into periods or eras. These are long stretches of time when people had similar lifestyles or used the same tools. For example, in your study of history you will come across the Pre-Colonial period, the Turko-Egyptian period, the Anglo-Egyptian period and the Post-Colonial period.

Exercises

1. Explain BC and AD
2. Put the following dates in order beginning with the oldest:
   1000 AD; 650 BC; 920 AD; 1966 AD; 450 BC; 960 BC; 29 AD: 990 BC.
   460 AD; 1821 AD: 1314 AD: 350 BC: 1935 AD: 90 BC.

3. In what century do these dates occur?

Date	Century
59 AD	
1972 AD	
565 AD	
1821 AD	
2005 AD	
65 BC	
1956 AD	

4. Which of the dates in the date column in Question 3 is (a) the second oldest? (b) is the date nearest to the year 1 AD?

Interpretation of history

Different interpretations/schools of history
1. Turko-Egyptian School:
2. Mahdist School
3. Anglo-Egyptian School
4. Northern Nationalist School
5. Africanist School

All the above schools of historians tackle history and write according to their lenses of interpretations. The Africanist school is a school of historians interpreting history from an African perspective.

The other schools of historians interpret history through the lenses of the North or through the views of foreigners. But also within one school of historians there may be different interpretations. Not all South Sudanese historians interpret history in exactly the same way. They may have different lenses depending on their ideological orientation, their ethnic background, if they live in exile or not etc.

As you will see in the next chapters, a historical event or a piece of historical information is not necessarily an undisputed fact. Due to different sources, different points of view, political positions, or sources that are vague or contradictory relating to a specific event, a historical narrative may offer different information about the same event. History is not mathematics with one right answer. Historians are often in disagreement about what has happened, how it happened and why it happened. The past is interpreted in different ways. A story about a specific event may be the conqueror's story or the loser's story. Sometimes historians seem to differ about early history because the historical sources are vague or contradictory. Why things happen is often more difficult to explain than what occurred.

However, sometimes people question events that undoubtedly have happened. For example some do not want to include the coming of Christianity to Nubia in the history books for schools even though it certainly happened. In this book you will find examples of how historical events are interpreted differently.

Some writers share their perception of people who lived and worked in Southern Sudan during the Anglo Egyptian Rule. These books were researched with the financial support of colonial governments whose intentions were to understand the people. Seligman's book, *The Tribes of Nilotic Sudan,* provides a comprehensive description of some of the main communities of Southern Sudan. Other books, like those of Geoffrey Lienhart and E.E. Evans-Pritchard, are specific for individual communities and they were written to help the British find suitable means of governing the Sudanese. This history book is based on interpretations of historians from different schools, but an attempt has been made to focus as much as possible on the history and the peoples in the South and to see the history from their point of view.

This is the first time a comprehensive history book for secondary schools about Southern Sudan is written, and it is very difficult to rewrite history that has been so strongly dominated by colonial British and Northern Sudanese nationalist historians in the past. The early history of the Southern Sudanese peoples in particular has not been thoroughly researched due to lack of written sources and because of the dominance of non-Southern Sudanese historians. South Sudanese historians will in the future generate new knowledge about the history of South Sudan. At the same time, pupils and students in South Sudan will play an important role in collecting stories about your people from your parents, grandparents and other elders in your community.

Another important issue is the role of women in history. Women in South Sudan have also been major contributors in agriculture, besides taking care of children. Women have often been overlooked as political actors, even though some have played major roles in the political and economic development of the region. Their reproductive function has been an important factor in explaining their modest role in politics. In addition, the patriarchal societies in South Sudan have been slow in opening up to female participation. Owing to the lack of historical sources in South Sudan, we are regrettably unable to discuss the contribution of women in detail in this book. Hopefully this issue will be addressed more comprehensively in later editions.

2
The Early History of Sudan

Introduction

Ten thousand years ago, East Africa and the Upper Nile region, which is now South Sudan, were much wetter than at the present time. The entire region, between the Congo basin, the Ethiopian highlands and the Nile valley and between the Great Lakes to Dongola in the North, was covered with forests. The present day Sahara region in North Africa was, however, covered with grasslands and trees and had many rivers and lakes. Sahara must have looked like the present day savannas in East Africa. A rich wildlife with elephants and hippos, lions and grass-eating animals roamed across North Africa and competed with human groups for survival.

The origin of human beings

According to archaeological evidence, groups of the first human beings survived and developed in East Africa and gradually spread to other parts of Africa and the rest of the world. Olduvai Gorge, in present-day Tanzania, is known as "The Cradle of Mankind". Homo sapiens (human beings) lived 17,000 years ago. We can safely assume that the first groups of human beings also migrated northwards from the Great Lakes of East Africa, to the Nile region between the Ethiopian highlands and the Congo basin, which is called South Sudan today. A very small number of archaeological excavations were carried out in what is now South Sudan in the 1970's and 1980's. The findings of the archaeologists indicate that humans lived in this area several thousand years ago.

Hunters and gatherers

These early people were hunters and gatherers and they lived together in small groups. They survived by gathering wild plants and berries, by game hunting and fishing. There are indications that some groups were organised by women, either by a group of related women (sisters) or by an elderly woman or matriarch. It is therefore possible that the first people who arrived in present day South Sudan were associated with the early women and men of East Africa. These people were pantheists and believed that all living things, plants and animals, have a spirit. Simple technology of stone scrapers, knives, spearheads and fishing hooks were used. A clear distinction between the first human groups and their more animal-related forefathers (primates) was that these groups could make fire and develop simple tools.

Questions
1. Where did the first human beings originate?
2. Describe the food and tools used by the people who lived several thousand years ago in the present- day South Sudan?
3. What distinguished human beings from other primates?

The Nilo-Saharan peoples

Between 10,000 and 5,000 years ago, people were living in the eastern region of what is known today as Sahara. These people are called the Nilo-Saharan peoples. They developed a way of living together and a common language in that region. Therefore today, most of the people in Eastern Africa, which includes South Sudan, are believed to belong to the Nilo-Saharan language family.

From gatherers to cultivators

The Nilo-Saharan people took an interest in the cultivation of grain, grasses and plants. They gathered seeds from grass, and from the roots and fruits of many different plants. They noticed that their seeds yielded a better harvest when sown in fertile soil and along the river banks. Some of them began to select and plant the biggest seeds in the more fertile areas. As well as using stone tools, they used tree sticks to help cultivate the soil. Grass of poor quality was burnt and cleared away to allow the good grass seed to grow. Through experimentation and innovation they developed new crops.

While some groups developed a mixed economy of cultivation and the rearing of animals, others specialised in animal husbandry and migrated seasonally with their cattle. Pigs, hens, donkeys and cows were common animals in Nilo-Saharan households. The people began to gather smaller animals around their homes instead of hunting them. Among these domestic animals were goats, sheep and dogs.

Fig (1)   The Nubian goat has elongated ears and a sleek coat.

New social and political organisation

As time went by people began to build permanent dwellings along the Nile shore. This demanded new forms of social and political organization. Between 3000 BC and 2000 BC the climate in North Africa slowly became drier and many more groups from Sahara flocked to the Nile. The increase of population along the river soon necessitated better regulation of rights to cultivate and feed from the river shores and of social responsibilities. As a result, kingdoms and royal dynasties developed along the Nile in present-day Egypt and Sudan.

In summary, ten thousand years ago, the people of Southern Sudan were hunters and gatherers but as they began to cultivate and to rear animals, their social and political system changed.

> **Questions**
> a) Who were the Nilo-Saharan people?
> b) Describe their economic development.
> c) Why did kingdoms and royal dynasties develop?

The Kush Kingdom in Nubia

Where is Kush?

For hundreds of years, the banks of the Nile River were home to two different cultures, Nubian culture and Egyptian culture. The Nubians lived along the Nile to the south and the Egyptians lived along the Nile to the north. Nubia was a true African country whose black kings and Nubian civilisation is among the oldest in the world.

The Nubians were Sudanese nomads who originally lived in Sahara from 10000 to 6000 BC. Those Nubians were closely related to the people living in South Sudan today. Over the centuries, some Nubians migrated into Kordofan, the valleys along the Blue Nile, westwards to Darfur and to the South. All are Nilo-Saharans, related through their common ancestors in Nubia and the Sahara, together with those who live in Nubia and in east Sudan today.

Today, the land that was ancient Nubia is divided between two countries. The most northerly part is in modern Egypt but most of it is in Sudan. This dry region is still called Nubia. Ancient Egyptians and perhaps ancient Nubians as well, called it Kush. Some rocky rapids and waterfalls, called cataracts, break up the flow of the Nile as it passes through Nubia. The first cataract is at a town called Aswan today. Long ago, Aswan served as a border between Egypt and Nubia.

The Early History of Sudan 21

Fig. (2) **A cataract of the Nile.** Cataracts are formed by granite rocks that break up the flow of the river.

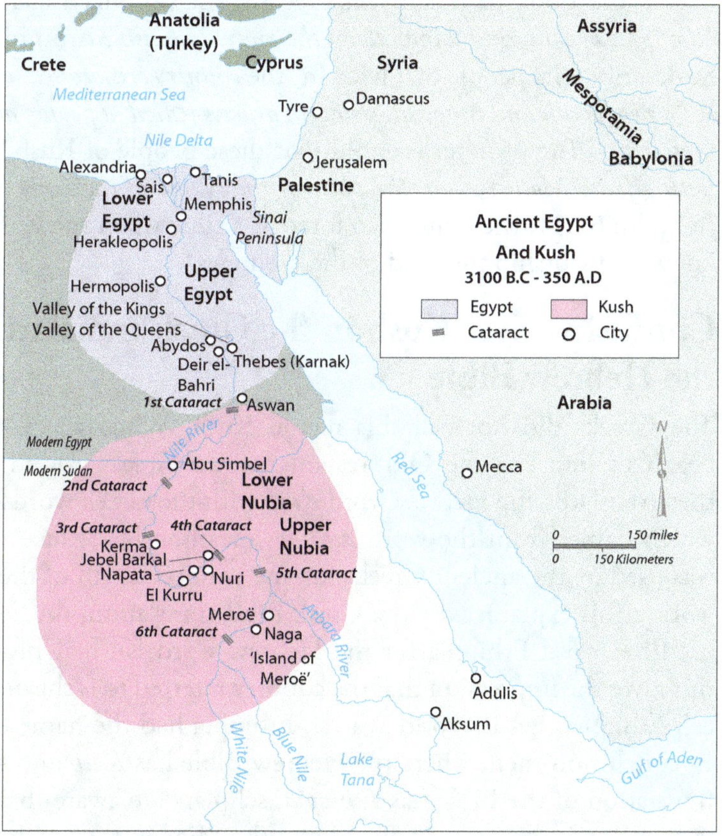

Fig. (3) Kingdoms of Egypt and Kush (*Dillon*)

Historians often divide Kush (Nubia) into different sections: Lower Nubia and Upper Nubia. Lower Nubia was to the north closer to Egypt. Upper Nubia was to the south because it is nearer to the starting point of the River Nile.

Kush in the Christian Bible

In ancient times, Kush was the name the Egyptians gave to the region directly south of Egypt along the Nile. At the time of the prophet Isaiah, Egypt was governed by pharaohs of Kushite origin and there is reference to Kush in the original Hebrew Bible. Kush is sometimes spelt Cush in English bibles.

In The Book of Isaiah, Chapter 18, the prophet Isaiah refers to *"the land of whirring wings along the rivers of Cush"*. Around 750 BC, he describes the people that lived in "the *country crisscrossed with rivers*" as "*a people tall and bronzed, a nation always feared, a people mighty and masterful."* The prophet foretold that these people of Kush*"will come with gifts to Mount Zion, the place of the Name of the Lord Almighty."* In Psalm 68:31, the writer also foretells a time when the Kushites will know and worship the God of the Hebrews.

Confusion over Kush in the Greek translation of the Hebrew Bible

The Greeks did not call this region Kush. When the Greeks first began to translate the Old Testament into Greek around 300 BC, they translated the Hebrew word *Kush* with the Greek word *Aithiopia,* which comes from the word *aithiops* meaning black face. The term was used by the ancient Greeks for any country south of their known world. This explains why the Greek Bible translation, the Septuagint, used the word Ethiopia for the Hebrew word Kush. Unfortunately, this gives the impression that the country referred to is the one we now call Ethiopia. Until World War II, Ethiopia had the name Abyssinia. In conclusion then, where the Hebrew Bible has *Kush* and the Greek translation of the Bible has *Ethiopia*, scholars are aware that the land in question is the country directly south of Egypt, the north of Sudan. This region was later called *Nubia*.

The foundation and growth of the Kush Kingdom

From 2000 BC, the Egyptians exploited Kush in search of gold and slaves and the Egyptians conquered Kush as far as the fourth cataract in the early 15th century BC. From then until the thirteenth century BC, Kush was governed by a viceroy or governor known as the "King's Son of Kush". He made sure that the Kushites paid an annual tribute of gold, slaves, cattle, ebony, ivory and ostrich feathers to the Pharaoh of Egypt. The Egyptian Pharaoh Thutmose III is said to have collected about 250 kg of gold annually from Kush.

When the Pharaoh of Egypt was in control in Kush, the Egyptians built temples like that dedicated to the sun god Amon at Napata. The Kushite elite worshipped Egyptian gods along with their own deities and used the Coptic language which was spoken in Egypt. In 1160 BC, Egypt became weak and Kush won back her independence. In historical records, nothing more is heard of Kush for the next 300 years.

The kings of Kush at Napata: c.750 BC – c.270 BC

In the 9th century BC, a Nubian monarchy began to emerge. Its capital was at Napata and it grew into a strong, prosperous Kingdom of Kush near the Fourth Cataract. It is the first Sudanese kingdom of which we have any detailed knowledge. In 730 BC, only a century after coming to power, the Kushite kings under their great Black Pharaoh, Piye, were strong enough to conquer Egypt as far as the shores of the Mediterranean Sea. For about sixty years Egypt was ruled by the kings of Kush.

They were impressive pharaohs. They built many monuments and encouraged a revival in literature and the arts in Egypt. This came to an end in 671 BC when the Assyrians invaded Egypt. With their superior iron weapons, they defeated the armies of Kush under king Taharqa. By 654 BC, the Kushites had been driven back to their capital Napata.

Although the Kushite reign in Egypt lasted just over 60 years, the Nubian civilisation far outlasted the Egyptian. The kings of Kush continued to rule the middle Nile for another 1000 years. Soon after they retreated from Egypt, Meroë became the capital of the Kingdom of Kush. Before we go to Meroë, let us look at the political, economic and social life at Napata.

Fig. (4) The Black Pharaoh of Kush, Taqarta, younger son of king Piye, was king of Kush and Egypt during the time of the Kush Kingdom at Napata. (*National Geographic Magazine*)

Political organisation of the kingdom of Kush at Napata

It was a strong kingdom from at least the 9th century BC. From the 8th century, the Kings of Kush came from the same family. Historians believe that these Nubian kings were brought up in the culture and customs of Egypt. Their political organization was similar to that of Egypt. It emphasized a strong monarchy based on the belief that the king was a god. The king was an absolute monarch. He had a standing army and he was its commander in chief. The king's wealth came from tribute of his chiefs and from his control of trade.

Economic life at Napata

The Kushites at Napata were cattle keepers. Many were cultivators who grew crops such as sorghum, millet and date palm. They hunted the lion, leopard, elephant and ostrich and the Black Pharaohs of Napata had many horses. The Kushites raided weak societies, e.g. the Berbers and the Beja. Many Kushites were soldiers, famous for their skills with the bow and arrow. Other Kushites worked in the gold mines. Indeed, the wealth of the Kushites flowed from the mines and grew with their control of the trade routes.

They did business with their own people and their neighbours, the Egyptians, Greeks and the Romans. They traded in gold, cattle, ivory, ebony, slaves and ostrich feathers, animal skins, frankincense and plant oil. The kings of Napata imported juniper and cedars from the timber traders of Lebanon. Fishing was also carried out on the Nile for domestic consumption and for internal trade.

Social life at Napata

The society at Napata had different groups. There was the royal family, the priesthood families, chiefs, commoners and slaves. Historians believe that the royal families and the priesthood families intermarried.

Egypt greatly influenced the architecture, paintings and beliefs of Kushites at Napata. When a king died, his tomb was marked with a pyramid. King Piye was buried with his 4 horses.

Fig. (5) Today Sudan has more pyramids than Egypt. Great pyramids of the Napata kings are found in El Kurru, Nuri and Meroë. This photograph shows the pyramids of the Kushite rulers at Meroë today.

Gods of the Kushites at Napata

The Kushites worshipped the Egyptian god Amun in many temples with their own deities. They feasted and offered sacrifices to these gods and asked their protection before leaving for battle. The Egyptians believed that Amun was born at the foot of the holy mountain Jebel Barkal near Napata. On the pinnacle of the rock face of Jebel Barkal, the Kushite king Taharqa had his name inscribed in gold leaf to bedazzle those who passed by!

Fig.(6) The last standing pillars of the temple of Amun at the foot of Jebel Barkal.

When the capital of Kush was moved southwards from Napata to Meroë between the 5th and 6th Cataracts around 350 BC, the influence of Egyptian culture was weakened and the Kushites were increasingly in contact with the long-established African cultures farther south.

Questions
1. Explain why the Egyptians raided Nubia for centuries.
2. Describe the political organisation and religion of the Kushite Kingdom at Napata.
3. Outline the economic activities of the Kushites. Which of these activities brought most wealth to their Kingdom?
4. Describe two great achievements of the Kush kings at Napata.

The Kush Kingdom at Meroë: 350 B.C-350 A.D.

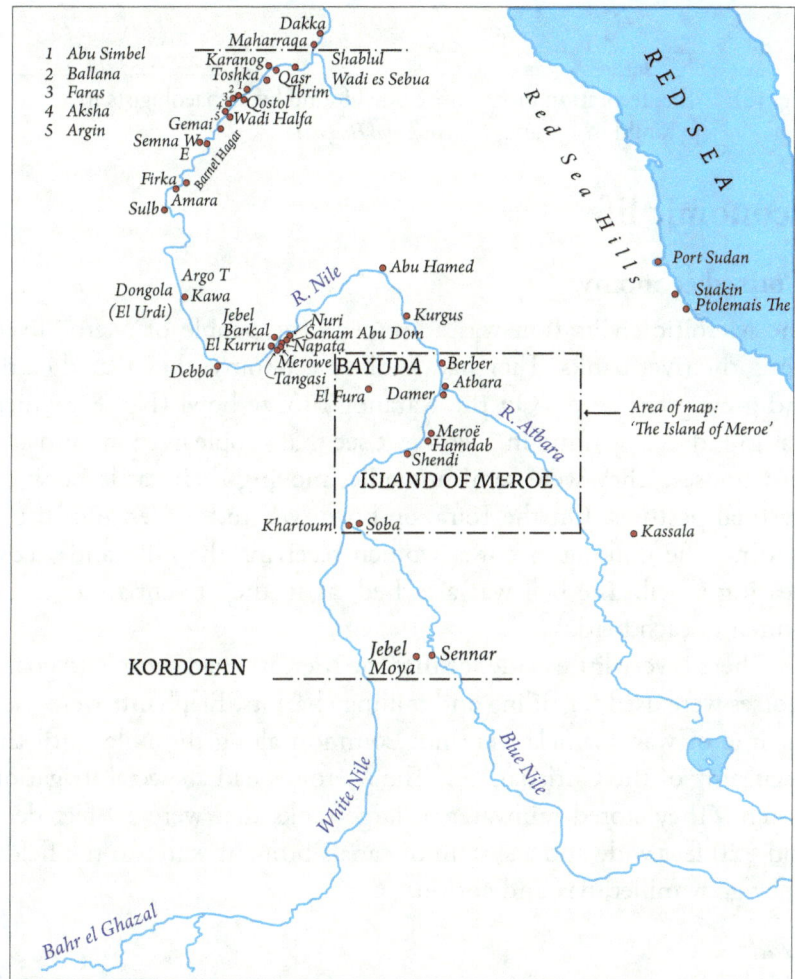

Fig. (7)   Map showing the Kingdom of Meroë (*Thames and Hudson*)

The kingdom of Meroë was situated in a fertile plain along the Nile. Nubian culture flourished there from the 4th century B.C. to the 4th century A.D. It included most of Nubia and areas far south of present day Khartoum.

This interesting artefact below tells us much of the way of life of some people in Meroë.

Fig. (8) The decoration on a bronze bowl found by archaeologists in a pyramid in Karanog. (*Thames and Hudson*)

Economic life

A mixed economy

The Meroitic civilisation was advanced. The people of Meroë lived along the river banks. They had a mixed economy: they reared cattle and grew grain crops. On the Karanog bronze bowl (Fig. 8), which was found in a pyramid in Meroë, we see that people lived in mud and reed houses. They were semi-nomadic, moving their cattle between seasonal pastures. On the Karanog bowl, we find evidence of cattle herding, the milking of cows, women receiving the milk and a cow wearing a bell. The bell was attached, as in the present time, to an animal in each herd.

There is very little evidence that the Meroites had sheep and goats. Horses were used for riding and pulling chariots. Elephants were used in time of war. Camels were not common along the Nile until the beginning of the Christian era. The Meroites had a special irrigation system. They stored rainwater in large tanks that were 50 feet deep and 820 feet wide and a system of canals brought water to the fields. They grew millet, flax and cotton.

Trade

Meroë was a centre of international trade. Just north of the Fifth Cataract, traders could cross the desert to rejoin the Nile above the Second Cataract so they could avoid the dangerous stretches of the Nile in between. Many routes went eastwards to the Red Sea, where the Romans had developed ports to encourage trade. In this way, the people of Meroë exchanged goods with the people of Greece and Rome, the near East, southern Arabia and Abyssinia. Scholars believe Meroë had trade connections with India and China.

Iron tools
Iron tools for hunting helped the Meroites to produce trade items such as ivory, leopard skins and ostrich feathers. They also provided iron tools for sale in distant markets. Archaeologists have found many bronze and silver artifacts at Meroë that are evidence of trade with Greece, Rome, Egypt, Assyria and Persia.

Iron working
About 350 BC the people of Napata moved to Meroë probably because there was iron ore and wood there. The Assyrians taught the Meroites how to smelt iron and to make hoes, spoons, and weapons such as arrows, knives, and spears. Meroë was one of the centres from which the use of iron tools and iron weapons spread to Central and East Africa. In these places, better tools especially the axe and the hoe, allowed people to produce more food, so the land could provide for larger populations.

In other areas, such as Ghana and Mali, better weapons led to the establishment of a central authority by a king. These great kingdoms depended on iron weapons to keep control over their neighbours.

Pottery

Fig. (9)   These beakers were found in a tomb in Faras. Made of fired and painted clay, they are typical of the art of Meroë in the 2nd and 3rd century AD (*Dillon*)

The Meroites were excellent in the making of pottery which has been found in Nubian graves and temples and believed to be among the best in the ancient world. Men made wheel turning pottery which was very like the pottery made in Egypt and also shows the influence of the Mediterranean. The pottery made by the women was made by hand and was truly African.

Jewellery

Some Meroitic jewellery is like the jewellery of Egypt. Most of this jewellery has been found in graves of queens who wore gold earrings, collars, amulets and many bracelets, and rings set with precious stones. Gold and silver beads and circular ostrich egg shell beads were common then as they are in Sudan today. Engravings of flies and rams heads were often on the jewellery.

Fig. (10) Gold earrings taken from the pyramid tomb at Meroë show the head of the goddess Hathor, who was shown as having the ears or the horns of a cow. Hathor was believed to be the divine mother of all pharaohs. (*Dillon*)

Gods of the Meroites, Amun and Apedemak

Fig. (11) The god Amun (*Dillon*)

In the early years of the Meroitic civilisation, the Meroites worshipped the same gods as the Egyptians, including Amun. The ram was recognised for its fertility in both Egypt and Nubia but only in Nubia is Amun shown as a ram with a man's head.

By 225 BC the Egyptian ram god Amun had been replaced by the Meroitic god, Apedemek. He is often shown as a man or as a snake with a lion's head. Sometimes he has three faces and four arms. The Meroites liked to engrave African animals such as ostriches and giraffes, lions and elephants. Some historians believe that living elephants may have been kept at the Temple of Apedemek.

Fig. (12) This container was found with many others in a tomb at Faras, near Meroë. (*Dillon*)

The lion head represents Apedemek, the god of the Meroites. The pottery of the Meroites shows both the Mediterranean and African traditions in Meroitic culture.

The Meroites used their own language known as Meroitic and invented their own writing. It was different from the language of the Egyptians and probably originated from the Nilo-Saharan languages. No one has yet been able to make sense of this language.

Political organisation at Meroë

The king of Meroë was an absolute monarch. To be selected as ruler of the Kingdom, one had to have the support of all nobles and priests for an unpopular ruler could be removed. Women could also be rulers and sometimes queens ruled the Meroitic Kingdom. The King's mother or the Queen mother was greatly respected as in many other African cultures.

The king, the government officials and the professional craftspeople lived in towns. The chief town was Meroë. The king governed the area around the town of Meroë and his lesser kings governed the areas that were further from Meroë. The king's wealth came from the tribute of his lesser kings and from his personal control of trade.

The kingdom of Meroë came to an end in 350 AD when the King of Axum took possession of the Island of Meroë. Today historians agree that Meroë was one of the most important cities of Africa and that the Kushite civilisation of Meroë was perhaps one of the greatest Africa has ever known.

Questions
1. Describe the life of a farmer in Meroë, his crops, animals and agricultural methods.
2. Explain why it is believed the Kushites moved their capital from Napata to Meroë.
3. Describe three artefacts that help you to understand the work of the people of Meroë.
4. Outline the economic life in Meroë in the period 350 BC-350 AD
5. Explain the impact of the iron-smelting industry on Africa.
6. Compare the religion of the Kushites at Meroë with the religion of the Kushites at Napata.
7. Observe god Amun in Figure 11. Are the features African or Arab?
8. How was Meroë governed?

The three Kingdoms of Christian Nubia

In 350 AD, an Axumite army captured and destroyed the city of Meroë, ending the kingdom's independent existence. By the sixth century AD, three states had emerged as the political and cultural successors of Meroë. Warrior aristocracies ruled in all three kingdoms.
a) Nobatia in the north, whose capital was at Faras in present day Egypt;

b) Maqurrah, at Dongola on the Nile, 150 km south of modern Dongola;

c) Alwah, (Alodia) in the middle of old Meroë, whose capital was at Sawba.

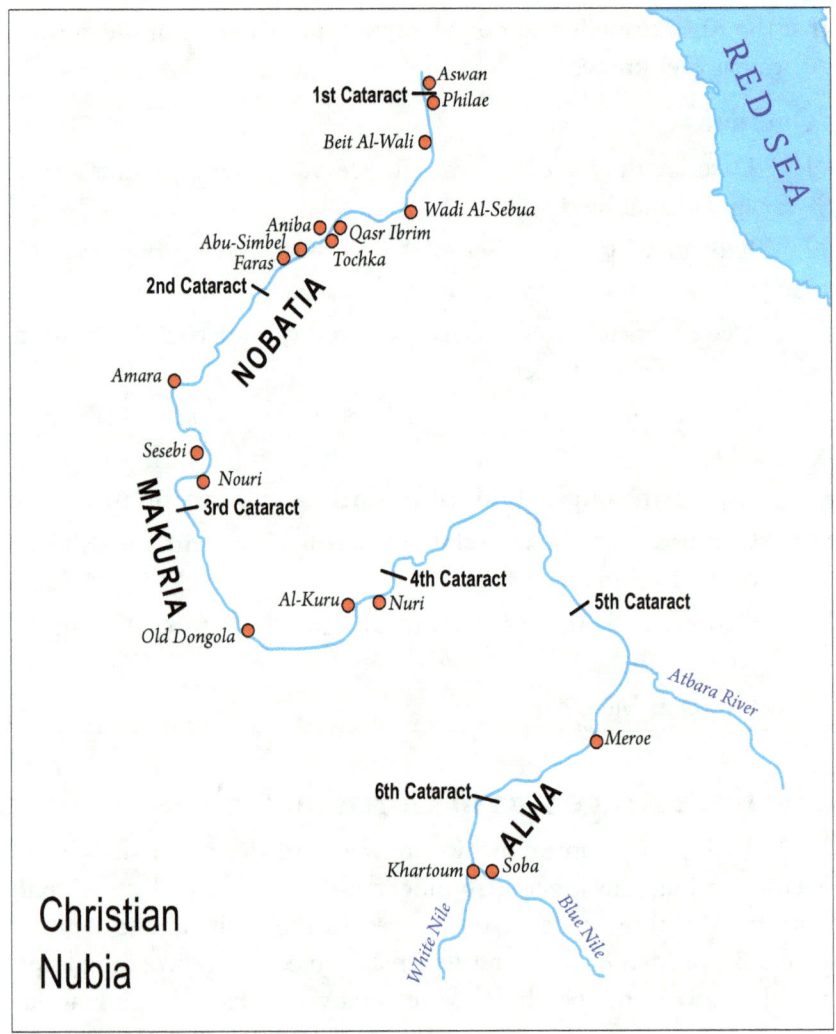

Fig. (13) The Three Nubian Kingdoms, Sixth to Sixteenth Centuries
(*Paulines Publications*)

The coming of Christianity to Nubia

The earliest references to these successors of the Meroitic kingdoms are found in accounts by Greek and Coptic writers of the conversion of the Nubian kings to Christianity in the 6th century. But there were Christians in Nubia long before that time. Three hundred years earlier, in the third century, when Christians were persecuted by Roman emperors, Christian monks and hermits fled into northern Nubia from Egypt. There was trade between Christian Egypt and Nubia and at Faras, the capital of Nobatia, there was a growing Christian community in the 5th century. There was also a Christian community in Soba in the 6th century. Missionaries had come there from Ethiopia, known as Abyssinia at that time.

Fig. (14) Empress Theodora (mosaic from Ravenna) (*Paulines Publications*)

In the middle of the sixth century, Empress Theodora, the Egyptian born wife of the Byzantine Emperor, sent Julian, a missionary bishop, from Constantinople to Nobatia. The Nubian kings became Christian.

They accepted the spiritual authority of the Coptic Patriarch of Alexandria in the Nubian church. After some years, Nubians were ordained priests and Nubian men were named and consecrated bishops in Egypt by the Coptic Patriarch.

The church in Alexandria was Greek speaking and Greek was used in Nubian church services. As the Bible was not translated into the Nubian languages for many years, Nubians did not have a deep understanding of their faith.

The Nubians lost contact with the mother church in Alexandria in Egypt in the 7th century when Egypt was conquered by the Muslim Arabs. This weakened the young Christian church in Nubia from the beginning.

However for a thousand years, from the 6th to the 15th century, the Nubian kings were Christian and Christianity was the official religion of the three Sudanese kingdoms.

Architecture, art and learning in Christian Nubia

One result of the spread of Christianity was the development of building and painting and hand crafts such as pottery. After the eighth century, cathedrals were built with the help of Byzantine architects and artists. These cathedrals were great works of architecture and art. They were entirely decorated in the interior with brilliantly painted frescoes of scenes from the Old and New Testaments. The spectacular frescoes in the excavated cathedral at Faras, the capital of the Nobatia kingdom, show the influence of the Byzantine church.

Nubian Bishop Marianos under the protection of the Virgin with Christ Child - Faras (*Warsaw, National Museum*)

Detail of Bishop Marianus

Fig. (15) In this fresco from Faras, the 11th century Nubian Bishop Marianosis dressed like a Byzantine bishop at a religious service.
(*Paulines Publications*)

Fig. (16) Example of a 14th century Nubian reddish brown earthenware chalice and paten found in Banganarti church ruins, 10 km from Old Dongola. This shape of vessel was typical of chalices and patens found in Nubia by archaeologists. A black stripe runs around the upper rim and the foot edge.

Another result of the spread of Christianity was the growth of literacy in Nubia. The church encouraged literacy in Nubia through its Egyptian-trained clergy and its cathedral schools. The main languages used were the Coptic language of Egypt and Greek. The Bible and other religious texts were translated in Nubian languages and a Nubian script was developed.

Fig. (17) Here is an example of beautiful Nubian book decorations.
(*Paulines Publications*)

Monasteries were also centres of learning and of prayer. These were very important for the Nubian church. Archaeologists have located remains of over thirty monasteries in Nubia. They were found in all the major towns as well as in remote lonely places. Most of the monks were Nubian or Egyptian.

Fig. (18) The columns of the ancient church of Dongola. (*Publishers EMI*)

Why did Christianity disappear in Nubia around 1500 AD?

1. Christianity disappeared because there was an absence of active Christian leaders. As time went on, it became common practice for bishops and priests to hold leadership positions in the government of Nubia. They neglected to give spiritual help to their people so the Christian church was weak.

2. Christianity disappeared because Christianity was closely related to the Nubian kings. These kings were fighting among themselves around 1500 AD. As the Christian kingdoms became weak and fell, the practice of Christianity also crumbled and gradually disappeared.

3. Another reason was that the clergy failed to establish the Christian faith among people outside the towns. The clergy did

not have close relationships with the common people, who were not literate. Many of the clergymen in Nubia were foreigners, from the Egyptian Coptic church and from Greece. They used their mother tongue which was only understood by those who were educated.

4. Finally, when asked, the Abyssinians gave no help. In 1450, six men from Alwa went to the king of neighbouring Abyssinia, present day Ethiopia. They begged him to send them priests and monks to teach the people of Nubia but they did not.

The history of Christianity in Sudan shows that Christianity has been in Sudan for a very long time and was introduced to the Sudanese long before the coming of Islam. It is important to remember however, that although many South Sudanese are Christian, this does not mean that there is a historical, unbroken link between the Christian kingdoms in the north and the southern Christians of today. The growth of Christianity in the South is due to a much later development in the 19th and 20th centuries. We will learn more about this in chapter 3.

Questions

1. Name the three Christian kingdoms in Nubia.
2. Who brought Christianity to Nubia in the first century A.D.?
3. Who converted the Nubian kings to Christianity in the 6th century A.D.?
4. What evidence is there that the Christians in Nubia were skilled craftsmen?
5. Explain why Christianity did not put down deep roots in Nubia after the 6th century.
6. Outline why the Christian kingdoms were weak in the fourteenth and fifteenth centuries.
7. Do you think the history of these kingdoms is relevant for you as a South Sudanese?

8. In many school history books about Sudan the history of Sudan starts with the coming of Islam. Why do you think the history of Christianity in Nubia has been left out of many history books?

The coming of the Arabs to Sudan

Not long after the death of Mohammad in the seventh century, Arab armies left Arabia and went westwards into North Africa. It took the Arabs only 75 years to have political control over North Africa. They carried Islam with them.

The Arabs came into Sudan by two main routes. Most of them came quietly from Egypt through the desert into eastern Sudan. They did not come in by the Nile valley, because they were afraid that the Nubians would see them. Some Arabs came to Sudan across the Red Sea, either through Abyssinia or directly to Sudanese ports such as Badi and Suakin.

The reasons for the migration of Arabs into Sudan in the 7th century

Before the 7th century, there was contact between the Nubians and Arabs.

- Arab nomads often came into the region looking for fresh grazing land for their cattle.

- Arab traders also traded in spices and slaves in Red Sea ports.

- The Arabs wanted to trade. Africa already had distant trade routes and they saw great opportunities for trade.

- The demand for slaves was growing in Arab countries and the Arab merchants hoped to find slaves in Sudan.

- The overpopulation of Arabia forced Arabs to go beyond their borders to find work.

- In the middle of the 7th century, the Arabs in Egypt wanted to stop Nubian attacks on the Nubian-Egyptian border.

The migration of the Arabs into Nubia in 641-651 AD

Arabs had migrated to Sudanese ports along the western coast of the Red Sea by the mid 7th century. There they developed a trade centre for spices and slaves. These Arabs were Arabian refugees who had been given protection by Abyssinians.

When the Arabs took over Egypt as far south as Aswan, the Nubians attacked the Egyptian border. When this happened, the Arab governor of Egypt ordered attacks on Nubia. The Arabs invaded Nubia in 642 AD and again in 652 AD. The Nubians defeated them. The Arabs had to accept a peace agreement and had to remove their army. This resulted in a very unusual treaty, called a *baqt*, in the history of Islam.

Treaty/*Baqt* between Egyptian Arabs and Christian Nubia: 652 AD

The treaty shows that the Arabs realised the commercial advantages of peaceful relations with the people in Nubia. So in the *baqt* the Arabs and the Nubians agreed not to raid each other's territory. They also agreed that neither would defend the other in the event of an attack by a third party. As a gesture of good will, Christian Nubians gave slaves to Muslim Egypt every year in exchange for grain.

Course of migration and settlement of the Arabs

The early migration and settlement of the Arabs in Sudan was made possible, first and foremost, by this *baqt* of 652 AD between the Arabs and Nubians. Although the agreement was sometimes broken, this treaty (*baqt*) and the other treaties that revised it, kept peace between the two peoples for more than 600 years.

- **The *Baqt* advanced the migration and settlement of Arabs in Sudan.**

  This treaty gave Arabs a privileged position in Nubia. Under the terms of the *baqt* for example, Arabs were allowed to buy land from the Nubians south of the frontier at Aswan and Arab merchants were able to set up markets in Nubian towns. The Arab merchants exchanged grain for slaves. They traded horses and manufactured goods for ivory, gold, gems, aromatic gum and cattle. The Arabs brought these goods to Egypt or shipped them to Arabia. The treaty also gave Arab engineers the right to supervise the gold and emerald mines east of the Nile.

Another result of this *baqt* was the spread of Islam. By the 9th century, there were mosques and Muslims officials collecting alms in the land of the Beja. The Beja were Nubians and their land lay between Aswan and the Red Sea.

The *baqt* of 652 AD also ensured the expansion of trade and peaceful travel for the Arabs in Sudan. Conflicts between the Arabs and Nubians were continually settled by referring to the spirit of the *baqt* of 652 AD. In the 9th century, for example, the Beja agreed to respect Islam and its mosques and in return they were allowed to travel and trade freely in Egypt. In other treaties, the Beja allowed Muslim pilgrims from North Africa to travel safely to Mecca through their lands.

- **The gold mines encouraged the migration of Arabs into north eastern Sudan.**

The *baqt* of 652 AD gave Arab engineers the right to supervise the mines east of the Nile. There the Arabs used slaves to extract gold and emeralds. In the 9th century, many Arabs migrated from Egypt to the mines of eastern Sudan. The Beja resented so many Arabs coming to the gold mines in their land and they tried to stop them mining. But in 855 AD the Arabs defeated the Beja and from then on the Arabs worked the gold mines.

In the **13th century**, when the gold mines fell into disuse, Arabs migrated to Alwa in search of work because there was a peaceful Islamic community and mosque already established there.

- **Intermarriage with the ruling Nubian families advanced the migration and settlement of Arabs in Sudan**
  From the 7th century and the 16th century, the Nile valley was arabized. It happened gradually. The Arabs did not use force to conquer it nor did they compel the people to adopt Arab culture. After the 7th century, Arabic became the language for commerce. Little by little, the Arabs married into ruling Beja families and so benefited from the matrilineal succession, which was established all over eastern Sudan, and their children became chiefs of the Beja. According to some historians, through this custom, land gradually was passed into the hands of the Arab tribal community and so the Arabs gained status and importance.

- **Arabs settled in Sudan to avoid heavy taxes from the Mamluks.**
  In the second half of the 14th century, the Mamluks of Egypt were putting very heavy taxes on the Arabs who were trading along the Egyptian frontier. So Arab tribes from Upper Egypt migrated towards **Meroë, the Gezira and Kordofan.** Some remained as nomads and kept their own tribal system unbroken. Through marriage, others spread Islam in the society.

- **After 1504, Islamic teachers migrated from Egypt.**
  We know from the 18th biographies of the holy men of the Funj, known as the Tabaqat, that when the Funj came to power there were no schools for teaching the Qur'an in the kingdom and that most Muslims were not instructed in it teachings. The Funj kings welcomed Islamic teachers who migrated from Egypt and North Africa and instructed the Funj people in the Qur'an. The schools they set up deepened the Islamization of North Sudan.

Some effects of the Arab migration on the people of Sudan

- When the Arabs first came, Nubia was Christian. The Arabs converted Nubians to the new religion of Islam. By 1317, the rulers of Christian Nubia were Muslim kings. By 1504, the kingdom on Alwa became the Islamized kingdom of the Funj.

- Arabs intermarried with Sudanese and over the years were integrated into Sudan. In eastern Sudan land ownership passed to the children of Arab fathers and Beja mothers.
- The Arabs made a treaty (*baqt*) with the Nubians which lasted for almost 600 years. It ended with the fall of the Fatimid regime in Egypt around 1160 AD. However, from the beginning, the Arabs brought slave raids to Sudan and exploited the gold and emerald mines of eastern Sudan.
- The migration of the Arabs into Sudan took over 1,000 years. During the Funj regime (1504-1821) large numbers of Islamic teachers migrated from Egypt and North West Africa and preached Islam on a large scale. So Northern Sudan was united by Islam.
- During the Arab migrations the Arabs saw the lack of unity among the southern peoples. The slave traders, the Egyptian government, the Mahdists and the British all used this disunity to divide and control Sudanese.
- Many Muslim Arabs regarded themselves as superior to the non-Muslims. This led to racial and cultural hostility between the northern and southern part of Sudan. This legacy continues to influence perceptions of race and social status in North Africa today.

Questions

1. State and explain the causes of the Arab migration into Sudan 641-651 AD.
2. Outline the reasons that brought the Arabs to migrate and settle in Southern Sudan between the 7th and the 19th century.
3. Assess the impact of the coming of the Arabs on the people of the Sudan.

The Kingdom of the Funj: 1504 AD–1821 AD

Who were the Funj?

They were a non-Arab and non-Muslim people. It seems likely that they were black African and descendants of the ancient kingdom of Alwa. We do not know for certain where the Funj came from. They may have descended from the Shilluk of Upper Nile region or from cattle nomads from the Ethiopian border.

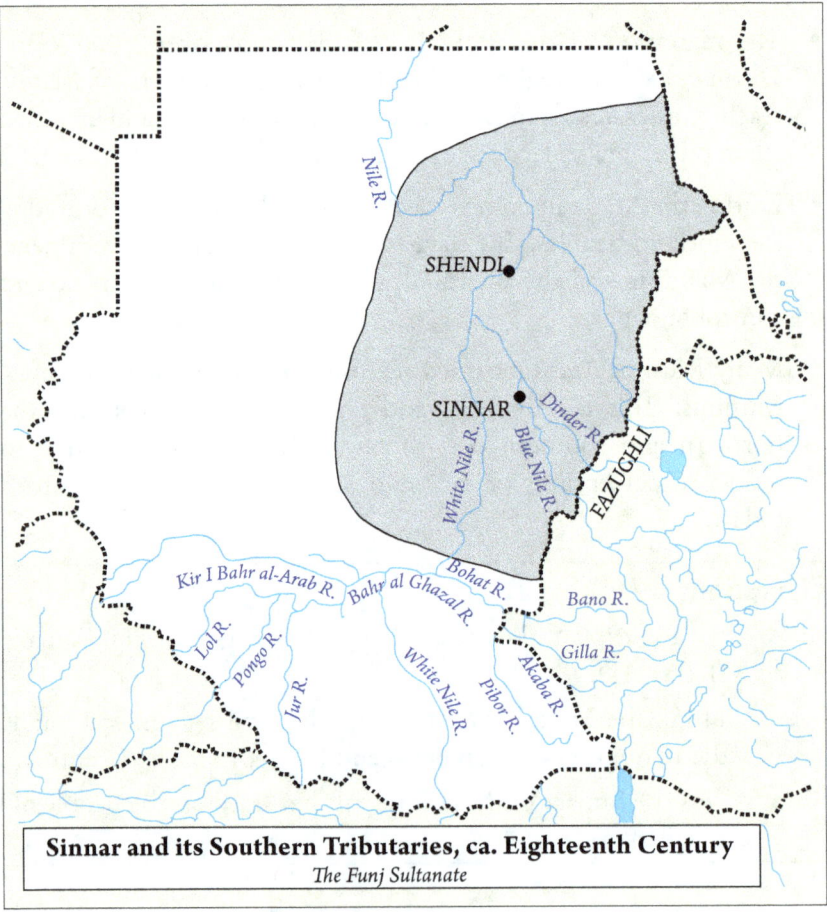

Fig. (19) The Kingdom of the Funj in the Eighteenth Century.
(*University of Rochester Press*)

Foundation and expansion of the Funj Kingdom

The Funj Kingdom was founded in 1504 by Amara Dunqas who was the first mek, sultan or king. The capital of the Funj Kingdom was Sennar, south of the present-day city of Wad Medani.

Within a hundred years the Funj had pushed the Arabs back to the third cataract. In the 1700s the Funj Kingdom was very powerful. It controlled Al Gezira and the gold rich areas of Fazughli. It had a border with the Shilluk Kingdom and fought the Fur over Kordofan. The Funj Sultans had a five storey palace in Sennar. Slavery was the cornerstone of Funj wealth and power. The Funj Kingdom fell in 1821.

We have four written historical sources that tell us about the Funj.
1. The Funj Chronicle on the origin and the last 100 years of the Funj.
2. The Tabaqat- biographies of holy Muslim men that are not historically accurate.
3. 18th century Land Charters show the power of the Islamic teachers.
4. The writings of 18th century travellers, Bruce and Burckhardt and missionaries who passed through on their way to Abyssinia.

Fig. (20) Scottish explorer James Bruce 1730- 1794

Social life of the Funj

Religion

The Funj originally practised a combination of traditional African religion and Christianity, but in **1523** the Funj upper class publicly converted to Islam. They had been instructed in Islam by of a small number of Islamic missionaries (jurists) who came from the larger Muslim world. However they continued to live by their traditional African customs and remained nominal Muslims. The second half of the 16th century many teachers came from the Muslim world to teach the Shari'a and the Arabized Nubian people became devout Muslims.

Groups in the Funj society

- **The Sultan and his court.** The Sultan had a council of 20 elders, the chief minister, court officials as well as secretaries and treasurers. Slaves worked in the court as treasurers.
- **The provincial sheikhs** and their courts: The army and civil servants of the sheikhs were almost all slaves and they lived within the compound.
- **The teachers of islamic law (fakis) were given special privileges in the society.** Some were exempted from taxes and others were given grants of land. In the early 18th century, particular families of fakis set themselves apart as the only teachers of Islam. The fakis had power and influence. They educated their followers well and helped to place them in the highest positions of government which allowed them to spread Islam.
- **The people** who were traders, cattle keepers, cultivators and builders.
- **The slaves.**

Customs: Every day at sunset there was drumbeating at Sennar and at Qarri and when people heard the drum they stopped what they were doing and shouted praise for the Sultan.

The Funj at war: It was the Sultan who led the army into battle. The army of the Sultan were horsemen drawn from the nobility, who wore chain mail and helmets made of iron or copper. They carried broadswords and shields made of elephant, giraffe or buffalo hide. The horses were covered in copper head-guards and thick blankets. Women carried delicious food for the Sultan on their heads and marched with the slave foot soldiers.

Economic life of the Funj

Taxes were paid to the Funj Sultan: The Funj Sultan, his Sheikhs or provincial governors used their horses to tax the settled cultivators and the cattle nomads of the Gezira. When the pastoralists were moving their herds between winter and summer grazing land they often stopped them at river crossings and forced to hand over some of their cattle as tax.

Cattle keepers: During the Funj Sultanate, herding of cattle continued as a way of life the nomads of the Gezira and in the southern rainforests.

They were traders and they controlled trade routes: The Funj traded in gold, ivory and ebony wood of the White Nile, ostrich feathers and rhinoceros horns. They also traded in slaves who were captured from weaker communities of the southern border. Traders in southern Nubia traded herbs and spices from Egyptian Gallaba (travelling merchants) in return for gum and incense. From the 15th century, the peoples in the north of Sudan who controlled the long distance caravan routes leading to Egypt and the Red Sea ports grew rich and powerful. In the 17th century, the Funj king controlled important trade routes. Goods of high value passed through the Funj Kingdom and the Funj King levied taxes on all trade. By the 18th century, West African Muslims travelled through the Funj Kingdom on their pilgrimage to Mecca. In those years, Sennar was a hub of international trade. The missionary and traveller, Theodore Krump, describes Sennar in 1701:

> **In all Africa…Sennar is close to being the greatest trading city.** Caravans are continually arriving from Cairo, Dongola, Nubia, from across the Red Sea, from India, Ethiopia, Darfur, Bornu and other kingdoms. This is a free city and men without any nationality or faith may live in it without a single hindrance. After Cairo, it is one of the most populous cities. Every day a public market is held in the public square.

There were towns in the Funj Kingdom: These were visited by caravans of merchants so historians believe that there were **many sedentary people and cultivators.**

The Funj were builders: Around 1600, they made a permanent settlement in Sennar. The *Funj Chronicle* states that Sultan Irbat started to build a mosque at Sennar. His son finished it and built a five storey palace.

Fig. (21) **The Palace of the Funj Sultans at Sennar.** Taken from a drawing made by F. Cailliaud and published in *Voyage a Meroë, au Fleuve Blanc* (1826-7)

The sheikhs in the provinces lived in palaces made out of stones and earth and surrounded by walls with three or four storey towers. Why do you think the Funj built four and five storey palaces?

Political organisation of the Funj

- The Funj Kingdom was not a centralised state but was feudal in character.

- The Funj sultan was the high king. The Sultan had power and wealth. He had power to give out land. In the 17th century, he controlled important trade routes, got a share of the ivory and gold that was traded. He received his share of the slaves captured in Kordofan and Nuba Mountains.

- The kingdom was divided into a number of provinces. Each province had a sheikh or a provincial governor and these sheikhs had much of the power.

- In the north of the Funj Kingdom, the strongest of these sheikhs was the Sheikh of Qarri. Known as the Abdallabi, these Arabs ruled with a great deal of independence.

- In the south, the heart of the Funj Kingdom, it was the sultan who appointed the provincial governors/sheikhs.

- Each year all the sheikhs had to report to the Sultan to show that they were still loyal to him. In 1701, the tribute of the Sheikh of Qarri was *"several hundred slaves, horses and camels, and a large sum of money"*.

- These sheikhs of the provinces received tribute from their own lesser chiefs, (who had the non-Arabic title of *makk*).

- Council of 20 elders: As a ruler the sultan never made decisions alone. The sultan had a council of 20 elders and a chief minister, the Vezir, helped him make decisions on important matters.

- Responsibilities of the sheikhs of the provinces: They looked after law and order in the country. They tried cases. The people paid taxes to them on crops and on the use of the water wheel. The people also built houses for the sheikhs and provided food for them and their army when they were travelling.

- The sheikhs married from noble families of other provinces, not from their own province.
- Their sons were brought up at the court at Sennar.

The decline of the Funj Kingdom

Slavery was the cornerstone of Funj wealth and power. In the 18th century, the Funj rulers built up a military division of slaves from foreign lands who were loyal only to themselves. By the mid 18th century, these Funj rulers were very powerful.

The tribal sheikhs became very strong in the areas which lay far from Sennar. In 1762, the Hamaj sheikhs of Kordofan led a revolt against the Funj king. The king lost his power to the Hamaj because the aristocracy did not approve of the growing importance of slave soldiers in the kingdom. As a result, subsequent Funj kings were just puppets of the chief minister.

The Funj Kingdom was greatly weakened by a series of succession disputes and revolts within the royal family. There was also internal rivalry between the powerful provincial rulers. When the regent was murdered in 1821, the kingdom fell apart. In 1821, the Funj kingdom was conquered by armies sent by Muhammad 'Ali, viceroy of Egypt.

Questions

1. Describe the social life of the Funj in the 17th and 18th centuries.
2. Outline the economic activities of the Funj.
3. The government of the Funj was feudal. What is the difference between a feudal government and a centralised government?
4. Describe how the Funj Sultan governed the Funj Kingdom.
5. Outline some challenges the Sultan would have in governing his kingdom.
6. Explain why the Funj kings lost their power in the 19th century.
7. What lessons can we learn from the decline and fall of the Funj Kingdom?

The main languages of South Sudan

Scholars agree that four great language families include all the languages spoken in Africa. Three of them, Nilo-Saharan, Niger-Kordofanian and Afro-Asiatic are represented in Sudan. Each language family is divided into groups and divided into sets of related languages. We will look at each of these language families in turn.

Nilo-Saharan languages

One of the great language groups on the African continent are the Nilo-Saharan languages.

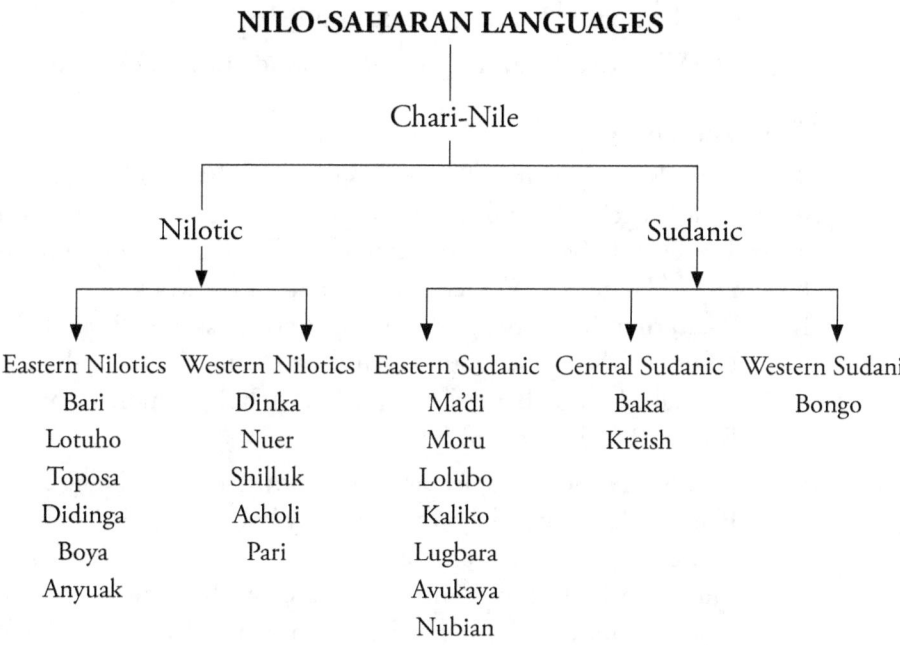

Fig. (22) The Classification the some of the Nilo-Saharan Languages of South Sudan

Nilo-Saharan languages stretch across the Saharan belt and have 6 subgroups. The largest of the 6 subgroups is called the Chari-Nile. Within the Chari Nile sub group we find the Sudanic and Nilotic languages of South Sudan.

Sudanic languages

The Sudanic languages are divided into three groups, Eastern Sudanic, Central Sudanic and Western Sudanic.

(i) The **Eastern Sudanic** languages include the Moru, Ma'di, Lulubo, Avukaya, Lugbara, Kaliko and Nubian. Most of these languages are spoken in Western Equatoria and Bahr el-Ghazal with the exception of Ma'di which is spoken in Eastern Equatoria, and the Kaliko, Lugbara and Lolubo which are spoken in Central Equatoria.

(ii) Among the **Central Sudanic** languages spoken in South Sudan are: the Bongo, Kreish, Mundu and Baka.

(iii) The Western Sudanic languages are found outside South Sudan.

Nilotic languages

The Nilotic languages are a large subgroup of the family of Nilo-Saharan languages. The Nilotic languages are spoken by those who live in Upper Nile basin and its tributaries. There are two groups in this family of languages, Western Nilotic and Eastern Nilotic.

(i) **Western Nilotic** peoples are also known as the River Lake Nilotics. The main groups include the Dinka, Nuer, Shilluk, Anyuak, Luo of Bahr el-Ghazal, the Acholi, Buuor, Belanda-Buuor, Pari, Lango and Jur.

(ii) **Eastern Nilotic** peoples are also known as Para-Nilotics or Plains Nilotics and they were formerly known as Nilo-Hamites as the language has strong features of the "northern zone" now called Cushite. The main groups are the Loi speaking Bari, Pojulu, Kuku, Kakwa. Nyangbara and the Mundari. Other Eastern Nilotics, who are not Loi speakers, are Murle, Didinga, Toposa, Lotuho, Lopit, Dongotono and Lango.

Niger-Kordofanian languages

A second language group on the African continent is the Niger Kordofanian language group.

The Niger-Kordofanian language group has two main branches. One branch is Niger-Congo and the second is Kordofanian.

a) **The Kordofanian languages** consist of about 30 to 40 languages spoken in the Nuba Mountains and its environs.

b) **The languages of the Niger-Congo** are called Bantu Languages. These languages spread across Africa eastwards and southwards from Cameroon and the Congo Basin. The largest Bantu group is the Azande of Western Equatoria and their language belongs to the Adamawa-Eastern division of Bantu languages. Smaller ethnic groups in Bahr el-Ghazal such as the Feroge, Golo, Ndogo, Belanda-Bviri, Togoya, Bai and Sere, also speak Bantu languages.

However, linguists and historians have not yet classified the Azande language with certainty, but they have generally agreed that it belongs to Ubangian language family which is spoken in Central African Republic, Congo, Cameroon and Western Equatoria State in South Sudan. It has been adopted and spoken by many Bantu and non-Bantu ethnic groups in South Sudan.

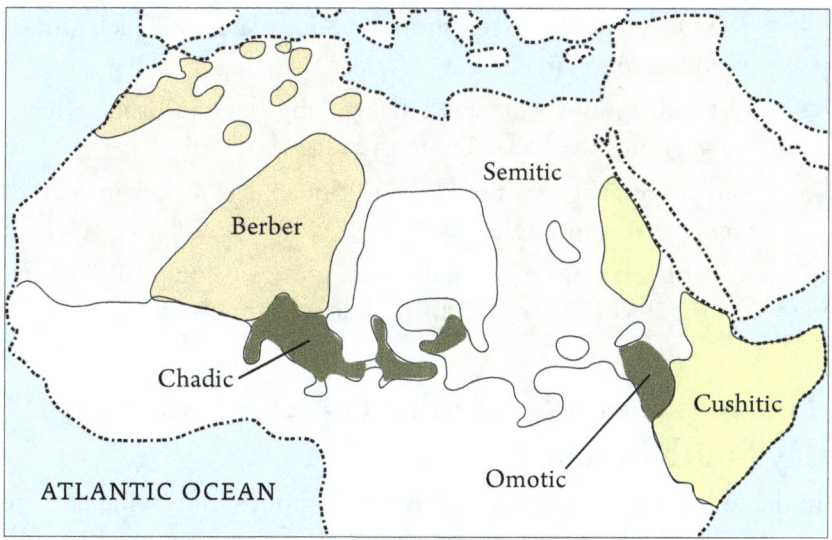

Fig. (23) Map of Afro-Asiatic languages in Africa and the Middle East
(*www.webspace.ship.edu/cgboer/languagefamilies.html*)

Afro-Asiatic languages

A third language group on the African continent is the group of Afro-Asiatic languages. The **Afro-Asiatic languages** are spoken across North Africa. These languages have a number of sub-groups today.

The Semitic languages are a largest subgroup of the family of Afro-Asiatic languages and are spoken by more than 460 million people across much of North and East Africa and in the Middle East. In Africa, this includes Morocco, Algeria, Tunisia, Libya, Egypt, Sudan, South Sudan, Kenya, Tanzania and Somalia.

Arabic is the most widely spoken Semitic language today with an estimated 206 million native speakers. In South Sudan people living in commercial centres speak pidgin Arabic.

Questions
1. State the two great language divisions found in South Sudan.
2. Name 3 groups of people from Eastern Nilotic, Western Nilotic and Sudanic peoples and state where they live in South Sudan.
3. Name a Sudanic language that is spoken in Eastern Equatoria.
4. The Dinka are the largest group in South Sudan. Which group are the second largest?
5. List four groups who speak Bantu languages and state where these groups live today in South Sudan.
6. Which language group of South Sudan has its origin in the Central African Republic?
7. To which language group do these groups belong: (i) the Bari (ii) the Beja (iii) the Kreish (iv) Luo of Bahr el-Ghazal?

The migration of Sudanic peoples to the present day South Sudan

In the following sections we discuss ethnic groups from some of these language families. Due to the vast number of ethnic groups in South Sudan it is only possible to select a very limited number of ethnic groups. The Ma'di has been selected as an example of a Sudanic people, the Bari as an example of Eastern Nilotics. To represent the Western Nilotic peoples, the Dinka and the Nuer are included as these are the most numerical in South Sudan today. Finally, the Shilluk (Chollo), the Anywaa and the Azande are also described here as these groups have a king.

Archaeological and language studies indicate that three of the main language groups came into Southern Sudan in the following order.

The central Sudanic peoples

The first people to arrive in Upper Nile and Western Equatoria were the Sudanic peoples, namely the Moru, Baka, Bongo, Kreish, and Avukaya. According to some historians, pioneering groups of these Sudanic people migrated southwards from Sahara into the forests of the south in the pre-Christian era as the Sahara was becoming a desert. In addition to animals, they brought knowledge of fire. With iron technology they changed their new environment. They gradually cleared the forests into savannas, so their new homeland became similar to what they had left behind in Sahara. It is likely that these Sudanic people were mixed farmers around 1000 BC and integrated the care of cattle and sheep with the cultivation of sorghum, sesame, pumpkins and gourds. Nowadays these former cattle herders are farmers.

We will now look at social, economic and political structures of the Ma'di, one group of the Sudanic people of South Sudan.

The Ma'di

The Ma'di means "human being". The Ma'di speak Ma'di tongue which is a Sudanic language related to the Moru, Lugbara, Kaliku, Logo, Lolubo and Avukaya, which provide evidence of their common origin.

Fig. (24) Ma'di women

Migration history

Some claim that the Ma'di people occupied a large area extending from Southern Sudan to Lake Albert. As time passed, they were invaded from all sides at different times. The Nilo-Hamites migrating from the Ethiopian highlands pushed the Ma´di southwestwards; The Luo from the north pushed them southwards; the Azande invaded them from the west and the Bunyoro from the south. As a result of conflict, the people were divided into different groups.

The Ma´di oral tradition, on the other hand, tells about a disagreement between two brothers at Amadi. One departed and travelled to the east until he and his Ma'di followers reached the River Nile. The brother who was left behind in Amadi formed the Moru group in the present day Western Equatoria around Mundri. On the arrival of the Eastern Nilotics, the Madi settled by the river bank and intermingled with the Bari until they migrated southwards. In addition, the Ma'di tradition claims that the Acholi and the Alur of Uganda are a result of intermarriage between Luo and Ma'di. Today, the Ma´di people inhabit the southwestern part of Torit district where the Nile River makes a sharp bend into Uganda. Ma´di people are also living in Uganda.

Political organisation

The Ma'di were traditionally known for their rainmakers and there used to exist more than 45 rainmaker centers among the Ma´di. Today some of the rain maker families can be identified but they do not practice it anymore. The Ma'di believed that the 'rain stones' come with the rain from the sky. By making use of a special set of stones, the rainmakers were believed to produce rain when it was needed. The Ma´di are organized in chiefdoms headed by a hereditary chief known as the Opi who had both political and religious powers.

Religious beliefs

Since the Ma'di believe that everything is born from the earth, Mother Earth plays a central part in daily life and also during traditional ceremonies, festivities and rituals. Ancestors are important, because they are believed to intercede directly with God in human affairs. The Ma'di attribute every trial and trouble to the anger of a spirit. In the event of a misfortune or illness, they consult a spirit-medium (ojjo or ojjogo) to find out which ancestor is behind the suffering. Sacrifices are then offered to the particular spirit in order to prevent it causing harm to the living. The dominant families among the Ma'di were believed to have powerful ancestral spirits to help them.

Economic and social life

The Ma'di were probably mixed farmers already around 1000 BC, and as well as caring for cattle and sheep, they cultivated sorghum, sesame and gourds. However, tsetse fly depleted the livestock population at the end of the nineteenth century and now the Ma'diare farmers with few cattle. In the past, cattle was used in the payment of a dowry but as cattle dwindled out, dowry payments were made in goats, sheep, arrows and hoes. The metal for the hoes was traditionally obtained from iron ore in the river beds. Today, instead of hoes and arrows, money is used in the payment of a dowry.

Fig. (25) Map showing where the Ma'di, Nuer and the Dinka are located today

> **Discuss in class**
> 1. In the text rainmakers and ancestral belief seem to be common among the Ma'di. What is the role of the rainmaker? Are there rainmakers in your tribe?
> 2. In your opinion do the ancestors play a role in societies in South Sudan today?

The migration of Eastern Nilotics

The Nilotic groups arrived in Southern Sudan after the Sudanic speakers, perhaps from 1000 AD onwards. The first people to arrive in Eastern and Central Equatoria were the Eastern Nilotics, also known today as Plains Nilotes or Nilo-Hamites. One group of these arethe Loi speaking Bari, Pojulu, Kuku, Kakwa, Nyangbara and the Mundari. Loi means nobles. Another group are the non-Loi speakers: Murle, Didinga, Toposa, Dongotono, Lopit, Lango and Lotuho.

The original home of these Eastern Nilotics was north of Lake Turkana in modern day Ethiopia. Their route to Equatoria was to the east and along the Nile between the Ethiopian highlands and the Sudd. Many Bari, for example, had begun their migration from Ethiopia in the mid 1600's when the Oromo invaded their territory. The Bari, Lotuho and Toposa arrived in Equatoria between 1500 and 1800 in different migrations. Many believe that they found the Madi already living in Equatoria.

The civilisation of the Nilotes

Eastern Nilotics carried with them a new form of political organization: the clan system and the early form of kingdom or rule by the rainmaker. They were considered the "lords of East Africa", with a lineage system of hereditary rule.

The Eastern Nilotics had above all the new warrior system of age sets developed from all the clans living together in an area or village. The warriors were controlled by a group of elders, wise men who controlled the wealth or cattle and the social order. Thus there was a balance of power within the groups, between the elderly and the young and between different clans.

A separate class was formed by the blacksmiths. They had some supreme powers and spirits, and although they were considered the lowest class in the society, they were feared and respected. The elders were the custodians of the customary law and when crimes were committed, they decided what compensation had to be paid.

Many of the Nilo-Hamites lived in family clusters in villages or small towns which were surrounded by wooden fences. There was an open area and meeting place in the centre. Here the king or rain maker lived with his wives, and surrounded by gates and enclosures for the close watch and control of the cattle. When attacked by their enemies, the Nilo-Hamites retreated to the mountains with the cattle and the women, while the warrior class stayed on to defend the village.

The Bari of South Sudan

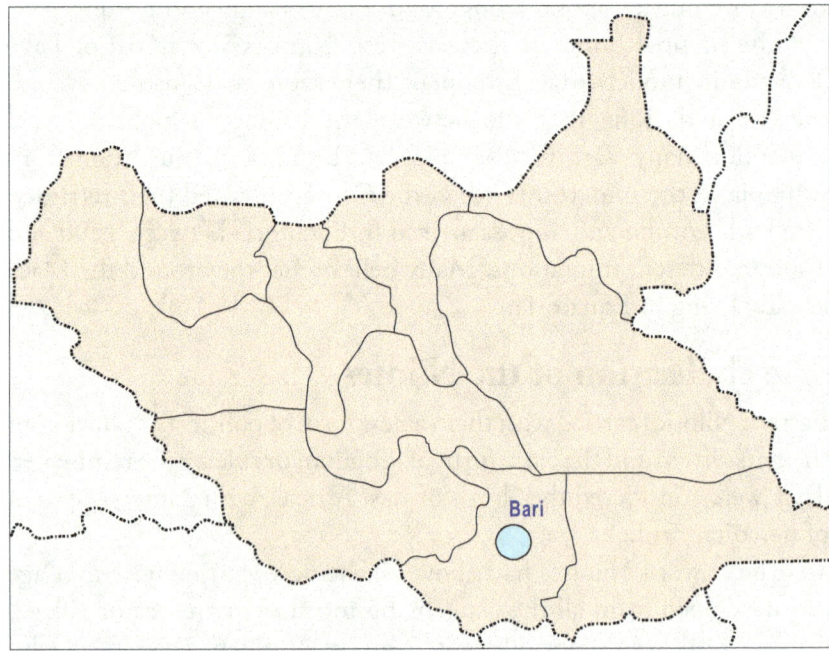

Fig. (26) The location of the Bari in South Sudan

Migration history

The Bari are an example of an Eastern Nilotic group. Their history dates back to the 15th century when the Bari came from Northern Abyssinia (Ethiopia) in large waves. The Bari probably arrived in their present location around the middle of the 17th or in early 18th century. According to oral tradition, their search for new settlement was caused by the Oromo, one of the largest Abyssinian tribes, who invaded their territory. Today, the population of that area of Ethiopia have the same physical appearance as the Bari of South Sudan. Linguistic studies tell us that the Bari came from Bahr al Jabal, that they moved southwards and westwards and settled in their present homelands.

Economic life

Slave traders caused suffering and depopulation: Since their arrival in the new land, the Bari people have been plagued by war and conflict, especially from slave raiders and from the Dinka and the Azande. Even before the 19th century, the Arabs and Turks involved in the ivory trade raided slaves from the Bari to supply domestic needs of their home communities and to sell them in the markets of northern Sudan and beyond.

Subsistence farming: Today, the Bari ethnic groups occupy the savannah lands of the Nile Valley around Juba. They are subsistence farmers whose main crops are sorghum, cassava, maize, simsim and groundnuts. They raise cattle to supplement their diet.

Social and political organisation

In the past there were two distinct groups in the society, the *lui* or free men and the *dupi* or serfs. The *lui* were the chiefs and the fathers of the soil and the *dupi* were those who had a trade e.g. ironmongers, fishermen, blacksmiths. The *dupi* were a hereditary class of serfs who had to give their services to the *lui*. Before colonial times, the Bari had the fathers of the land and the rainmakers who belonged to certain hereditary clans and they exercised both spiritual and secular power.

As Eastern Nilotes, the Bari today are divided on the basis of rank or status: young boys: young girls, initiates, warriors and elders.

> **Questions**
> 1. How would you describe the Bari? If you are not a Bari, how will you describe the relationship between your ethnic group and the Bari?
> 2. Describe the difference between the mixed farming of the Bari and pastoralism. Would you prefer to marry an agriculturalist or a pastoralist?
> 3. Many Bari live in and around Juba, the capital of South Sudan. What do you think are the advantages and disadvantages by living close to the capital city?

The migration of Western Nilotics (or River Lake Nilotes)

Linguistic studies strongly suggest that the cradle land of all Nilotic people is in central Sudan and archaeological studies support this evidence. However, with the exception of the Dinka, most Western Nilotes can remember only a residence in Southern Sudan.

The Western Nilotics such as the Dinka, Nuer, Shilluk, Luo of Bahr el-Ghazal, Anywaa, and Acholi arrived in Southern Sudan after the Eastern Nilotics. The Sudanic groups had settled in Bahr el-Ghazal from the first century AD.

According to oral tradition, the main group of Dinka and Nuer came to Bahr el-Ghazal in the period between 1400 to 1700 in different migrations southwards. Their route was west of and along the Nile. The Dinka migrated from the Gezira in the 15th and 16th centuries and the Nuer from the dry area of Kordofan in the 18th century. One cause of these migrations was drought. Another reason was to escape from Arab and Nubian slave raids. The Western Nilotics easily settled on the savannas made by the Sudanic groups.

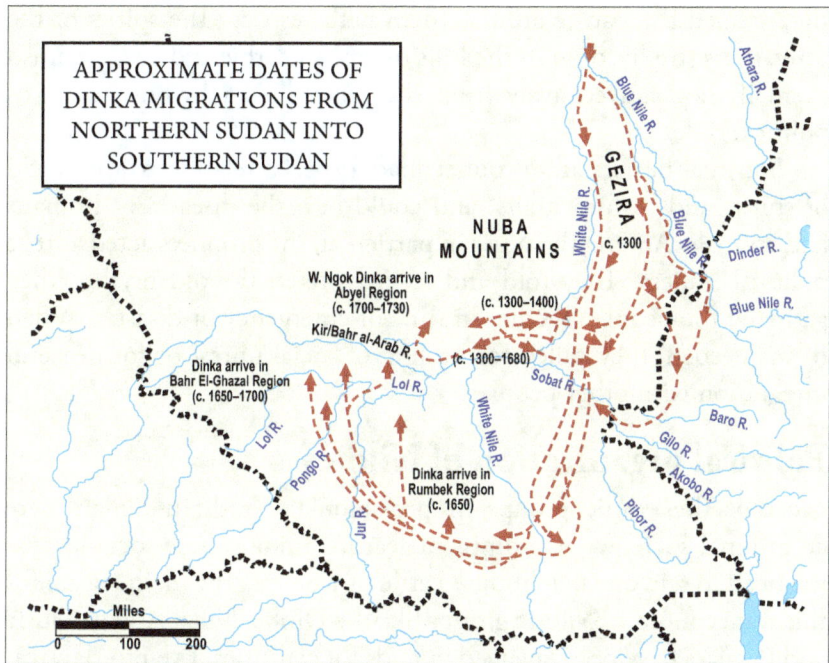

Fig. (27) Dinka Migrations according to oral traditions (*Rochester Press*)

The Luo groups among the Nilotes

From around 1500 the different Luo groups moved further from Bahr el-Ghazal to many parts of this region. These Luo groups are theShilluk, Anyuuaa,(Anuak) the Pari of Lafon, Acholi and Lango. They also moved into Uganda and north-western Kenya. The Luo were welcomed in many areas as friends and rulers because they could organize the defense and make peace with neighbouring groups through trade and negotiations. They were ruled by the Rethamong the Shilluk or by the Rwot among the Acholi.

Beliefs of Nilotes

Back in Nilo-Nubian times, Nilotes may have had a notion about a supreme god, the spirit of Jok. They had a highly developed sense of spiritual belief. For Nilotes, all living things had spirits, and therefore they treated the nature around them with respect. The spirits of the forefathers still lived on in the hills or rivers nearby, and could punish them if they strayed away from the established religious, social or political order.

Spiritual healers and prophets had a special relation to the world of spirits and to forefathers, and could heal the diseases of humans and animals. Among the Nuer in particular, the prophets acted as true political leaders. They told and re-interpreted the old myths. They gathered the people together in time of emergency or disaster. When it was needed, they called for healing of social unrest or for peaceful integration with other peoples.

Political organization of Nilotes

Most of the ethnic groups in pre-colonial Southern Sudan were communal societies. A prominent feature among these societies was the need to raid one neighbour's cattle or women. The main reason for this was economic. Nilotic groups like the Dinka, Nuer, Atwot, Murle and Baggara have been engaged in raids for centuries. Even to-day, this is common among the Didinga and the Toposa in Eastern Equatoria. Women were also important and were raided for agricultural and household help.

Economic life of Nilotes

With different combinations and emphasis, the Nilotes grew finger millet and bulrush durra (sorghum), yams, pumpkins, cow peas, and sesame. They reared goats, sheep, hens and cattle and also had donkeys and dogs. Some groups had the old African cattle from the green Sahara region and others brought in the Indian cattle with humps. The new open grasslands, which were developed by the Sudanic people in Southern Sudan during the first millennium after Christ, facilitated cattle keeping. Among the Western Nilotics, cattle symbolised wealth and social position and cows were deeply rooted in their culture and identity. They managed to control the animal diseases, especially the sleeping sickness derived from tsetse flies, originally living in forest areas near water. The Nilotes also picked wild berries, fruits and roots and ate fish.

> **Questions**
> 1. State four examples of Central Sudanic peoples.
> 2. Explain the effects of the migration of the Central Sudanic people from the Sahara to Southern Sudan in the pre-Christian period.
> 3. Why are the Bari, Pojulu, Kuku and other Nilo-Hamites called Eastern Nilotics?
> 4. Outline the effect of the migration of the Eastern Nilotics (Nilo-Hamites) in the pre-colonial period in southern Sudan.
> 5. List five western Nilotic groups.
> 6. Explain two reasons for the migration of the Western Nilotics (River Lake Nilotes) in the 15th and 16th centuries.
> 7. What does it mean to be a communal society?

The Shilluk (Chollo) Kingdom of the White Nile

Fig. (28) A Shilluk warrior

Fig. (29) A Shilluk girl in 1950

Origins and migration of the Shilluk (Chollo)

The name Shilluk is a corruption of Chollo, who are the main group of the Shilluk clans. Oral tradition states that sometime in the 15th century, Nyikang, the founder of the Chollo nation, separated from other Luo groups somewhere in Bahr el-Ghazal. According to oral tradition, Nyikang led his followers north along the Nile in rafts and canoes, searching for a suitable place to settle. They arrived at their present location at the junction of the Nile and Sobat rivers around 1500 A.D. and settled near Malakal. They fought several wars with the Funj and defeated them.

Language and formation of the Shilluk (Chollo)

The Shilluk speak a Nilotic language of the Chari-Nile branch of the Nilo-Saharan family. They are the only Nilotic people to honour a king called *reth*. They are the largest group of the Western Nilotic group (sometimes called Luo group) that lives today on both banks of the White Nile in South Sudan. In the 16th century, the small group spoke the Luo language and incorporated Funj, Nuba and some small ethnic groups. Tradition has it that Nyikang's son, Dak, was the most influential in the establishment of the kingdom. In the second half of the 17th century, these groups with different cultures and economic traditions came together to form the Shilluk or Chollo Kingdom. By then they were sedentary agriculturalists.

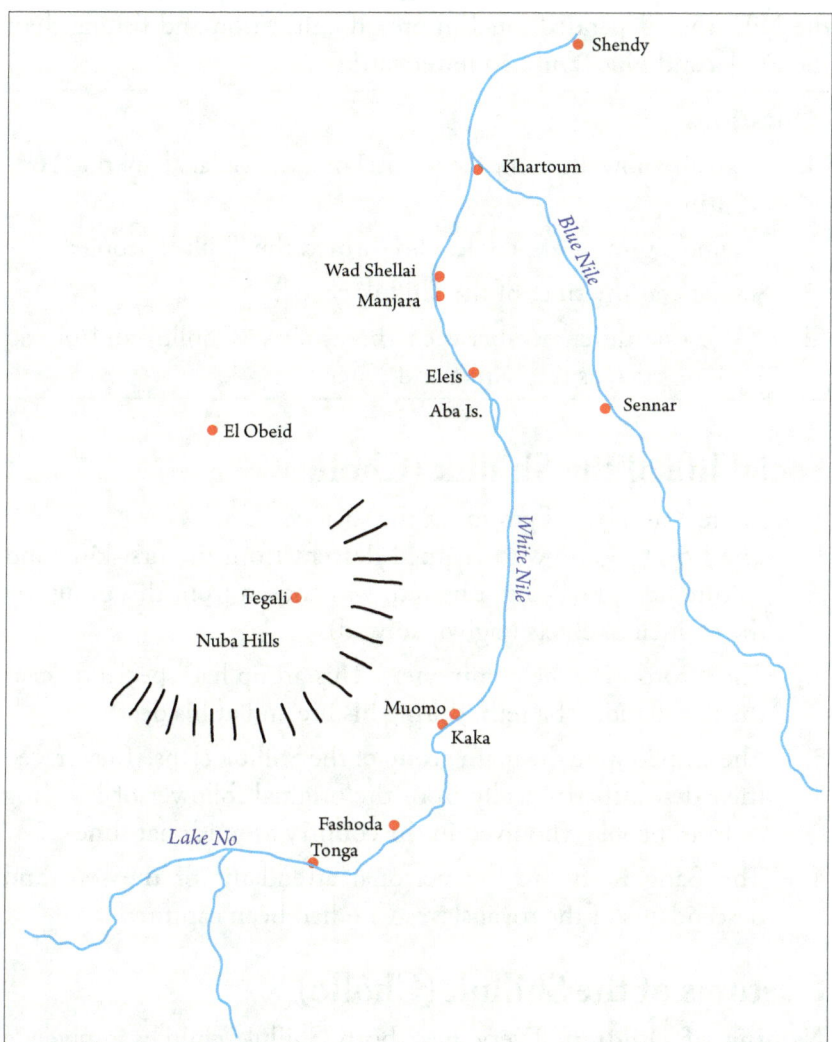

Fig. (30) Map of the Shilluk heartland.

Settlement of the Shilluk (Chollo)

The Shilluk settled along the west bank of the Nile between Lake No and latitude 12°N in the south of the Sudan, just north of the point where it becomes the White Nile. With easy access to good land along the Nile, they depended much more on cultivation and fishing than the Dinka and Nuer and had fewer cattle.

> **Questions**
> 1. Explain how Luo speakers got land in Malakal in the 16th century?
> 2. Name 3 groups of people who formed the Shilluk people?
> 3. What was the ruler of the Shilluk called?
> 4. Give one difference between the Shilluk (Chollo) and other Nilotes such as the Dinka and Nuer.

Social life of the Shilluk (Chollo)

There were a number of groups in the society.
1. The Royal House who claimed descent from the first king and culture hero, Nyikang. The reth was chosen from this group by the council of chiefs (jagiwipadiwad).
2. The Ororo were the commoners. This group had special tasks at the installation of a reth, during his life and at his death.
3. The Chollo were the main group of the Shilluk clans. They traced their descentpatrilineally from the original followersof Nyikang or from people who lived in the country around that time.
4. The Bang Rethwere the personal attendants of the reth and descendants of the royal slaves who had been captured.

Customs of the Shilluk (Chollo)

Naming of children: Every new born Shilluk child was given a milk name, the meaning of which may relate to the experience or circumstance of the parents or close relative e.g. Okach or Nyakach refers to famine; Oyoo or Nyayoo having been born on the road. A child could be named after some important person including a departed Reth. In this case, the child was taken and offerings made on that person's grave or shrine of the Reth. The Shilluk by tradition don't name a child after a living person.

Initiation ceremonies: There was a dance ceremony for initiating boys into adulthood. For the first time, the young man wore dance regalia consisting of a leopard skin and wild-cat skin, beads made from shells of ostrich eggs and a necklace made from tail of giraffe. The young man began to prepare his own sorghum field and to organize his marriage.

Marriage: Marriage was the ultimate goal of every adult male and female. However, marriage to blood relatives or in-laws was not permitted. Courtship could last for up to a year or more. Once marriage had been decided on, the girl informed her mother who then informed the father or paternal uncle in case the father is deceased. Once the man had been accepted and announced, the initial bride price was paid. The Shilluk dowry was a minimum of ten cows and thirty sheep and goats. Divorce was rare but if it happened, the dowry was returned.

Beliefs of the Shilluk (Chollo)

According to Shilluk tradition, the Shilluk king is the reincarnation of Nyikang, the original leader and hero of the Shilluk nation. The reth is the one who intercedes for the people with God called Juok. So the reth is the central figure in Shilluk religion as well as a symbol of political unity.

Economic life of the Shilluk (Chollo)

The Shilluk engaged in various economic activities. These included:

Crop cultivation: The Shilluk were sedentary agriculturalists. Both men and women did agricultural work. Some of the common crops were maize, durra, beans, sesame and pumpkin. The Shilluk became important producers of African gum.

Livestock: The wealth and social position of the Shilluk were estimated in cattle. Sheep and goats were kept and cows were highly regarded. The Shilluk lived beside the river so there is no need to migrate to cattle camps for summer grazing. In the summer the cattle were taken across to islands and the youths accompanying them built temporary cattle camps. Men hunted, herded and milked the livestock. Boys and old men milked the cows. Women were not allowed to milk.

Fishing: Fish were speared and the hippopotamus was harpooned.

Hunting and gathering: The Shilluk hunted by surrounding an area and speared the animals as they attempted to escape but game obtained from hunting was only a small part of their diet. The Shilluk women and children also gathered wild fruits and leaves of certain trees.

The Shilluk were excellent craftsmen. The blacksmiths manufactured jewelry, spears for hunting and fighting, daggers and agricultural tools. They made their dug-out canoes were small as their only wood was the *doleib* palm tree and small rafts like the reed rafts of the ancient Egyptians. Their thatching of the royal shrines was among the best along the rivers in Sudan. As well as making pottery, women decorated clothes with beads, made baskets and mats from woven grass and produced smoking pipes from bamboo and clay.

Shilluk trade was not highly developed. The Shilluk carried out small scale barter with the Arabs and other neighbours. They traded strips of hippo-hide for making whips. They traded spears and pots, hides and various vegetables for cattle, salt, iron, grain and cloth. The Shilluk did not have the important commodities of salt and iron. For salt, most Shilluk substituted cows' urine. The purchase of iron must have been the most important element in Shilluk trade with neighbouring peoples.

River raiding: From the seventeenth to the nineteenth centuries the Shilluk were known as river-raiders who dominated the White Nile and often raided sedentary Arab peoples living to the north as well as the Dinka, Nuer and Anywaa. The Shilluk fortunes changed in 1861 when their territory was attacked by Muhammad Kheir.

> **Task:** Imagine you are a young man of the Shilluk. Describe your life among your people. Your answer should include reference to the role of Nyikang in your culture, your initiation rite, bride wealth, diet, occupation, trades and skills among your people.

Political organisation

Since their first wars with the Dinka between 1600 and 1650, the Shilluk (Chollo) people have been a centralized monarchy, and thus unique among the Western Nilotic peoples. The kingship grew out of the need to control conquered non-Luo peoples. The divine king (reth) was chosen from the sons of previous kings. His duty was to perform the sacrifices to Nyikang and he made sure that the shrines of Nyikang were maintained. He was the symbol of political unity.

The Shilluk Kingdom was divided into two principal political divisions: the north (Gar) and the south (Lwak). It was divided into 15 provinces, each under a paramount chief. A province consisted of eleven settlements with clear boundaries and common grazing and fishing areas. These settlements were under the administration of a chief who was directly responsible to the reth.

> **Questions**
> 1. Most Nilotics do not have centralised political organisation. Can you think of any advantages of a centralised system?
> 2. What are the disadvantages of decentralised organization?
> 3. Describe the political organisation of the Shilluk (Chollo).

The Anywaa

Known by the neighbours as the Anywaa the language the language of the Anywaa is close to that of the dhok- Shilluk (Chollo) and dho-Luo of Bahr el-Ghazal.

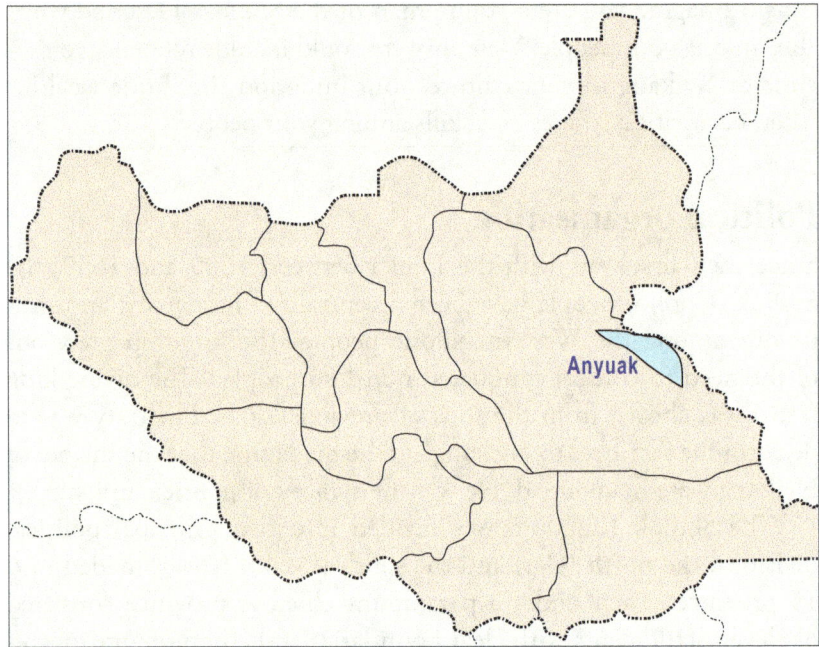

Fig. (31)   The location of the Anywaa in South Sudan

Origin and migration history

Like the Shilluk (Chollo) the Anywaa trace their origins to the "country of Dimo". Nyikango, and his brother Gilo with their followers moved northwards from Bahr el-Ghazal with other Luo people. They journeyed towards Khartoum before returning to the Shilluk area around Malakal. Nyikango, whom the Anywaa call Akango, settled there and Gilo led the majority of the people northwards and eastwards up the Sobat. It is not known which peoples they dislodged during these migrations.

At the beginning, the people were ruled only by traditional chiefs. Usually they were leaders of kindred people and had hereditary powers. According to tradition, Gilo's grandson, Cuwai was the first king of the Anywaa and the descendants of his children became the Anywaa people. With the arrival of kingship, the Anywaa had a stronger system. It brought law and order. Often the kings were tyrants, so people migrated and settled elsewhere.

Among the Anywaa, the most scorned people are the Nuer and Murle. The Anywaa lost control of the Sobat region about 1840 when they were invaded by the Nuer and cut them off from their closest relatives, the Shilluk. They continued to be pushed eastwards until the early twentieth century. In addition, the Anywaa raided the Murle for cattle, women and children and Murle raids brought intolerable instability to the agricultural Anywaa. These raids caused many of them to migrate and settle some distance from their traditional Anywaalands. Today the Anywaa live in Pochalla and Akobo counties along the banks of the river Baro, Gilo and Akobo-Piborrivers extending into western Ethiopia.

Social organisation

The Anywaa society is communal. Inter-village relationships are marked by solidarity and the sharing of resources especially in times of disease and famine is compulsory.

There are no ceremonies related to birth or the passage to adulthood. The Anywaa are polygamous. At time of marriage, dimui beads with a few cattle are paid to the girl's family. In recent times, money is exchanged instead of dimui beads. The Anywaa wear many beads and other ornaments such as the tail of giraffe.

They have a strong belief in spirits.They believe they can communicate with those of have departed through a medium.Juok has the same role as among the Shilluk (Chollo), but prayer and sacrifice is usually offered directly to Juok in time of illness.

Political system of the Anywaa

Anywaa-land is really a federation of villages under a High King. The village is the largest political unit. Each village is self sufficient and has its own government and its own court of justice. Each village has its own headman and the line of a headman in one village cannot be replaced by the line of another headman.

These village headmen are under the sub-chiefs who administer the villages on behalf of a Nyie. Since the Anglo- Egyptian period all the Nyie reportto he who is the highest Nyieof the Anywaa, he who is in possession of the royal throne and the bead.

The Anywaa respect the Nyie (king). The investiture of an Anywaa king is similar to that of a Shilluk *reth* but the death of the Nyieis different to that of the *reth*. When his life is nearing an end, he tells his people that his spirit has returned to the river from which he came. His anointed son succeeds him. His body is buried in the ordinary way. The people do not cry but they play drums and blow trumpets and praise the deeds of dead king.

Economic life

The Anywaa are predominantly agriculturalists and are an industrious people. They grow sorghum, maize, simsim, beans and tobacco. They have some cattle, goats and fowl. They fish and hunt. They trade with other villages especially in tobacco. In the past, they were involved in slave raids against their neighbours and exchanged slaves for guns from the people of the highlands. According to some sources, Anyuua youth pan for gold today near Dima and Maji and exchange the gold for dimui beads or other goods with Ethiopian highlanders.

Questions
1. Where do the Anywaa live today in South Sudan?
2. Give one difference and one similarity between the Anywaa and the Shilluk?
3. Look at the picture of Anywaa beads in Chapter 1. Describe the role of beads in the life of the Anywaa. Are beads important in your culture?

The Nuer

The Nuer call themselves Naath, meaning human beings, and they are one of the biggest ethnic groups in South Sudan and Western Ethiopia. In South Sudan they live mostly in Unity State and the Upper Nile Province. They are located around the junction of the Nile River and the Bahr el-Ghazal and Sobat River and along the Sobatacross the border into Ethiopia.

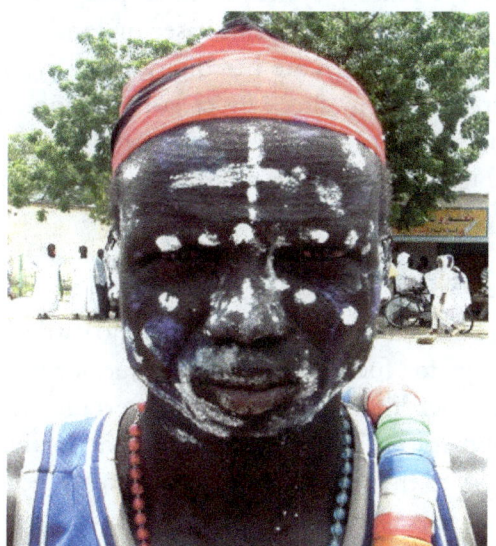

Fig. (32) A man from a Nuer tribe with traditional marks on his forehead and colorful painting on his face.

Migration history

Oral tradition indicates that the Nuer migrated south from the drought ridden area of Kordofan around 1700 and arrived at the rivers of Bahr el-Ghazal. As a result of the Baggara slave raids into Bahr el-Ghazal in the 18th century, the Nuer initiated a mass migration east of the Nile. They occupied a vast Dinka and Anywaa territory and increased their territory fourfold. In this process, many Dinka were absorbed into the Nuer culture so that the Nuer people are similar to the Dinka in aspects of culture and language. While many scholars state that most Nuer have a Dinka background, others believe that Nuer have a Luo origin, like the Anywaa and Shilluk. The split into different ethnic groups probably occurred due to disputes over cattle and they have been in regular conflict over the last 300 years.

Political organization

The Nuer have no centralized political organization, instead their society is kin-based. The kinship system includes people related both by descent and marriage. When a society is based on kinship, generally it means that family relationships are hereditary through the father's side. The Nuer keep conflict in check by creating alliances that vary according to the context: those who are one's enemy in one situation are one's ally and supporter in another situation because of lineage alliances.

Economic life of the Nuer

Like the Dinka, the Nuer culture is organized around cattle. The cattle are not primarily kept for food, although the Nuer drink milk. An animal is sacrificed when the Nuer meet at important celebrations. Due to their location in the Upper Nile valley, fish, particularly the Nile perch, is also an essential part of their subsistence economy. In addition, vegetables and millet are important parts of their diet, but are not produced for sale in the market. In some areas of Nuerland, the millet supply seldom lasts the whole year, and when it is exhausted, the people are dependent on milk and fish. The Nuer remove blood from their cattle, which is a supplementary diet in the dry season.

Discussion question

Sometimes there are conflicts between pastoralists and agriculturalists. Why is this in your opinion?

The Dinka

The Dinka are the largest ethnic group in South Sudan. They call themselves Moinjaang, "People of the people." In the broader Nilotic family, the Dinka languages are most closely related to the Nuer.

Migration history

We mentioned that the Dinka migration from the current Gezira areas to the hot and humid swamplands of the Bahr-el-Ghazal region of the Nile Basin was caused by drought and by slave raids of Nubian slave raiders. They were one of the last groups to arrive in modern day South Sudan. Before them were the pastoralist Shilluk, Anyuak, Nuer, Luo and Atwot.

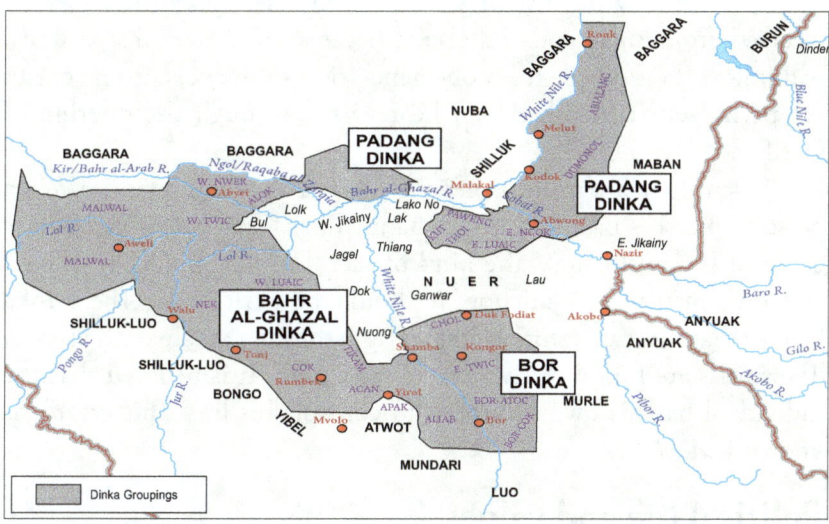

Fig. (33)   Location of the Dinka in twentieth century Southern Sudan.

Slave raids into Dinka territory is a recurring feature of life in Dinka oral history and memory. The Islamic Sennar Sultanate in the 16th and 17th century and the Islamic Baggara in the 18th century led massive slave raids into Southern territory. In Northern Sudan they cemented an impression of "Southerners" as inferior, as slaves, and as infidels. Due to this attitude Northerners seldom marry southerners: 'you do not marry a slave', and in the Dinka community one is not expected to marry a slave trader. The experience of slave raids may be one reason why the Dinka did not convert to Islam. Today the Dinka people are located in the greater Bahr el-Ghazal and Upper Nile regions.

Religious beliefs of the Dinka

The beliefs of the people are centred in the origin of their ancestors. There are many myths surrounding the creation of the first ancestors and each clan has its own stories about the origin of its ancestors and their own totems. Some clans have their own gods such as Mayual or Malondit.

The Dinka think that the past misdeeds of their ancestors affect their present way of life. They believe that the curses the ancestors received from their gods or others because of their transgressions, will follow their people from one generation to the next. Some curses are permanent and others can be reversed through the offering of sacrifices.

When there are misfortunes the head of the family visits a *tiet*, a person who sees past and future happenings. The *tiet* will relate the cause of the misfortune, the kind of sacrifice that should be offered and give instructions on how it should be performed. The Dinka believe that their ancestors send messages through dreams and visions. The spirits are found in rivers, lakes and trees. It is believed that the individual has his own creator who controls his life. This creator is known is *Achiek*.

Political life and values

The Dinka have no centralised political authority, instead they have many independent and interlinked clans. Each Dinka clan has very many sub-clans. Each clan has its own paramount chief who is assisted by an assistant paramount chief and by chiefs of the sub-clans to keep order. The responsibility of the paramount chief is to receive the taxes collected by the sub chiefs for the government. The paramount chief sometimes instigates development projects and negotiates the establishment of schools and clinics.

The chief of the sub-clan is responsible for the sub-clan. He is elected by all the sub-clans in the community. He must be informed of all activities and disputes among them. He is usually very much to the fore in the settlement of disputes and he is known to arbitrate by peaceful persuasion. He is not a political ruler but a spiritual leader whose power rests on his wisdom. The chief should be upright man and a model of virtue and in Dinka terms "a man with a cool heart" who depends on persuasion and consensus rather than coercion.

The numerical dominance of the Dinka has been easily accomplished for they are polygamous and observe levirate marriage. In the past, their first wives were prominent Dinka women and all subsequent wives were obtained at the lowest possible bride price.

Despite the warlike profile of the Dinka, their moral values emphasise the ideals of peace, unity, harmony, persuasiveness and mutual cooperation. These values are summarized in a concept known as *cieng*. *Cieng* is the Dinka way of living together. At the core of *cieng* are the values of dignity and integrity, honour and respect, loyalty and the power of persuasion. *Cieng* does not only encourage unity and harmony but it involves helping one's fellowmen and women. Good *cieng* is the opposite to coercion and violence. The Dinka also believe that solidarity, harmony and mutual cooperation are more fittingly achieved voluntarily and by persuasion. *Cieng* applies equally to men and women and to all age groups.

Fig. (34) A Dinka, delighted with his cows near Rumbek, South Sudan.

Economic life

The main economic activity is nomadic pastoralism. The cow is deeply rooted in Dinka culture and identity. A Dinka will kill and even risk his life for a single cow. Proud of their vast herds, the Dinka believe that their wealth is the envy of other pastoralist peoples. The Dinka rear cattle for dowry and prestige as well as for beef. A girl's bride wealth is usually between one hundred and a hundred and fifty cows. Cattle are also central to social events such as marriages, funerals and the settlement of disputes.

As well as cattle keeping, the economy of the Dinka includes agriculture and fishing. During the rainy season, the young men and girls stay in the cattle camp with their cattlewhile the parents and some of the young people cultivate at home. The main crops grown for subsistence include groundnuts, sorghum, millet and simsim. After the harvest, if the family have more than ten cows, the entire family usually go to the cattle camp. They move from one cattle camp to another in search of pasture. During this season they depend on fishing and on their cattle for milk. The main methods used in fishing include the use of hook and line (*agoor*), the gill net (*abuoi*) and the fishing spear (*bith*). Fish are dried or smoked to preserve them and any surplus is sold. To earn money, some also sell milk in nearby towns. The Dinka also keep sheep, goats and poultry. Some practice blacksmithing and carpentry.

Questions
1. Describe the economic life of the Dinka.
2. Outline the tasks and values of a Dinka chief.
3. How many differences can you find between the Dinka and the Shilluk (Chollo)?

The Kingdom of the Azande

A Bantu group in South Sudan

While the Nilotic peoples dominated the Bahr el-Ghazal region of Southern Sudan, the non-Nilotic Azande, Moru-Ma'di and others, settled in Equatoria. The Azande are a Bantu group who occupy the largest part of the south western region of South Sudan.

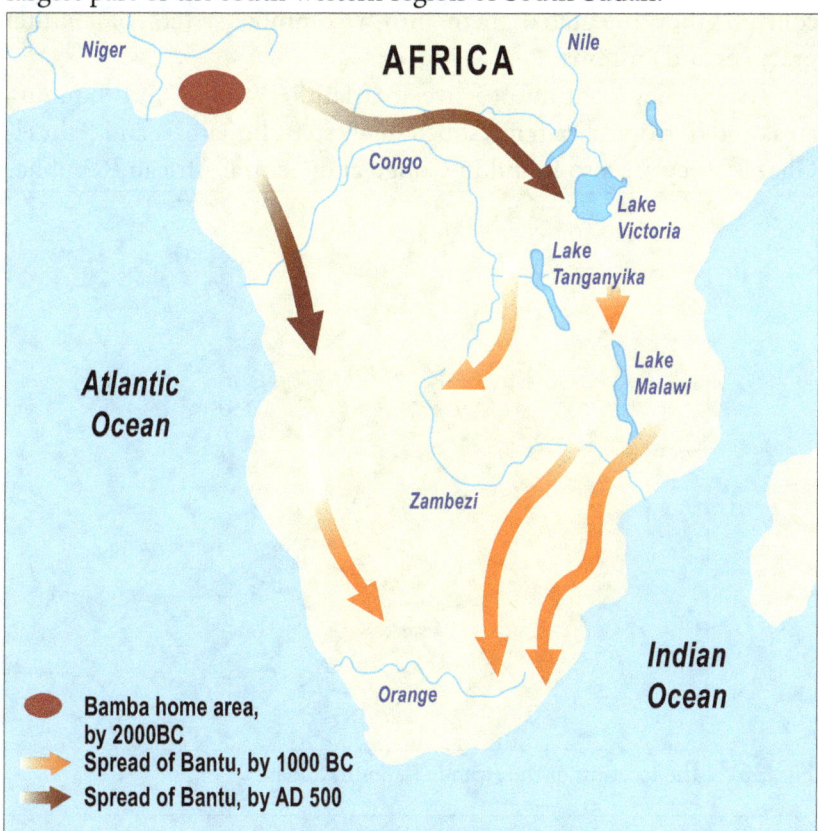

Fig. (35) The Bantu migrated eastwards and southwards

The Azande are the largest nationality in South Sudan after the Dinka and Nuer clans. Originally they came from the west and migrated into Congo in the 17th century. They were the last major group to arrive in south western Sudan from the Congo basin in the latter part of the

18th century. The name *Azande* means "the people who possess much land".

In the second half of the 18th century, the Avungara leadership with the help of the Ambomu people whom they had conquered, began to move into south western Sudan from the Central African Republic. Without superior technology, they succeeded in bringing many culturally diverse groups under their military and political control. They integrated them into a common system of cultural practices and customs.

Today, they continue to live in Maridi, Yambio and Tambura areas and in tropical rain forest belt of Western Equatoria and Bahr el-Ghazal. They are also found in Congo and Central African Republic.

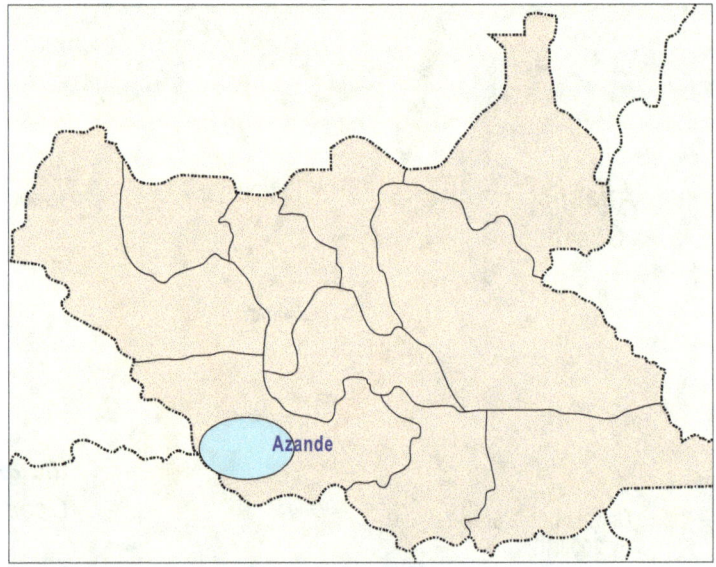

Fig (36)   The location of the Azande in South Sudan.

Questions
1. Where do the Azande live today in South Sudan?
2. Name countries outside South Sudan where the Azande are found today.

Social organization

Traditionally, the kingdoms were independent of each other and governed by a king or paramount chief. The king or the chief headed their own military forces. Being a deeply hierarchical society, the paramount chiefs, the Avungara royal family, were on top. The Avungara are the descendants of their great King Gbudwe and his two sons Yambio and Tambura. Next there were the Ambomu, whose cradle land was the valleys of the Mbomuriver in Central African Republic. They fought under the leadership of the Avongara when there was war. The third group of people were the Auro, the conquered people who were the majority. The slaves, captured in war were at the bottom of the social hierarchy. The headman of each clan was under a prince or a chief.

Traditional beliefs

Prayers were addressed to the Supreme Being, Mboli, who was given great respect. They believed that Mboli is the Creator of all. Mboli had no special dwelling place. They prayed and offered sacrifice to Mboli to avoid evil caused by spirits. Some prayed to Mboli many times a day to protect them as they went about their work. Professional rainmakers did not exist among the Azande.

The Azande religious system plays a very important part in the support of theAzande moral values. They have chiefs who act as judges and spiritual leaders. They do not believe in natural death, there has to be a reason and someone who has caused the misfortune. There is a strong belief in witchcraft. The Azande believe that anyone is able to cause misfortune to another human being by ill will toward that person, even if he was not aware of so doing. Through use of oracles, the Azande find out who was the guilty of bewitching his neighbours. The Azande contact the oracle by rubbing two wooden sticks together as the names of different suspects are called out. When the pieces stick together, instead of rubbing smoothly against each other, the guilty one is identified.

Customs around birth and married life

Pregnant women do not eat certain foods, for example, the meat of the waterbuck, and some kinds of sweet potato. Four days after the child is born, a fire of green leaves is lit at the entrance of the house. The mother sits in the smoke of the fire with the child in her arms for half an hour. This is said to make the child strong. In the past, dowry of about twenty spears was paid to the girl's family when she married.

Gender roles are clearly marked among the Azande.. When a woman serves food to her husband, she does not eat in front of him. She draws water and breaks off fire wood for him and hoes his father´s cultivation. Azande men are polygamous, which means they can have many wives. Traditionally men were allowed to beat their wives.

Political organisation of the Azande

The Azande had many kingdoms. Traditionally, the Azandeempire was divided into a number of kingdoms, each founded by a chief or noble of the Avungara. Each kingdom was independent and governed by a king or paramount chief and had its own army.

Fig. (37) The Azande prepare for battle in the early 20th century.

The provincial governors: These kingdoms were further divided into provinces, each province was administered by a governor, who was usually a younger brother or son of the king, or by a few wealthy commoners appointed by him. The early Avungara provided ruling kings and nobles, but they did not set up an inclusive, centralised state. It was the Ambomuconquerors who brought culturally diverse groups under their control and taught them a common system of cultural practices and customs.

The Local chiefs: The provincial governors ruled through local chiefs. They used witchcraft and oracles to administer justice to thieves, and those suspected of adultery as well as to those who murdered through bewitching. Many of these punishments were very severe in the past.

Succession practices: It was not superior military technology but the pattern of succession that caused the Azande to increase the size of their territory. Succession to the office of chief was usually by the elder son or another son selected by the father. A man succeeded to his father's throne only when he had conquered those of his brothers who chose to compete for it. At the time of the selection of a new king, one or more of the brothers, a prince without land or people but with followers looking for the fruits of conquest, undertook to find and to rule a previously unconquered group.

Economic life

Agriculture: The Azande have always been gatherers and agriculturalists focusing on subsistence agriculture. Their staple crop is finger millet and they grow maize, rice, groundnuts, sweet potatoes, soya beans and cassava. They cultivate fruits such as mangoes, pineapples, and bananas. They grow coffee, oil bearing palm and sesame plants. Non-food crops such as jute, tobacco and cotton are common. They are not pastoralists, because of insects who caused sleeping sickness in the country. Some families keep goats and sheep.

Hunting and fishing: The Azande engage in hunting and they fish in the streams. **Forestry:** Much of the country is covered with forests and those involved in forestry grow hard wood trees such as teak, mahogany and cinderella.

Handicraft: The Azande make excellent barkcloth, baskets woven from bark and leaves of palm. They produce different types of wooden goods, tables and chairs.

Ironwork: Blacksmiths make bows and arrows and special iron knives and swords.

Gender roles are marked among the Azande.

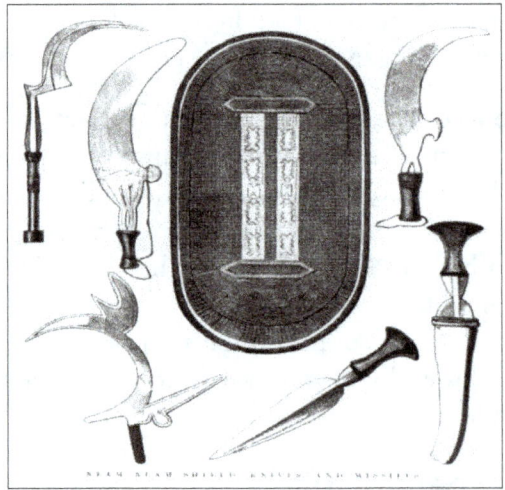

Fig. (38) and (/39) Picture of pottery and knives and a shield of bark cloth

Questions

a) What does a hierarchical society mean?

b) It is stated in the text that the Azande do not believe in natural death, and that there has to be a reason for it, for example, bewitching. What is the situation among the other peoples in South Sudan? Is bewitching common among your people?

c) In the past, the Southern Sudanese groups governed themselves and practised their beliefs. Outline three similarities and three differences between a Nilotic group and the Azande.

d) Outline the social, economic and political organisation of the Azande.

Questions on the peoples of the present day South Sudan

1. State the two great language divisions found in the present day South Sudan.
2. Name 3 groups of people from Eastern Nilotic, Western Nilotic and Sudanic peoples and state where they live in South Sudan.
3. Which language group do you connect with the area north of Lake Turkana?
4. Name a Sudanic language that is spoken in Eastern Equatoria.
5. The Dinka are the largest group in South Sudan. Which group are the second largest?
6. List four groups who speak Bantu languages and state where these groups live today in South Sudan.
7. Which language group of South Sudan has its origin in the Central African Republic?
8. To which language group do these groups belong: (i) the Bari (ii) the Nubians (iii) the Beja (iv) the Kreish (v) Luo of Bahr el-Ghazal?

3
Nineteenth-Century Turning Point

Introduction

The 19th century could be called a turning point for what is now called South Sudan because of the great consequences the Turkish invasion had on the territory. Before 1850 different clans and peoples migrated across the South, and there was a gradual extension of pasturelands and cultivation. The region was well populated, cultivated, with large herds of domestic animals. From 1850, however, this development was broken by the activities of different governments. As a result of slavery and disease an extensive depopulation took place in the valleys west of the Nile,

Economic and social development in Southern Sudan by 1850

The Sudanic zone extends from Upper Egypt down to the Great Lakes. The inhabitants of this zone had interacted among themselves in terms of migration, settlements and marriages for a long time. The people here had their political, social and economic ways of life. Politically, most of these societies were egalitarian, like most Nilotes. Few of them were monarchical like the Shilluk (Chollo) and Azande kingdoms.

The population in Southern Sudan must have grown steadily since 1500, when the last groups started to arrive in this region. All the major river valleys were densely populated around 1800, especially the Nile tributaries. Social and political orders were well established and broad based economies facilitated steady growth of the population.

Land was communally owned by the local groups, and its use was regulated according to custom and yearly needs.

Fig. (1) Materials for hut building. (*Universitetsforlaget*)

Some of the first European travellers and missionaries coming to the southern part of Sudan at around 1850 were surprised to find vast open cultivated fields and pasture land. Great flocks of cattle were watered in regulated order at the Nile shores and other rivers. Population growth even resulted in lack of good land for cultivation and animals in some areas. Some agrarian groups, like the Lango, may have developed elaborate cultivation techniques to increase the crops. Some pastoral groups pressed into neighbouring areas in search of more grassland. The southern part of Sudan was plagued by many diseases and natural disasters such as tsetse flies that carried sickness for both humans and cattle. Many water borne diseases were found here and recurrent droughts, floods and locust swarms regularly destroyed the crops, as did elephants and myriads of birds. Still the population in the region thrived well and established sustainable local communities, larger political kingdoms and clan-based systems. It would be reasonable to explain this positive development by the combination of a broad based mixed economy of agriculture and animal husbandry, a well- established social order and flexible ways of coping with natural disasters. One way of coping was to trade and exchange food and people with neighboring groups. Another method was to save the surplus of the production in the form of domestic animals, mainly cattle.

> **Work in pairs**
> 1. What are the differences and similarities between South Sudan then and now?

Political groups in the South in the 19th century

Over the centuries some ethnic groups in the present-day in the present-day South Sudan established control over their neighbouring peoples through various means. The Loi or Bari speaking groups used the concept of rain and drought making to win the peoples' obedience. The Azande, on the other hand, used conquest and assimilation. Such expansion of certain population groups may have been the result of natural population growth, but may also have been due to drought or conflicts. In Equatoria the Bari and Azande expanded their areas of domination into the areas west of the Nile (later Western Equatoria). The Azande kings established firm control in most parts of south-west Equatoria with their strong warrior classes. The Ma'di and others had to acknowledge Azande kings and their domination.

These were some of the reasons why people lived in big, dense settlements and in thickly fenced villages. Thus kingdoms that grew up among Acholi, Bari, Lokoya and Ma'di became bigger and more powerful. Larger political units grew out of military alliances, ethnic and linguistic similarity and became the "tribal groups" of Acholi, Ma'di, Didinga, Bari and Lokoya etc. The migration and raiding led to widespread contact between the different groups and cultural ideas, goods and plants were dispersed.

In Bahr- el -Ghazal and Upper Nile the Nuer started to move eastwards in the late 1700s and early 1800, and absorbed many Dinka groups on their way towards the Ethiopian highlands. Nuer prophets made possible this mix of people in peaceful ways. Many

Dinka groups acknowledged Nuer supremacy and adopted the Nuer language and way of life. At the same time, other Dinka groups in Bahr el-Ghazal pressed southwards and westwards and came to dominate other peoples living in Bahr el-Ghazal, such as the Moru and many other smaller groups. This has been called the "Dinkaization" of Bahr el-Ghazal.

The Shilluk (Chollo) kingdom ruled from the Nile/Sobat confluence to El Ais. Until 1838 the Shilluk (Chollo) conducted numerous wars against the Dinka, who were migrating from the west to east across the Shilluk (Chollo) kingdom. The Dinka who lived in the area between Akobo to Bor, were also in constant warfare with the Murle, a pastoralist people. The Dinka were pressed westwards towards Bor and the Nile.

> **Question**
> 1. List the main political groups/divisons in Southern Sudan by 1850.
> 2. Explain briefly how each of these groups gained political control.

Political organization of Sudanic and Nilotic societies in the 19th century

As mentioned above the Shilluk (Chollo) and Azande had kingdoms with a centralized system of government. The kings were symbols of unity and presided over all functions of the kingdoms. They had standing armies to defend the kingdoms from outside invaders, and used locally produced military equipment like spears, arrows and shields for protection.

The sedentary societies were organized under their respective chiefs and spiritual leaders who could mobilize men in cases of attacks. They also had a well-coordinated security network. Most of these societies were Sudanic and Nilotic language speakers.

Fig. (2)   Moru archers (*DuMont Buchverlag*)

Some groups such as the Lokoya, Didinga, Lotuho and Lopit adopted the age-class system in the struggle for pastoral communities. As boys entered manhood they had an age-set ritual to celebrate the transition.

The different clans from the same community lived together for a period, learned defensive skills and followed the cattle flocks when they trekked away from the villages. They learned the songs and stories about heroes of the past and the great deeds of their forefathers, and in Nilotic societies they praised the favorite bulls in songs. Just as young men went through traditional ceremonies to enter manhood, young women went also through processes of learning female skills and were taught respect for cultural and social behaviour.

> **Work in pairs**
> 1. Describe the transition ritual for boys and girls in your ethnic group at the present time

Economic organization in Southern Sudan around 1850

The societies which spoke Sudanic and Eastern Nilotic languages were economically well organized. The fertile arable land yielded crops such as cereals, sesame, and groundnuts. Agriculture was mainly practiced by fairly permanently settled communities. Iron ore was discovered and mining was developed to support industrial and agricultural growth. Iron and stone tools such as hoes and axes were used in agriculture and blacksmiths played a great role in this industrial development. Besides agriculture, communities alongside the River Nile practiced fishing mostly for home consumption and hunting and honey harvest also took place. Cattle, goats and sheep were kept for prestige, marriage, milk and meat. Intra-southern trade (i.e. trade between various areas in the South) had been common for a long time. The Bari were famous blacksmiths and made iron goods that were traded, along with ivory, salt, cereal and cattle. Trading took also place between the Dinka and the Islamic Baggara who sold the goods to Northern Sudan.

> **Work in pairs**
> 1. Briefly explain the economic organization of Sudanic societies in the 19th century.
> 2. Describe the economic life of Southern Sudanese societies in the nineteenth century. Your answer should include agricultural life, iron-working, fishing, hunting, animal husbandry and trade.

Social organization and women's role

Socially there was intermarriage among the communities. Marriage was seen as a community celebration and an expansion of clans. Celebrations such as traditional dances were normally organized on such occasions. Rain makers performed their traditional duties. In case of drought, they would approach the rainmaker to request him/her to make rain. Women could also exercise these spiritual powers.

Queen mothers played important roles among Eastern Nilotic (Nilo-Hamitic) societies. Queen Ikang of Tirangole is one of the longest ruling persons in Lotuho history. She reigned from 1886 up to 1936, when she abdicated because of old age.

As is seen in the example above, women could ascend to the highest level of government in the South, but that was a rare occurrence and usually it was men who dominated the political field. Local communities were governed by a group of elderly men or by a rainmaker-king or by clan leaders of men. Women worked in the home and in the cultivation fields. Reproduction of children was a main obligation and task. Rich men could marry several wives, and a bride price of more than one hundred cows for a woman of good descent was not unusual around 1850. Women worked together in groups and supported each other in cases of illness, food shortage, births and childcare, natural disasters or social situations. Women also organized working parties where they engaged large parts of the village community to undertake tasks like the clearing of forests and hoeing and weeding of fields. The working parties were served beer and food and success depended on good organizational skills and management of the harvest.

The average lifespan of women was probably quite short, perhaps between forty and fifty years, but the lifespan of men was even shorter. There were few elderly women to be seen in the South before 1900, with Queen Ikang a notable exception. But the women constituted the backbone of the production and reproduction in the South, and their work resulted in thriving communities and growing, prosperous populations.

Fig. (3) Women grind flour (*Universitetsforlaget*)

Summary: **After 1500** the population in the south of Sudan increased steadily and around 1850 there were many thriving and sustainable communities. Small kingdoms thrived in the first half of 19th century. Major droughts led to widespread migration and conflicts between groups. Queens such as Ikang ruled among the Lotuho, but this was the exception as women were almost everywhere dominated by men.

Work in pairs

1. What was special with Queen Ikang of Tirangole?
2. Imagine you are living in the South during the 1800's. List the occupations of women in your village?
3. Does the role of women to-day differ from the role of women in the 19th century. Explain your answer.

The Turko-Egyptian conquest

Muhammad 'Ali became governor (wali) of Egypt in 1805. He wanted to increase Egypt's influence both in the Mediterranean and the Near East through conquest. He fought against Sudan, Syria, Hijaz and the Osmanian Sultan.

Fig. (4) Muhammad 'Ali (1769-1849)

Mohammad 'Ali was the son of a lower Ottoman officer and was of Albanian stock. When Napoleon Bonaparte invaded Egypt in 1798, Muhammad 'Ali led a contingent of Turkish forces in 1800 against the invaders. Thereafter he became the governor of Egypt because of intrigues and able military leadership. On his way to power he defeated the leading warrior class, the Mamluks and he was given the title viceroy by the Sultan of Istanbul, Turkey. He was called wali. Under his rule Egypt underwent large economic development and administrative reforms

Before 1820, Southern Sudan was unaffected by the activities of Egypt. The Shilluk had their capital at Fashoda on the White Nile, and the Dinka who lived along the Kiir, the White Nile and the Sobat successfully halted their progress.

It was Mohammad 'Ali rather than the Ottoman Sultan who prepared for the conquest of Sudan in 1820-21.

Why did Muhammad 'Ali want to conquer Sudan?

1. **Muhammad 'Ali wanted to make Egypt a strong international power.**

    He saw Egypt as the natural successor to the decaying Ottoman Empire. He summed up his vision for Egypt as follows:

> "*I am well aware that the (Ottoman) Empire is heading by the day toward destruction...On her ruins I will build a vast kingdom... up to the Euphrates and the Tigris.*"

He needed a strong army and money to carry out his plans so Mohammad 'Ali planned to conquer and colonize Sudan.

2. **Muhammad 'Ali wanted to recruit soldiers to rebuild his army.**

   Many of his soldiers had been killed in the military campaigns between 1811 and 1818 against the Wahhabis in Arabia. (The Wahhabis are a conservative Sunni Islamic sect and the dominant form of Islam in Saudi Arabia.)

   Muhammad Ali decided to rebuild his army with slaves from Sudan because he believed that a slave-army would be loyal to him personally and therefore would not be a threat to his power. In the past, Egypt had obtained slaves from Sudan through the slave trade. Muhammad 'Ali believed that he would not be able to buy all the slaves he needed in the slave markets. He decided it was better for Egypt to conquer Sudan in order to capture slaves directly through slave-raids.

3. **He wanted to exploit the gold of Sudan.** He planned to extract the gold from its mines to use the revenue to build and equip his army and to modernize agriculture and industry in Egypt.

4. **He wanted to strengthen his own position.** His dream was to find the gold and build up a strong slave army so that he would be more secure in his position and independent of the Ottoman Sultan.

5. **He wanted to break the power of a group of Mamluks** who had escaped from Egypt to Sudan in 1811. Muhammad 'Ali saw the Mamluks as the enemies of Egypt. He feared that the Mamluks might reorganize themselves with the support of the Sudanese, invade Egypt and overthrow him. His aim was to conquer Sudan and prevent this from happening. In the beginning of his time as Wali (Governor) of Egypt in 1805, his most dangerous

opponents had been the Mamluks. The Mamluks were the survivors of the military and governing elite whose chiefs had been the real masters of Egypt in the previous century.

By massacre, he succeeded by 1811 in breaking their power in Egypt, but a section of the Mamluks had escaped beyond his control to Sudan. There they built a walled town for themselves in the state of Dongola on the west bank of the Nile where they were dealing in slaves. In 1820, the Sultan of Sennar informed Muhammad 'Ali that he was unable to comply with his demand to expel the Mamluks. In response Muhammad 'Ali sent 4,000 troops to invade Sudan, clear it of Mamluks, and incorporate it into Egypt.

Discuss in pairs
1. Who was Muhammed 'Ali?
2. List the various reasons why Muhammed 'Ali wanted to control Sudan.

Discuss in class
1. To what extent was the search of slaves an important reason for conquering Sudan?
2. Is the slave issue important today in Sudan and South Sudan? Explain your answer.

The conquest of Sudan

The peoples of Sudan from Nubia, Sennar, Kordofan and the Red Sea were the first to be conquered by Muhammed 'Ali's youngest son, Ism'il Kamil Pasha. While the Egyptians were equipped with modern firearms and artillery the various Sudanese rulers were not. They had inferior and traditional weapons. The indigenous kingdoms were conquered quickly. The Funj kingdom collapsed after more than three centuries of existence on June 12, 1821. Kordofan was conquered in a pitch battle at Bara in late 1821.

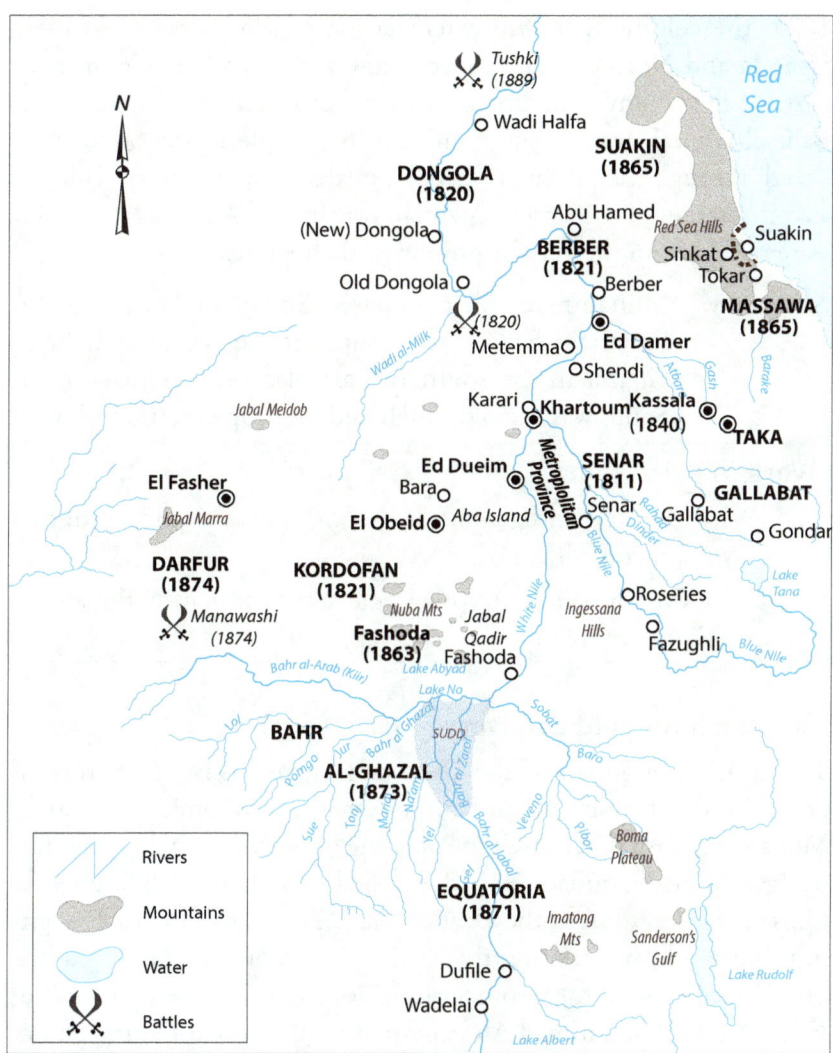

Fig. (5) Sudan at the time of the Turkyia (*Cambridge University Press*)

By October 1821, Egypt had established a vast colonial territory in Sudan, which was divided into the provinces of Dongola, Berber, Sennar, and Kordofan. The colony continued to expand, however, with the annexations of Eastern Sudan in 1840-1865 and Southern Sudan in 1869-1871. And with the conquest of Darfur finally in

1874, the colony in its full extent encompassed parts of Northern Uganda and Northeastern Congo. However, Egyptian rule in many parts of the colony, and especially in the provinces of Equatoria and Bahr el-Ghazal, was largely nominal. The people in the South were 'taxed' through the raiding of people, cattle, corn and ivory. This was a continuation of the Turko-Egyptian rule in the North, as areas there were raided from the very beginning of the regime.

Summary: Muhammad 'Ali conquered Sudan in 1821, but the Egyptians had no real control in Equatoria or Bahr el-Ghazal in the southern part of Sudan.. However, the South was taxed through raids of people, cattle and ivory.

Work in pairs
1. Why did the indigenous kingdoms fall so quickly under Egyptian control?
2. Why do you think Egyptian rule was nominal in Equatoria and Bahr el-Ghazal?

The search for gold and ivory

The invasion of Sudan by the Turks and Egyptians is a great turning point in the history of Sudan. It was the economic interests of Muhammed 'Ali that caused the opening of the White Nile to modern navigation. Muhammad 'Ali had travelled to Sudan in 1838 to see for himself what resources the country had. He even went to Fazughli to inspect gold prospecting there. The visit to Sudan convinced him of the need to look for resources in regions as far as the source of the Nile. In fact, Muhammad Ali believed that the equatorial region had minerals and so urged his officials in Sudan to go there for that reason. Ivory was also another resource he wanted to explore those regions. Thus, it was not by accident that the expeditions to the White Nile began soon after Muhammad 'Ali's visit to Sudan.

The opening of the White Nile to trade with the outside world

Fig. (6)   Sailors from Dongola played a leading role in the opening up of Southern Sudan (*Weidenfeld and Nicolson: London*)

The first government expedition in 1839 did not go much beyond the *Sudd*, but the second expedition broke out of the Sudd to discover beautiful wooded parklands, densely populated with huge herds of cattle, cultivated fields, and huge numbers of elephants. This expedition sailed down the Nile to Equatoria and reached Gondokoro in January 1841. This may have been the first time that Equatorians had direct contact with the outside world in the context of peaceful trade. Before the expeditions Equatorians had been in indirect trading contact with the outside world. Those who travelled and lived in the region had reported seeing items which originated from places outside Africa, for example cowrie shells, beads, and Indian cotton cloth.

The results of opening the White Nile to ships from North Sudan were:
- Explorers and traders came from Europe, Egypt and from the north of Sudan to Southern Sudan.
- Southern communities were raided for slave soldiers and for domestic slaves for sale in the markets of Cairo for the cotton industry, for domestic use and for agricultural work.
- Herds of elephants were killed and their ivory was sold to European traders.
- Muhammad 'Ali realized that there was no gold in Southern Sudan.

> **Work in pairs**
> 1. What were the reasons opening the White Nile to modern navigation?
> 2. What natural resources of Sudan did Muhammed 'Ali want to exploit?
> 3. What is the evidence that there had been trade contacts between Equatoria and the outside world before the expeditions of Muhammed 'Ali on the White Nile?

Slavery

A slave is a person who is owned. **Slave trade** is all actions involved in capturing of another person in order to exchange, sell or dispose of him or her.

Slavery has existed for centuries in the indigenous communities in Southern Sudan. In ancient Sudan, slaves were used as sacrifice or in exchange of goods by Sudanese kings. In the late 17th century the Funj kingdom opened up to commercial relationship with the Mediterranean world. The urban middle class who appeared during the 18th century used slaves not only for domestic use, but also in agricultural production. Slaves were taken from the people south-west of Darfur and traded in the commercial center of Shendi. In the

18th century Islamic slave traders from West Africa raided for slaves in Southern Sudan and in Nuba Mountains. In the 18th century the Islamic Baggara took advantage of the rise of the Sultanate in Darfur and supplied it with slaves. However, the trade in slaves was mainly local until the 19th century when the slave trade started to flourish owing to growing demand for slaves from the Muslim world.

Fig. (7) Slaves in Eastern Africa during the 19th century

One of Muhammad 'Ali's motives for conquering Sudan was to obtain slaves for conscription into his army as well as for use as cheap labour in his modernization program. Upon completing the conquest, the government embarked on extensive slave-raids both in Nuba Mountains and Upper Blue Nile and in the South. The people in the North from Nubia, Sennar, Kordofan and the Red Sea were forced to collaborate with the Egyptian army in these slave raids, mostly against the peoples in the South: the Dinka, Nuer and Shilluk Victims of these raids were captured by the hundreds. The people who lived in the Sudd were protected by the great marshes and were the least affected by the slave raids.

Females, children, and males judged unsuitable for the army or in excess of the number needed for the army, were sold to get money from the government, or were used as "salaries" to pay soldiers and other government employees. Slaves judged suitable for the army were conscripted and taken to Aswan where they underwent military training. Upon graduating, they were distributed among the regiments in Sudan as *jihadiyya* (slave-soldiers). It was therefore ironic that these slave-soldiers, most of them of Southern Sudanese and Nuba backgrounds, would be the ones most used in the slave-raids.

While this might seem surprising at first sight, it should be noted that the Turko-Egyptian state was only using a system long-established by previous Muslim states in Northern Sudan such as Darfur and Funj sultanates. The Baggara had been coerced to pay taxes in slaves to the Islamic kingdom of Wadai (Chad), and they often raided Dinka populations in order to get slaves. Some of them migrated to the Sultanate of Darfur where they continued to engage in the slave trade, now more voluntarily. The heavy taxation in the North by the Turko-Egyptian regime also meant that the people in the North needed more income to pay their taxes, and therefore the slave-raids were intensified.

Fig. (8) Slave raids in Southern Kordofan (*Weidenfeld and Nicolson: London*)

The slave raids in the South created an atmosphere of domination and subjugation, establishing the big divide and gap between the North and the South. Since slaves from the South also were used as domestic slaves in the North, blacks were often called slaves by the man in the street in the North, a situation which still exists. The Southerners were not passively looking on as their people were carried away. There were many cases of them fighting back and taking slaves from among the slave raiders. There were also cases where they ran away vacating the villages. This tragic history of slavery and slave-trade has contributed significantly to the deep distrust, hostility and bitterness felt by the Southerners to the North until the present day.

Officially government-sponsored slave-raids stopped in the early 1840s, but slave-traders (jallabas) with their private armies continued with the practice. Slave traders like Zubeir Rahma Mansur established himself as the principal slave trader in the western part of Bahr- el Ghazal resulting in the sparse population we find today in the state of Western Bahr el- Ghazal. The conqueror, Muhammad 'Ali, died in 1849.

Summary: The White Nile was opened to modern navigation in the 1840's. Muhammad 'Ali saw possibilities of acquiring minerals such as gold and ivory from Sudan. This opened up new and peaceful trading possibilities between the North and the South. However, slave raiding became the order of the day and erased the possibility of peaceful trade and co-existence. The Turko-Egyptian government sponsored slave-raids between the 1820's and 1840's and encouraged the Northern population to engage in the slave trade which was the beginning of the tense relationship between the North and the South.

Work in pairs
1. Discuss how the slave raids were conducted. How and why did Northerners take part in the slave raids?
2. Why did slave raiding increase during the Turko-Egyptian period?

Discuss in class
"The tragic history of slavery and slave-trade contributed to the tense relations between Northerners and Southerners."

The coming of the Christian missionaries to the South

Among the outsiders to come to the South after 1841 were Christian missionaries who came to convert Africans to Christianity. The Roman Catholics were the first to come. Hearing of the new route to central Africa, the Pope created the Vicariate of Central Africa in 1846, with Khartoum as its headquarters. The first group of priests arrived in Khartoum in 1848, but they could not establish themselves in Gondokoro in the South before 1851. In the Bari area they were well-received by Nyigilo and Subek of the Bilinyang royal house. Father Vinci (1819-53) was the first Christian to live among the Bari. He made two journeys on the White Nile, the first in 1849 and the second in 1850-51. Here is an excerpt of Father Vinci's diary from his encounter with a Bari chief:

> *On 24 February 1851, I arrived safely at Mogiri, a large Bari village lying on both banks of the river, between 4 and 5 degrees N. As soon as I landed, I asked the whereabouts of their chief Nyigilo, whose acquaintance I had made during the first expedition. In answer, I was told that Nyigilo had gone off to Lotuka to exchange the few beads given to him by (an) expedition, for oxen, rams and other things. At last, Nyigilo arrived.... (and) took me to see his aged mother, so that I could give her some beads. In addition, I presented Nyigilo with all sorts of things I had with me. I gave him a good Arab dress, many beads, two brass bells, a mirror, and other trinklets, which pleased him very much. This was proved by the fact that, in addition to the two oxen he had presented to the crew of the boat, he forced me to accept four beautiful elephant-tusks.*

Unfortunately, in 1854 only one of the five priests was alive; the rest had perished due to lack of immunity to local diseases, among them Father Vinci. The lone survivor abandoned Gondokoro and founded a new mission station of Holy Cross, one hundred and fifty miles downstream of Gondokoro, among the Dinka.

Gondokoro was, however, reopened in 1855 when three priests arrived in Gondokoro and built a mission station consisting of several house brick structures and a school, all encircled by a brick wall. The priests then settled down and for two years concentrated on translation work and teaching basic reading and arithmetic to a handful of interested pupils. But once again, death destroyed their work, prompting the lone survivor, Morlang, to travel to the Yei River region in 1859 in search of a more hospitable place for the mission. Although his impressions about the Yei River region were positive, Morlang returned to Gondokoro, where he stayed for several months more before finally abandoning it by the onset of the rainy season in 1860. Another failed attempt was among the Shilluk (Chollo). A large party of Franciscans arrived there in 1861, but high death rates forced them to withdraw. By 1863, missionary efforts in Southern Sudan were abandoned. They now concentrated their efforts in the Nuba Mountains.

Three problems contributed to the failure of early missionary efforts in the South. The first and largest problem was the lack of immunity to local diseases, which resulted in the death of the vast majority of the missionaries. The second problem was one of communication. The missionaries were not familiar with the languages of the people, nor with their attitudes and values. Southern Sudanese on the other hand refused to change their culture and to be converted to Christianity. The third problem was due to the presence of foreign traders in Gondokoro: the local people did not often distinguish between the missionaries and the White Nile ivory and slave traders. Both came together, possessed the same weapons and were identical in colour. So missionaries were often blamed for the misdeeds of the traders and were viewed with suspicion and distrust.

Summary: Missionary activities in the South started in 1851, but the missionaries abandoned the region in 1863.

> **Discuss in pairs**
> 1. When and how did the missionaries arrive in the South?
> 2. What is your impression of Father Vinci's encounter with Sudanese? Give reasons for why the missionaries did not manage to settle permanently there.
>
> **Discuss in class**
> 1. The text does not say much about the reasons for missionaries coming to Southern Sudan. Why do you think they came?
> 2. The missionaries took many notes of the life and language in the South at that time. Do you think this is of any value to Sudanese to-day? Why/why not?

The White Nile trade after 1841

The opening of the White Nile to modern navigation introduced the White Nile trade which attracted foreign traders to the South. From 1841 to 1852, the White Nile trade was dominated by government trading expeditions. The government sent trading expeditions every dry season as far as Gondokoro. Private traders were not allowed to participate during this period because ivory was the monopoly of the government. The expeditions traded with the local peoples along the Nile for ivory and other valuable items. But government trading expeditions ended in 1852 and the trade was taken over by private traders.

European traders and Khartoumers (Arab and Muslim traders resident in Khartoum) dominated this phase of private trade, and like the previous government expeditions, the trade was confined to the river. Without local operators and networks in Southern Sudan itself, however, that trade could not have continued for long. The networks penetrated from the Nile deep into the interior, with many local operators and middlemen involved. Some of the middlemen worked independently, while others were contracted by the Khartoumers.

When the trading season ended, the White Nile traders, also called Khartoumers, would leave the unsold merchandise to selected local middlemen. Most of these middlemen were chiefs or people of high standing in their societies. The middlemen would then continue selling the goods to local customers. Sometimes they even travelled to the interior to sell the goods. Good examples of these local middlemen among the Bari were Nyigilo of Bilinyang (former missionary contact person) and Lungasuk of Mokido. Nyigilo frequently travelled to Lokoya, Lafon and Lotuha on trading missions. Lungasuk, on the other hand, went on trading mission to the Yei River region.

Elephant hunters become wealthy

Another result of the White Nile trade was the emergence of professional elephant hunters. For instance among the Bari, Kakwa, Kuku, Pojulu, etc. there were professional hunters called *ligo* (singular *ligotot*). Before the coming of the ivory traders, these professional hunters were well regulated by the land lords in that they could only kill so much in a season which ensured conservation. When the traders came this traditional practice was abandoned as the *ligo* could no longer adhere to cultural norms. Indeed some of the *ligo*, through direct sale of ivory to the traders, became richer, more powerful and more famous than the traditional rainmakers or land lords. This disrupted the hierarchy of traditional authority.

Questions
1. What was the most important trade item?
2. Why were the local middlemen necessary?
3. Who were the Khartoumers?
4. How was the traditional authority disrupted by ivory hunters in the South?

The *zaribas*

However, by 1857 in Bahr el-Ghazal and by 1861 in Equatoria, the traders began sending their own trading missions directly to the interior, thereby removing the middlemen. By 1863, they went a step further and established trading stations (*zaribas /zara'ib*) in the interior. This coincided with the withdrawal of European traders by 1863, partly due to the growing international criticism of the slave-trade, but largely because of hostile government policies toward their business. This opened the way for Arabs, Northern Sudanese, Egyptians and Syrians to dominate the trade.

As mentioned above the change to *zaribas* occurred first in Bahr el-Ghazal and later in Equatoria. Most of the *zaribas* in Bahr el-Ghazal were in the area inhabited by the Luo, Bongo, Ndogo, Kreish, etc., but some were also found among the Dinka. The *zaribas* were not established among the Azande until the 1870's because the Azande were strong enough to protect their country from the traders. But all in all, Bahr el-Ghazal had the largest number of *zaribas* and Upper Nile had the fewest of them all.

The spread of violence

The *zaribas* acted as trading centers for the people around it. They also acted as stores in which merchandise were kept. Ivory and other items were also stored there before being taken to the Nile or Bahr El-Ghazal (Kirr) rivers for shipment to Khartoum. But more important, the *zaribas* acted as garrisons in which the private armies of the traders were stationed. Most of these armed bands were Danaqla and Shayqiyya from Northern Sudan. The establishment of *zaribas* brought widespread violence almost all over Southern Sudan. The violence was due to the fact that the *zaribas* used their armies to take by force things they needed or wanted: ivory and other trade items, food, and above all cattle and slaves. Ivory was still the main item sought by the Khartoumers, but the cost of trading continued to increase. The traders had to buy their goods, pay transportation costs, salaries, business taxes and other dues as well as food for their *zaribas*.

These increasing costs were happening while profits from ivory were diminishing, because money had to be borrowed at high interest rates.

One measure to reduce the costs was paying the salaries of their soldiers in kind (sugar, slaves etc.), and to require the *employees* to produce their own food. The soldiers in the *zaribas* were therefore potentially poor. They improved their situation, however, by preferring to be paid in slaves, because they could then sell the slaves for cash, or keep them for housework, farming, and other activities. In this way, slaves provided the soldiers with some material comforts and a sense of dignity. Thus, raiding for slaves, food, and other requirement resulted in widespread violence wherever *zaribas* were established. Some of the most notorious "Arab" ivory and slave traders included Zubeir wad Rahma Mansur in Western Bahr el-Ghazal, and Abu Su'ud in Equatoria.

It would not have been possible for the *traders* to do all these things had there been unity among Southerners. But the division of Southern Sudanese between mutually hostile tribal or other communal groups made it easy for the traders to take advantage of these local hostilities. That is, the traders allied themselves with one group against another, and then repeated the same tactics over and over again until they brought whole areas under their control. These alliances enabled them to capture slaves, ivory, cattle, and even food from "hostile" groups. Some of the slaves were also bought from the Azande leaders who had captured them as prisoners of war in their wars of expansion. Cattle were also captured in the conflicts and were used either for buying ivory from "friendly" people, or for the consumption by the people of *zaribas*.

One of the consequences of the violence was to reduce the local peoples into subjects who were required to pay tribute and to supply porters and food for the *zaribas*. Pastoral societies, such as the Nuer and the Dinka, fiercely resisted the traders and they had an advantage because of the marshy land in which they lived. Agricultural societies, on the other hand were worse affected. Many people in Equatoria retreated to the bush and forest again. One result was that the tsetse flies spread in many areas and made rearing of cattle impossible. This may perhaps have stopped the Dinka advancement into the South.

Of the agricultural communities, only the Azande maintained their independence until 1905. King Gbudwe was a powerful king who fought against the Arab traders, Egyptian soldiers and British colonizers. In 1882 he was captured by the Egyptian army, but was released by the Mahdi regime which regretted it when he exterminated all Arabs left in Azandeland.

Summary: Mohammad' Ali did not succeed in finding gold, but he had a profitable trade in ivory and slaves.
The trading was peaceful in the beginning, but quickly turned violent as trading parties fought against each other.

> **Work in pairs**
> 1. Explain the various types of the White Nile trade.
> 2. Who took part in the trade?
> 3. What was the *zariba* and what was the importance of the *zariba*?
>
> **Discuss in class**
> 1. Why did the Europeans withdraw from the White Nile trade and why did the Northerners not withdraw at the same time? Give reasons for your answer.

The impact of the slave trade on Sudanese during the Turkiyya

The Turko-Egyptian government put heavy taxes on the people they conquered. Taxes were put on the owners of slaves and flocks: $15 per slave: $10 per cow: $5 per sheep or donkey. (These were Spanish dollars, often called Marie Theresa dollars). This brought poverty and hardship to some Sudanese Muslims who were living in the North who struggled to pay the new taxes. Mohammad Ali also demanded a tribute in slaves from the people he conquered. Many were in debt and some turned to slave raids to pay their debts.

1821-1841: The Turko-Egyptian government increased slave raiding and slave ownership

Before 1821, it was the aristocracy of the Sudanic kingdoms who raided for slaves. After 1821, slave raiding was carried out by the government in North Sudan and slave raiding and the number of slaves taken was greatly increased. Slavery became a profitable trade accompanied by force and violence. Many of the indigenous people in the North were taken away as slaves. Excess slaves were kept by the raiders for their own use and domestic slavery became common through all of society in northern Sudan for the first time.

1826–1840: Northern Sudanese raided other Sudanese communities for slaves. The first people to be conquered were forced to cooperate with the Turko-Egyptian army to carry out slave raids into non-Muslim areas in the south of Sudan. We know that the Shaiqiyya, north of Khartoum, the Rufa of the Blue Nile and the Baggara along the White Nile and in the west, all took part in slave raids with the army. Some of these also organised raids of their own. The raiders kept excess slaves for their own use or for sale.

1841-1885: As time went on and especially after 1841, some of these northern **Muslims became wealthy slave owners.** So the economic policy of the Turko-Egyptian government in the north helped to cause the slave raids and suffering of Southern Sudanese.

Slave raids had consequences for the migration of peoples, depopulation and violence. In the 1820's Sudanese migrated from every province to save themselves from slave raids. Thousands of people from Blue Nile fled to Ethiopia for safety. Slave trading led to depopulation and threatened the falling apart of small communities as many also died during slave raiding. The Bari, for example, were nearly wiped out. Violence accompanied slave raids which led to wars between the slave traders and the local people and this caused violence, destruction and death.

Agriculturalists suffered more than pastoralists. Many agriculturalists in Equatoria left their houses and went into the forest but the spread of the tsetse fly made it impossible for them to keep cattle. On the other hand, the slave raids of the Turko-Egyptians also prevented the migration of people for the spread of the tsetse fly discouraged the Dinka from migrating further south and this gave more land to agriculturalists.

The slave trade of the Turko-Egyptian period deepened the racial divide between Northern and Southern Sudan. People were stratified according to race. The slave raids in the South created an atmosphere of domination and control by Northerners over Southerners, of Muslims over animists. After 1870, all the slaves who were in the north were southerners and in the mind of northerners, slaves, "blacks" and southerners were the same. Southerners were looked down on as people with low status. Even Southern Sudanese who became Muslims or achieved high rank in the army, were looked down on because of their slave origins. Deep distrust, hostility and bitterness is felt by the Southerners to their neighbours in the North to the present day.

Walled trading forts, known as *zaribas*, brought violence, fear and great hardship to the local people. Most of the *zaribas* were set up between 1863-1885 in Bahr-el-Ghazal by Khartoumers. By 1870, a powerful group of merchants had taken over all the smaller traders and organised the raiding and transport of slaves into a huge operation. The local people had to provide porters and feed these large communities.

The suppression of the slave trade and the annexation of Southern Sudan

> **Annexation:** capture, seizure, take over or occupation of territory. Annexation is the inclusion of a territory into another political entity. Often the territory which is annexed is the weaker part of the union.
> **International pressure** means demands being made on a person, group or country from other groups or countries.

By 1865, the international pressure against the slave trade in Sudan was so strong that Egypt was forced to act to suppress it. Egyptian responses to the outcry led ultimately to the policy of annexation of Southern Sudan and the setting up of an effective administration. Thus, in 1869 Samuel W. Baker was appointed by Khedive Isma'il to lead a large military expedition to annex the Equatorial Provinces. However, because of great communication difficulties, Baker was not able to reach the province's capital Gondokoro until April 1871. And on May 20, 1871, he officially proclaimed the annexation of the province as well as the abolition of the slave trade.

Fig. (10) Samuel Baker (1821-1893): British explorer, officer and writer. He was the governor of Equatorial Nile Basin from 1869-1873

But soon Baker had serious difficulties. He had problems getting supplies for his troops, and had opposition from the ivory and slave traders as well as from the local people. So by the time his contract ended in 1872, Baker had hardly achieved any of the goals of his mission.

Colonel Charles Gordon replaced Baker in 1873, and he stayed in office until 1876. The main achievement of Gordon was improvement in security, and this was due to the chain of stations he established along the Nile, including Lado to which he transferred the capital of the province. He also established some stations in the remote areas. Another achievement of Gordon was improved relations with the local people, although this took time to work out.

The improved relations made it possible for him to transport a steamer to Dufile (south of Nimule), where it was used for transportation between Dufile and Lake Albert. By the time he left office in 1876, Gordon had succeeded in establishing the government on a firmer basis. The slave trade was reduced, but still continued over land in Bahr el -Ghazal and in Kordofan and Darfur. It continued also east of Blue Nile into the Arabian Peninsula. Gordon complained bitterly that he was not able to control and stop the slave trade.

Fig. (11) Charles Gordon (1833-1885), governor of Equatorial province 1874-1876. General- Governor of Sudan from 1877-1880

The next important governor in Equatoria was Emin Pasha, who took office in 1878. Emin opened many more garrisons in the remote areas and this greatly increased the territory under government control. Discipline among officials continued to improve so that official cattle-raids were reduced considerably. One important contribution he made was replacing the *khuteriyya* (irregular soldiers, formerly the soldiers of the *Zariba*) with *tarajma* (militias recruited from local communities). All these contributed to the tranquility evident from Emin's travel reports about the province. Conditions improved considerably, and the province began for the first time to experience surplus in its accounts. But the Mahdist Revolution ended the Turkiyya in Khartoum and eventually in the province.

Fig. (12) Emin Pasha (1840-1892). Governor of Equatoria 1878-1885

Summary: As a measure against the slave trade, the Egyptian ruler Khedive Isma´il ordered Samuel Baker to annex Equatoria, which he did, but the area was not pacified until Emin Pasha´s rule (1878-1885).

> **Work in pairs**
> 1. Why and how was the slave trade suppressed?
> 2. Who were the main actors behind the suppression of the slave trade?
> 3. Who were the three governors in Equatoria and what did they achieve?
> 4. Write a short essay on the suppression of the slave trade.

Bahr el-Ghazal

Khedive Isma'il also sent another expedition in 1869 under Muhammad al-Hilal to annex Bahr el-Ghazal. The annexation of Bahr el-Ghazal proved even more difficult than that of Equatoria. The ivory and slave-traders there were more difficult to control than the White Nile traders because they used overland routes to and from Darfur and Kordofan. Secondly, Bahr el-Ghazal had the largest number of traders in Southern Sudan, with a combined *zariba* population of 55,000-80,000. The traders were also mostly Northern Sudanese organized under the leadership of Zubeir wad Rahma Mansur to defeat annexation. They became more formidable than Baker ever encountered in Equatoria.

Fig. (13) Khedive Isma'il (1830-1895) He governed Egypt-Sudan from 1863-1879. He was Muhammad Ali's grandson, and led an expansionist policy which resulted in great debts and European dominance

Tensions arose as al-Hilal negotiated for the traders' submission and eventually ended in hostilities at the end of 1871 in which Zubeir emerged victorious and Hilal died. Khartoum came to the conclusion that going to war with Zubayr was too risky and so in 1873 appointed him Governor of Bahr el-Ghazal. In 1874, Zubeir invaded Darfur and added it to his Bahr el-Ghazal empire. But Khedive Isma'il denied him rule over Darfur and persuaded him to return to Bahr el-Ghazal. Zubeir was so unhappy with this that he traveled to Cairo in 1876 to make a personal appeal to the Khedive where he was detained.

However the situation in Darfur and Bahr- el Ghazal was only superficially calm. A rebellion broke out in Darfur in 1877 with Sulayman, Zubeir's son, as a leader. Governor-General Gordon couldn't restore order before 1879, when Sulayman was defeated and executed.

Summary: Bahr el-Ghazal was not annexed until 1873, and Darfur 1874, 53 years after the Turko-Egyptian invasion. The area was not pacified until 1879.

Pair work:
1. Explain why the Turko-Egyptians found Bahr el-Ghazal difficult to control.

Apart from the impact of slave raiding and of the opening of the White Nile to trade with the outside world, the Turko-Egyptian rule had other consequences for the people of Sudan.

Political impact of the Turkiyya on Sudan

Mohammad Ali brought **centralised government** to Sudan. This type of administration was not there before 1821. The coming of Mohammad Ali brought an end to the Kingdom of the Funj and Northern Sudan was divided into 6 provinces. Provincial capitals, province boundaries and local councils were set up. The control and administration of the Turko-Egyptian government at local and provincial level gave Northern Sudan an experience of centralised government. This was not given to the people of the South, except among the Shilluk. This led to a difficulty of integrating the two regions during the Condominium years.

The **Sudanese Army** ranks and formation were first established in the 1820's. The Islamic judges of the Turkiyya sowed the seeds of the present religious system in Sudan and shari'a was very firmly established in North Sudan.

A **dockyard** was set up near Khartoum on the White Nile. The irrigation of the Nile was done by Egyptians who controlled the Nile irrigation. Egyptians had a fleet of boats on the White Nile.

During the Turkiyya, Sudanese began to go to Cairo in search of work and business and also for entertainment, for films and books in Arabic.

The high taxes and slave trading of the Turko-Egyptian government led to the **success of the rise of the Mahdi in the 1880's.** The Mahdi promised to drive out the Turks, the Egyptians and the British. The Dinka supported the Mahdi so that Turko-Egyptian rule would be brought to an end.

The Mahdist revolution

After Muhammad Ahmed ibn 'Abdallah publicly declared himself the Mahdi in June 1881, many in the Turkiyya probably dismissed him simply as just an ignorant religious fanatic. But the Mahdist rebellion scored one success after another in its confrontation with the government, even though its supporters were mainly armed with traditional weapons. Before long, garrisons began to surrender. By January 1883, Kordofan capitulated, the first province to do so. Other areas and districts followed soon, but probably the most demoralizing defeat was the annihilation of an Egyptian force of 10,000 men led by William Hicks at the Battle of Shaykan. From that point on, provinces began to fall, starting with Darfur, then Bahr el-Ghazal, etc. In January 1885, Khartoum itself fell, which was the end of the Turkiyya regime.

Fig. (14) Muhammed Ahmed (The Mahdi): 1844-1885. He proclaimed himself as the redeemer of Islamic faith (the Mahdi) on June 29, 1881. He was a Sufi sheikh of the Samaniyya order. He had great military success against the Turko-Egyptian regime, but died soon after his victory in 1885

Emin Pasha's Equatoria was the only province that had not fallen to the Mahdiyya. It was only during the expansion of Belgium to Equatoria that Mahdiyya started extending its powers on this land. So in October 1884, a Mahdist force under Karamallah Qurqusawi advanced on Equatoria from Bahr el-Ghazal, but they had insufficient ammunition and had to withdraw. The next Mahdist invasion of the province came in 1888, but by that time Emin's soldiers had reached a decision to abandon the province and return to Egypt through the East African coast. However, soldiers who were natives of the region refused to abandon the province, and this disagreement slowed down the withdrawal, giving the Mahdists opportunity to attack them. The fighting ended in a stalemate, however, and ultimately both lost the country to European colonial conquest.

Fig. (15) The Mahdiya (*Cambridge University Press*)

Why did the Mahdist revolution succeed?

There were a number of reasons.

Firstly, the Turko-Egyptian administration was weak. It often changed from centralisation to decentralisation and back again to centralisation. The Governor General spent very short periods in Sudan and as a result the provinces were weak and it was easy for the Mahdi to capture them. The Khedive of Egypt and Sudan were both weak rulers.

Secondly, the army was weak and untrained. There were not enough soldiers or arms. The army was stationed in remote areas and had transport problems.

Thirdly, The Urabi revolution in Egypt happened at the same time as the Mahdist revolution. This helped the Mahdists. Tawfic, the son of the Khedive of Egypt was trying to get rid of the Urabi followers so he refused to send troops to the Sudan.

(Urabi was a military officer in Egypt who forced Tawfic, the son of the Khedive of Egypt, to have an elected government. The Urabi revolution came to an abrupt end with the British invasion of the summer 1882).

The British were at war with Russia at that time. The British did not understand the Mahdist revolution so they did not take action at the right time.

Another reason for the success of the Mahdists was that they were supported by the Sufi sects of the Muslim religion. These sects were jealous that one section of Muslims, the Shakiyyya, (the Khatmiyya sect) were given privileges by the Turks.

The Dinka supported the Mahdi because the Mahdi promised to drive out all foreigners. The Dinka and other pastoralists hated the Turko-Egyptian rule because of the cruelty of Mohammad Ali and the Turkiyya in Southern Sudan, because of heavy taxes and the increase in slave raiding and violence during the Turkiyya and because of the great hardship that the people suffered because of the *Zaribas,* especially in Bahr el-Ghazal.

The slave traders supported the Mahdi because the Mahdi promised to drive out all foreigners. The slave traders wanted Baker and Gordon removed from Sudan because they were stopping their slave trade.

> **The Urabi revolution:** 1881-1882. Egypt was bankrupt, under European dominance and Tawfic (Isma'il's son) was a weak leader. The military officer Urabi forced Tawfic to consider an elected government which Tawfic accepted. The Urabi revolution came to an abrupt end with the British invasion in the summer of 1882.

What were the consequences of the Mahdi regime in the South?

1. The Bari people were the most affected by the Mahdi rule. Not only did the soldiers raid the livestock, but also women and children. Other parts of Equatoria were almost untouched by the Mahdi government, and the rule was left to local groups and jallabas.

2. Slave-raiding and slave trading decreased during the Mahdiyya.

3. Incursions into the South were almost entirely for plunder (raiding), for food during the great famine of 1888-1892, or for more slaves to add to the decreasing supply of domestic labour and military recruitment. The Southerners who suffered most under the Mahdi were the Bari people. The soldiers raided their cattle as well as their women and children.

4. Racial attitudes in the North towards the South were the same during the Mahdiyya as they were during the Turkiyya. In many ways the Mahdist state developed its own form of internal colonialism.

5. System of government: The Turko-Egyptian rulers had accepted the rights of the tribal and hereditary (traditional) Sudanic leaders. Under the Mahdists, Sudan was divided between the followers of the Mahdi, known as the 'Ansar', and unbelievers, whether Muslim or non –Muslim.

   The Mahdist state forced allegiance through religion and through the personal oath of loyalty to the Iman, the Mahdi, as the religious leader of the state and later to his Khalifa. Administrators of the government were appointed to rule the rural areas. During the Mahdist rule, these did not come from the local areas that they governed but they replaced or ruled over the local rulers and ruling families. This was clearly seen in Nubia, along the Anglo-Egyptian border, in the far west and in parts of the South.

Some Sudanese groups helped the rise of the Mahdi, but they were opposed to this Mahdist system of government. This explains why these same Sudanic groups helped the Anglo-Egyptians to bring the rule of the Mahdi to an end.

Summary: The Mahdi and his followers were successful in defeating the Egyptian army, and ruled over most of the country in 1885. However, most of the southern part of Sudan did not fall into the hands of the Mahdist government.

Timeline

1821: The Turko-Egyptian invasion.
1820s-1840s: Government sponsored slave raids.
1830s: Drought and famine caused migration and raiding.
1840-1865: The annexation of eastern Sudan
1841: The opening of the White Nile: First arrival of alien expeditions to Bari country.
1840s and 1850s: Arab and European traders come to the South and some established the *zaribas*.
1850: First Catholic missionaries arrive
1860-1871: Trade is converted to raiding and warfare.
1871: Turko-Egyptian government established in Equatoria.
1873: Annexation of Bahr el Ghazal by the Turko-Egyptian regime.
1874: Annexation of Darfur by the Turko-Egyptian regime.
1884: Revolt by the Bari
1885: The fall of the Turkiyya regime
1888-1898: The Mahdist and Northern Sudanese rule in Southern Sudan.
1896: Belgium gains control over Bari-land
1898: Anglo-Egyptian occupation of Sudan

Tasks

1. Arrange an interview with a leader in your community. Ask him/ her about the history of your people during 19th century. Present your findings to your class.
2. Imagine that you are a girl/ boy that is raided by slave traders and sold to a wealthy family in North Sudan. Write a story about your experiences.

Questions

1. Explain the reasons why Mohammad 'Ali Pasha invaded Sudan in the 1820's.
2. Outline the effects of the slave trade on the people of Sudan in the 19th century.
3. Outline the effects of Turko-Egyptian rule on the people of Southern Sudan.
4. "The Turko-Egyptian rule in the South can be summed in three words: Exploitation, oppression and resistance." Discuss.
5. Give at least four reasons why the Turkiyya failed.
6. Explain the reasons for the success of the Mahdist revolution in 1885 and its consequences for Southern Sudan.

4
Southern Sudan under the Rule of the Anglo-Egyptian Condominium (1899-1945)

Introduction

The Anglo-Egyptian occupation of Sudan at the end of the 19th century had major consequences for the development of what is now South Sudan. From 1899 to 1945, the Anglo-Egyptian rule introduced its administration in the South. The introduction of the Closed District Ordinance effectively separated the South from the North. This period also saw the coming of the Christian missionaries, and the introduction of mission schools, as well as the linking of the Southern Sudanese economy to the world markets. Although this period witnessed the end of slave trade which was a common feature during the Turco-Egyptian and Mahdia periods, the Southern Sudanese communities did not surrender in unison to the Anglo-Egyptians.

The Anglo-Egyptian conquest of Sudan

By the 1870's, slave trading in Southern Sudan had reached unprecedented proportions although the trade had been outlawed in countries such as the United States of America and Britain. As we have seen in chapter 3, the growing strength of the anti-slavery pressure, especially in Britain, made Egyptian rulers attempt to bring this trade to an end. As Governors of Equatoria, Sir Samuel Baker and General Charles George tried to suppress the slave trade. In 1882 Britain invaded Egypt in response to Tawfic's request, and the British took control of Egypt and Sudan's affairs.

However, soon after the Mahdia rebellion grew in strength and eventually resulted in the overthrow of the Turko-Egyptian rule in Sudan in 1885, and the subsequent killing of its Governor- General, Charles George Gordon. Gordon's death was unexpected, and changed the way that Britain regarded its imperial ambitions in Sudan. The British press put the blame of Gordon's death on the British prime minister, William Gladstone, and Gordon was initially perceived as an imperial martyr, the figure head of British imperialism. Gladstone, however, sympathized with the Sudanese who struggled to be free of Egyption oppression, and disliked Gordon's imperialistic and arrogant behaviour.

With the pressure from Christian fraternities at home, Britain was nevertheless forced to authorize Lord Kitchener in March 1896 to launch a campaign to revenge Gordon's death and to conquer the Mahdist Sudan. Britain provided an army and war materials, while the Egyptians financed the expedition. The Anglo-Egyptian troops overthrew the Mahdia in April 1898.

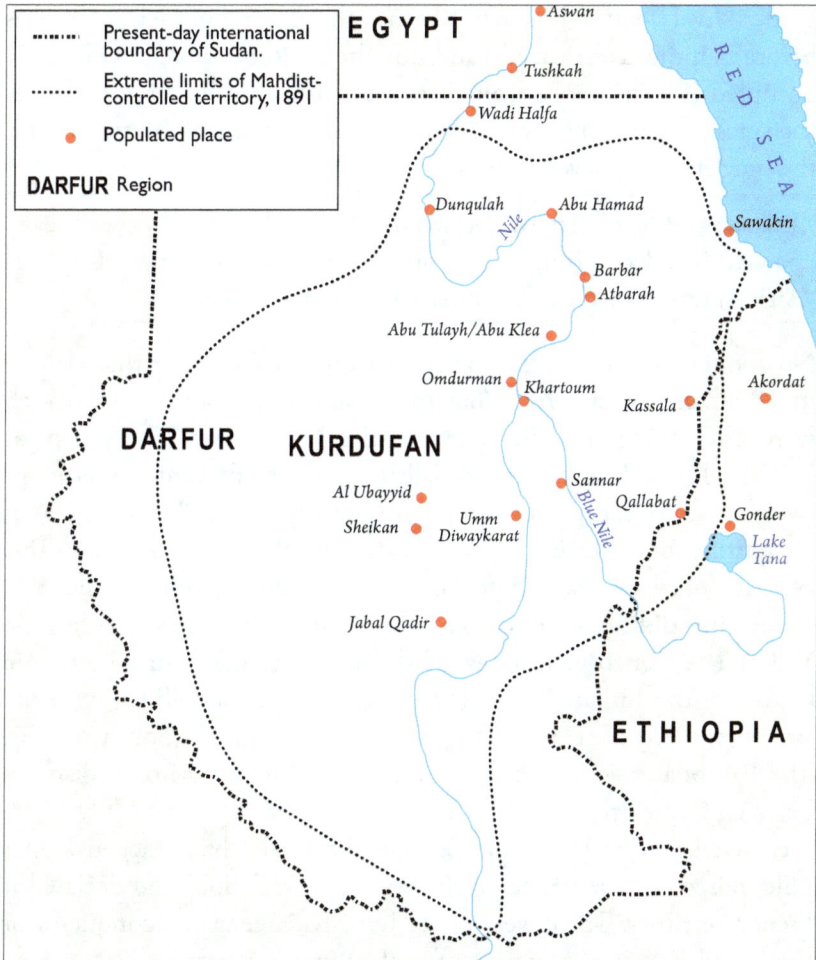

Fig. (1) Map of the Mahdist controlled area.

The Fashoda incident

During the late 19th century, the European powers were rapidly occupying Africa. Britain and France dominated the contest about Africa, although Italy, Portugal, Spain, Germany, and Belgium also participated. The Berlin conference was set in 1884-1885 to establish the rules for competition by which the European powers should be guided. Every nation had to notify the other powers of their intentions before claiming a territory. In addition the territory had to be effectively occupied (for instance through treaties with local leaders). However the rules were not always followed, and the European powers were on the border of war several times.

> **The scramble of Africa:** Between 1881 and 1914 the European powers invaded, occupied, colonized and annexed over 90 % of African territory. Only Ethiopia stayed independent.

No sooner had the Anglo-Egyptian troops overthrown the Mahdia in 1898, did Britain hear that there were European nations which were attempting to gain access to the Nile Valley. The policy of Britain's Prime Minister, Lord Salisbury was to prevent any attempt by other European powers to undermine Britain's authority in Egypt by cutting or diverting Egypt's water supply from the Nile. This British policy neutralized Italian and German interests in the Nile waters, but did not deter the French and Belgian interests in the Nile Valley. The French plans to establish a colonial rule from the Atlantic Ocean to the Indian Ocean (West-East) in Africa collided with the British wish to control Africa from "Cape to Cairo" (South-North). The Fashoda incident was the climax of colonial territorial disputes between Great Britain and France in Eastern Africa. On 12 July 1898, the French Major Jean-Baptiste Marchand, who had reached Upper Nile, raised the French flag in Fashoda (now Kodok) and declared it French territory. Three weeks later Lord Kitchener, the conqueror of the Mahdia, arrived to lay claim to the same territory.

With both armies wishing to occupy the fort at Fashoda, Kitchener and Marchand agreed that they did not want a military confrontation. They therefore agreed to fly the French, English, and Egyptian flags over the fort at Fashoda. The Fashoda incident brought Great Britain and France to the verge of war, but it ended in a diplomatic victory for Britain. The French realized that they could not win an imperial war and withdrew on 3 November 1898. The main consequence of the Fashoda incident was that the frontier between the two colonial powers was marked by the source of the Nile and the Congo rivers.

Southern Sudan under the Rule of the Anglo Egyptian Condominium (1899-1945) 133

Fig. (2) Kodok, former Fashoda, lies on the bank of the White Nile.

What were the reasons for the British-Egyptian attack on Sudan?

1. The British wanted to add the Sudan to its north African colonies.
2. Like the Egyptians, the British saw the Nile as the entrance to the fertile lands of East Africa.
3. Sudan was a means to connect British-controlled lands to the north and southeast of Africa.
4. Britain wanted control over Sudan to prevent the other European powers from gaining control over the Red Sea. They wanted to have control over that sea route to Asia through the Red Sea.
5. The British feared that if Sudan were a strong, independent country, it could be difficult for them to control Egypt.

6. Britain feared that France or Belgium would take advantage of a weak Sudan to seize land previously under the control of Egypt.
7. By 1896, the French were taking more and more land in Africa and they also threatened to go as far as the upper Nile, so the British decided to get there first.
8. Britain wanted control over the Nile to protect a planned irrigation dam at Aswan.
9. Britain had plans to build dams along the Nile.
10. The British wanted to increase the cotton growing areas to get profit for British factories.

The borders of Sudan were settled by 1914.

> **The Lado enclave**
>
> One border issue was the Lado enclave which was an enclave of the Congo Free State situated on the west bank of the Upper Nile in what is now the western part of central Equatoria and the eastern part of Western Equatoria and northwest Uganda. The Lado enclave was transferred to Sudan from Belgian Congo in 1910. On 10 June 1910, following Léopold's death, the district became a province of the Anglo-Egyptian Sudan. In 1914 the southern half was transferred to Uganda, then a British colony, while land in East Equatoria was transferred to Sudan. This meant that the whole of the west bank of the Nile in North Uganda became part of Sudan, whereas the whole of the later East Equatoria still was under Uganda. In 1914 the British administrations in Sudan and Uganda agreed to change the borders, and let the southern part of the Lado enclave (in present north west Nile in Uganda) be transferred to Uganda against a reciprocal transfer of land in East Equatoria to Sudan. Only after 1914 were the southern borders of Sudan finalised. But there was a discussion in London on the fate of the Equatoria region. Should it belong to Uganda (East Africa) or Sudan? In the end, the Uganda administration thought it was too much to administer, and Sudan took over. The fate of the Equatorians was, as we can see, decided more or less by chance in London, as for most other colonies.

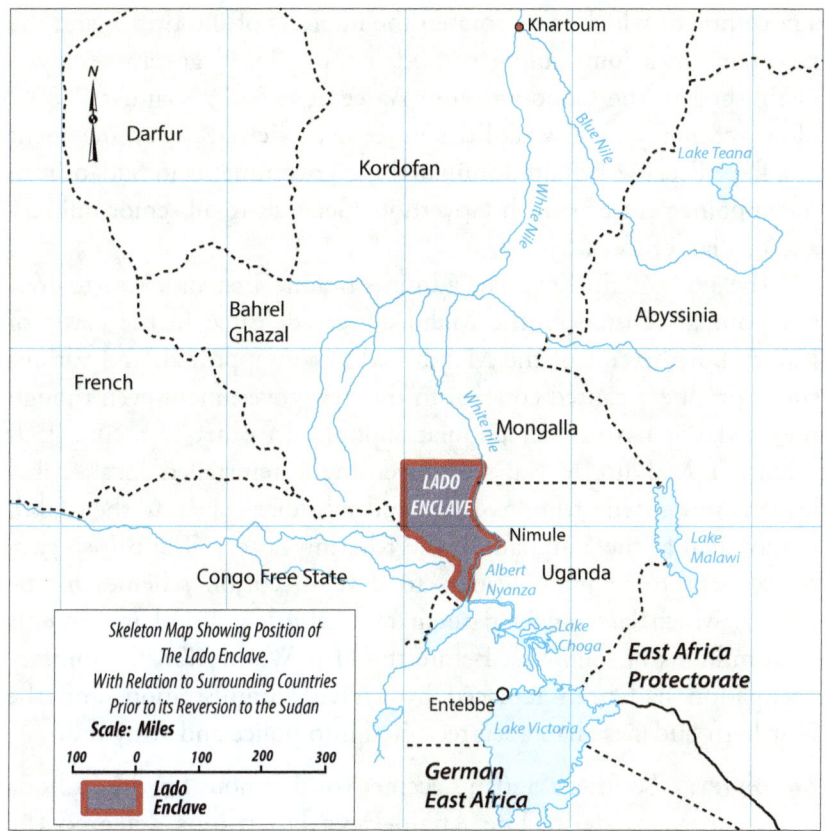

Fig. (3) Map of the Lado enclave (*Paulines Publications Africa*)

Condominium: A 'hybrid' form of government

Definition

Condominium: a political territory where two or more states formally agree to share sovereignty equally and to exercise their rights jointly, without dividing it up into 'national' zones.

To honour Egyptian historical claims and to safeguard British interests, Lord Cromer, the British agent and consul-general in Egypt, devised a "hybrid form of government". A "hybrid" form of government means a government which incorporated the interests of the British and the Egyptians in a joint ruling of Sudan. This 'joint' government was established in the Condominium Agreement of 19th January 1899. However, many observers of the Agreement viewed the arrangement as a farce because Britain dominated the governments in Sudan from the appointment of British Governor-Generals to all senior military and civilian officers.

The new Anglo-Egyptian administration's first task was to root out popular resistance. The Mahdist were defeated in the battle of Karari, but the cult of the Mahdi had not disappeared, and various small 'prophets' caused concern in the new government even though they did not have much popular support. In order to secure itself against a Mahdist revival the government reinstalled local, tribal leaders, supported orthodox Islam and subsidized rivals to the Mahdi family such as the Mirghani of the Khatmiyya sect. The British gave concessions to religious leaders to develop cotton schemes in the Gezira, which later enabled them to establish political movements with millions of followers. Before the First World War, the military occupation had been replaced by a civil administration, and the Northern Sudanese had been recruited into police and army units.

Summary: Southern Sudan became world famous for the Fashoda incident. The Anglo-Egyptian troops defeated the Mahdist and installed a Condominium regime in 1899.

Work in pairs
1. What was the Fashoda incident about?
2. Why did Britain/Egypt attack Sudan in the 1890's?
3. Explain what the Condominium Agreement was all about.
4. Why did the administration give concessions to the powerful families in North Sudan?

Fig. (4) Anglo-Egyptian Sudan

The British begin to rule Southern Sudan

The expansion of the condominium administration towards the South was delayed due to, amongst other things, shortage of resources (human and material). Despite limited investments in Southern Sudan, the Anglo-Egyptian government was able to lay claim over this vast region and its non-Arab, African population. Administrative posts were established here and there and were guarded by northern troops under British officers. However, this process of establishing colonial administration in the Southern Sudan was gradual.

From the Southerners' point of view, there was no distinction between the Turko-Egyptian rule and the Mahdist regime. The same administrative and military personnel were placed in the South under both regimes. The Southerners had not accepted the Turko-Egyptian rule and had risen against it in the 1880's. The inclusion of a few British officers in the returning Egyptian army just meant that they also were classified as "Turks". Naturally the coming of foreigners which included slave trading, and the looting of property was met with resistance. The forced labour and taxation without any social services in return caused the correct impression that condominium policies rested on the use of force and oppression. The Anglo-Egyptian government didn't see any need for negotiation with the chiefs in the South, partly because the Southerners were more decentralized than the Northerners, partly because there were no Mahdi-supporters who could have threatened the new rule.

Resistance to the Anglo-Egyptian rule in the various regions

The Yakanye resistance in Equatoria

Farmers in Equatoria who settled under the authority of traditional chiefs reacted and resisted the British pacification administration. However, the superior fire arms of the British suppressed the various resistances, and in 1909 the administration of the region came under British rule. But people were not content and around 1914, Rembe of the Yondu clan of the Kakwa people in Morobo moved all around asking people to resist the British rule. He had "holy water" which he administered to his believers with the purported idea that the water had spiritual powers which could repel or turn British bullets into water. Until he was hanged by the British in Yei in 1917, the Yakanye resistance of Rembe had created uprisings in Yei and in the West Nile region of Uganda.

A kakwa dirge (hymn)

Kakwa	English
Do sase Kenyi,	You sister of Kenyi
Do sase Anda,	You sister of Anda
Ado ku biriki'	Do not focus on
Ijijo na konyu	Grinding sesame
Ado ku biriki'	Do not focus on
Ijijo na kinyo	Grinding millet
Rembe lu amereki	Rembe has fallen
Indingi na Songodiro seku Liru	Between Songodiro and Liru
Rembe dio	Oh! Rembe
Lombe1 a tuwa	Lombe is dead

Challenges from the pastoralists in Upper Nile and Bahr- el-Ghazal

The pastoralists were difficult to pacify because they could flee rapidly into the remote areas, while the agriculturalists were more attached to their land and subsistence. The people who lived in the Sudd were also more protected by the marshes. Many pastoralist societies also lacked a centralized authority, which meant that the British had no recognizable leader with whom to negotiate. In addition the pastoralists were not used to accepting the authority of any paramount leader. The pastoralists with their vast herds of cattle only possessed ritual specialists and prophets. The best examples are the Nuer societies which were organized by "segmentary lineages" which settled disputes without an independent authority. The agricultural groups had more often a hereditary chieftainship.

Fig. (5)   Nuer chiefs captured (*Cambridge University Press*)

"In any new country you must establish law and order before you can develop either culture or trade, in doing so some eggs, as the saying goes, have to be broken." Arthur Vicars-Miles, a British administrator in 1934

The resistance of the Aliab Dinka

The Aliab Dinka struck in December 1919, when the Aliab under their leader, Kon Anok, ransacked the British station at Minghamman. A week later they inflicted a heavy defeat on the government expedition. The casualties included the Governor of the Mongalla Province, C. H. Stigand, and Major White, the force commander as well as 24 soldiers and porters.

The punitive action from the side of the British resulted in the death of 400 tribesmen, many villages were burnt and around 7,000 cattle were taken. Kon Anok surrendered and submittted to the condominium authorities, but later died of poison which presumably was self-inflicted.

Aliab Songs

Aliab	English
Wai die ke marol-jok	My spear on whitemen
Wo ce nak Acoli	We do not kill blacks
A ci wai lo kuara ee	The spear handle sounds *kuara*
Ci men cuor ke lei	Like lin with its prey
Akuen wa yok muor cuai ee	Akuen tell Muor Cuai
Rei die Apuot ke rewe	Apuote are thirsty
Ya wut ku ya yi	In the cattle camp
Apuk ma yok muor cuai ee	Apuk tell Muor Cuai
Riec die Apuot kecoke	Apuote are thirsty
Ya wut ku ya yi	In the cattle camp
Boluk ma yok muor cuai ee	Boluk tell Muor Cuai
Riec die Apuot ke coke	Apuote are thirsty
Ya wut ku ya yi	In the cattle camp
Akerma ma yok Muor cuai ee	Akerma tell Muor Cuai
Riec die Apuuot ke coke	Apuote are thristy
Ya wut ku ya yi	In the cattle camp
A nyai ne wath die thok	Why are you at my port
A nyai ne pim cie thok	Why are you at my watering point
Ya wut ku ya yi	In the cattle camp
Bor ma nyai rot yin ye	Bor get out
Ran kuc tong arerep	You do not know how to fight
Tong aba aroc a wer yei	I will castrate the Arab
Atuot ma nyai rot yin ye	Atuot get out
Ran kuc tong arerep	You do not know how to fight
Tong aba aroc a wer yei	I will castrate the Arab
Mundari ma nyai rot yin ye	Mundari get out
Ran kuc tong arerep	You do not know how to fight
Tong aba aroc a wer yei	I will castrate the Arab who commented upon this to be changed?

Fig. (6)   British-Sudanese troops in 1917

Challenges among the Nuer

There were rebellions among the Nuer (the Lou and the Gaawar) of the Upper Nile Province in 1927 and 1928. The government tried to capture the main leaders of the rebellions. The government sent troops throughout the Nuer country east of the Nile. According to Douglas Johnson: "The government planned a full scale settlement in 1929, aimed at concentrating the Lou and Gaawar in specified areas where they would be isolated from their Dinka neighbours and other groups of Nuer. The prophets were to be rooted out of their hiding places, and once military operations had been successfully completed, a vigorous new attempt to administer the Nuer would begin, with the building of roads, dispensaries, and administrative centres and the organization of the Nuer into a new administrative system under government appointed chiefs" (D. Johnson, 1982).

> **Definition**
>
> **Subsistence:** means of providing food for oneself
>
> **Segmentary society:** the society is organized in segments, or divisions, where the close family is the smallest segment where the members generally stand with each other. The family is part of a larger segment of more distant cousins and their families, who will stand with each other when attacked by outsiders. They are then part of larger segments with the same characteristics.

Cotton growing in Southern Sudan

The Southern Sudanese resistance to the condominium rule was also due to the introduction of cotton as a cash crop in the region in the early 1900's. The growth of cotton was foreign to the Southern Sudanese and was not popular. The cotton production involved the use of forced labour. Cotton growing started with experimental farms being established in Rumbek and Wau. It was proved that rain grown cotton could do very well in Southern Sudan and the Anglo Egyptian government went ahead by introducing cotton as a cash crop in places such as Upper Nile and the Nuba Mountains in 1923. By 1926, cotton growing as a cash crop had started in the Torit, Opari, and Kajo Keji areas, with ginneries in Torit and Sukole.

Despite the fact that the Southern Sudanese resisted the condominium regime in many areas, it should not be forgotten that one positive consequence of the new rule was that slave trade officially stopped after 1900, although it continued in reality until the 1920s. The *zariba* system came to a halt after 1900, and people could start rebuilding their lives.

Summary: The people in the South resisted the Anglo-Egyptian attempt to administer the region. Due to superior fire arms of the Condominium government they were defeated in the late 1920s.

Questions

1. What was the difference between the pacification in the North and the South?
2. What are the reasons for the different pacification processes in the South? Give examples.
3. What do you think were the consequences of the hard pacification towards the Nuer?

Condominium policy

Governors	Period
Lord Herbert Kiltchener	1899
Sir Reginald Wingate	1900-1916
Sir Lee Stack	1917-1924
Wasey Starry	1924-1925
Sir Geoffrey Archer	1925-1926
Sir John Maffey	1926-1934
Sir George Symes	1934-1940
Sir Hubert Huddlestone	1940-1947
Sir Robert Howe	1947-1954
Sir Alexander Helm	1954-1955

It is possible to divide the Condominium period into three phases where the authorities implemented different policies. The third phase, 1945-1955, will be dealt with in Chapter Five.

Phase one 1899-1920

The first Governor-General to be appointed under the terms of the Condominium was Lord Kitchener in January 1899. He only held office for one year. His successor Sir Reginald Wingate was to remain Governor-General until 1916 and became the major officer responsible for the pacification in the south. It was not until the 1930's that Southern Sudan really was under British control due to difficulties of transport and problems with the pacification process referred to above.

Fig. (7) Governor Wingate (1861-1953) served in the Egyptian Army from 1881-1898, where he had a central role in the reconquest of Sudan. He was appointed Governor-General in Sudan in 1899 and High Commissioner in Egypt in 1917. He retired from the Army in 1922 and died as a Baron in 1953

The government's concern in the first twenty years was the settlement of international borders, setting up the administration and an exploration of the conditions of the unknown South. During this period, the government did very little in terms of political, economic and educational development in the South. No construction work or services were implemented unless what was necessary for keeping government personnel there and for the maintenance of law and order. One exception was the sleeping sickness camps that were set up to cure and prevent the spread of diseases.

In the first two decades of the Condominium rule, the South was mainly regarded as a recruitment area for the "Sudanese" battalions of the Egyptian army which had settled in Sudan. Southern Sudanese refused to volunteer for military service, so conscription continued to be forced, reflecting the same exploitative pattern of the slave raids. The administration maintained their authority mainly by imposing payment of tribute up to the 1920's. The tribute consisted of land tax and herd tax.

Missionaries

As mentioned in Chapter 3, Catholic missionaries were in the Northern and the Southern Sudan from 1850. During the Mahdist era they operated from Cairo. Christian missionaries wanted to go to Sudan again after 1898, but the British administration was reluctant because of possible political unrest among the Muslim population in Sudan. Some were also afraid that conversion could ruin the tribal life. However, this policy was soon changed because of political and religious pressure. Christian missionaries were then asked to go to the South, but only a few concessions were given them in the North.

The Verona Fathers returned to the South after 1898 where their main focus was evangelisation and education. The Anglican Church Missionary Society (CMS) was given permission to work in Southern Sudan after 1898. The CMS educational focus was literacy and they did not teach technical skills. In 1901, the American United Presbyterian Mission (UPM) were allowed to open a mission to non-Muslim people in the South, and by 1911 they had established a cement block hospital among the Nuer.

The problems of the missionaries

To avoid competition for converts, as happened in Uganda, and for fear that conversion could lead to another Mahdist revolt, the government established in 1905 the "sphere system" or "spheres of influence", which meant zones for specific mission organizations. Both the Anglo-Egyptian government and the missionaries sought to limit the spread of Islam in the South and prepare the South for Christianity, but the missionaries were forbidden by the government to convert

Muslims for fear it might lead to another Mahdist uprising in the north. In order to spread Christianity the missionaries pressed on to make English the official language in Southern Sudan, discouraging the use of Arabic.

Fig. (8) Roman Catholic mission school in Wau (*Cambridge University Press*)

> As described in chapter two Christianity is not a new religion in Sudan. The Christian Nubian kingdoms, which survived for many centuries, achieved their peak of prosperity and military power in the ninth and tenth centuries. As mentioned in chapter three missionaries came to the South in 1851, but the missionaries had left the South by 1863.

Tropical diseases, poor transport, vast distances, lack of resources, the variety of languages, cultural factors, and little knowledge of the values and culture of the people made education a difficult task for the missionaries.

From the beginning of the Condominium period, the missionaries in the Christian churches in Southern Sudan competed for converts. This rivalry created misunderstanding and confusion among the Sudanese people as all were spreading the Christian message.

Another problem was that the people of the South were reluctant to send their children to mission schools. They feared that they would lose their cultural values at school. As a result of this fear, many of the bright children were denied the opportunity of schooling by their families.

Summary: The Anglo-Egyptian administration was more concerned about settling the borders and pacifying the peoples than in developing Southern Sudan. Eventually the Christian missionaries were allowed to go and open schools in the South.

Questions
1. What consequences do you think the pacification policy and the forced conscription had on the development of Southern Sudan?
2. What were the consequences of the Sphere System for the missionaries and the Southern Sudanese?

Phase two: 1920-1945

Indirect rule or "Native administration"

As we have seen the pacification of Southern Sudan was a difficult task. Indirect rule in Sudan was called "Native administration".

The British used indirect rule to avoid African resistance. Indirect rule used indigenous traditional leaders, who were loyal to Britain, to govern the people and to supply labour and tax. African chiefs were willing to cooperate on condition that their culture was not interfered with.

Indirect rule was Lord Lugard's idea. He believed it was cheap and would prevent African resistance because the people would be ruled through the local chiefs using indigenous structures, and indigenous laws and customs. The British lacked trained people to administer the territory. They also had little money to spend on administration and on the poor infrastructure of the territory. In the system of indirect rule, only a few British men were needed.

Some people believed that native administration would prevent the growth of detribalized religious or nationalist movements headed by educated men. Indeed, a disadvantage of the system of indirect rule was that it ignored the educated elite and did not recognise their ability to run their affairs without British supervision. The educated were distrustful of the illiterate chiefs appointed by the British.

In the North, the old families with authority under the Turko-Egyptian rule were reinstated and their chiefs were given specific judicial and administrative powers. In the South there was a much later assimilation of indigenous structures in the administration, mainly because there were few hereditary authorities such as those of the Shilluk (Collo) and the Azande. In many cases indirect rule caused a "tribalization" of people who had neither memory nor desire of tribal authority. The chief's courts for instance were just as much a colonial invention as an indigenous custom.

To establish chief's courts was not an easy task in areas where there were no indisputable leaders, for example, among the Nuer. Before this time, conflicts were mediated by the chief or religious specialists who relied on support from the community. Now, the chiefs and the elderly men were supported by the British and had a personal interest in upholding the law and order underwritten by the government. The election of these chiefs was monitored by British officials, and in the 1930's an increasing number of the chiefs had a military background.

> Tribalization was British policy both in the North and the South. Here is an extract from a conversation between the British inspector Blackley and Khidir Hamad, a Gordon College graduate (Sharkey 2003):
> Blackley: Khidir Effendi, what's your nationality?
> Khidir: Sudanese
> Blackley: I mean your tribe.
> Khidir: I don't recognize these tribalisms.
> Blackley: Fine, so what are these face scars?
> Khidir: To confirm that I am Sudanese

Fig. (9) A Kordofan tribal court (*Cambridge University Press*)

As mentioned above, the British tried to impose the system by force. They were successful with the Dinka of Bahr el-Ghazal, but failed with the Nuer of Upper Nile.

Two different models of administration were developed, one more mobile for the pastoralists in Upper Nile and Bahr el-Ghazal, and the other more bureaucratic for the sedentary agricultural communities in Equatoria and in Bahr al-Ghazal. Some scholars state that although the British promoted Native Administration, they really eroded tribal custom and authority in the South. The problem of relying on traditional leadership was that indigenous authority was contested and diversified. Other scholars claim that the British discussed with the locals how they should be represented and often chose someone with authority. At the same time the chiefs made sure that tribal customs were respected.

Work in pairs:
1. How did the native administration cause and sustain a "tribalization" of people?
2. Do you know from your own environment that tribalization took place in the past?
3. Do you think that Native Administration was a democratic system?
4. What power do you think the educated people in the community had?
5. How is your community ruled now?

Discussion in class:
1. Did the Native administration erode traditional leadership or did it reinforce it?

The policy of separation

From the very beginning of the Condominium period the government had wanted to prevent Islam from spreading to the South. After the First World War steps to strengthen this policy were taken, in conjunction with the Native Administration policy.

The Milner Report in 1920 recommended that Sudan should be divided into two distinct territories and the frontiers should be drawn along the rivers Baro, Sobat, White Nile and Bahr el-Ghazal (Kirr). It was also recommended to arrange annual meetings of the three governors in the South, and not with the other governors of the North.

"Closed District Ordinance"

A consequence of the policy of separation was the "Closed District Ordinance" in 1922. Under the provision of passports and permits in 1920, Southern Sudan was classified as "closed districts" resulting in the exclusion of the Northern staffs and traders, Moreover, it prevented the Southerners from traveling north to find work and education. All

Egyptian and Northern Sudanese Muslim officers were withdrawn from the South and local Southern Sudanese were recruited instead. Southern Sudanese who lived outside the closed districts (Kordofan, Darfur, parts of Kassala and the White Nile provinces) needed a special permit to live and work in these areas. Arab-style dress and names were prohibited. This law was designed to abolish the internal slave trade and to halt the spread of Islam to non-Islamic parts.

> 'I should like to lay stress on the undesirability of an Arab-Nuba blend ... The result is always an undisciplined, drunken, half-caste Arab who has no background and no tradition to keep him up to the mark.' A.L.W. Vicars-Miles, British administrator.

It was also suggested that the South should be assimilated into Uganda and East Africa. In 1930 the civil secretary reinforced this thinking by declaring that the South should be developed according to 'African' rather than Arab traditions, and that the South possibly should belong to East Africa in the future.

Fig. (10) James Milner (1854-1925) made a report about British-Egyptian relations which had great influence on British policy towards Sudan

Why did Britain promote a policy of separation?

One reason was a change of attitude after the First World War towards the colonized people from domination to development in cooperation with the missionaries. Another reason was the fear of Sudanese and Egyptian nationalism, and an attempt to prevent linking the South´s future with the North. The fall of the Ottoman Empire in 1914 made Egypt pursue the goal of an independent Nile Valley which comprises of Egypt and Sudan. The attempt of a united Egypt-Sudan was aborted by the British, and as early as 1919 there was a British plan for political independence of the South from the North of Sudan. Britain's intervention in the plans of a united Egypt and Sudan led to several independent insurrection incidents in Sudan, the most important in 1924 led by Ali 'Abd al-Latif.

Fig. (11) Leaders of the White Flag League (*Cambridge University Press*)

> Ali 'Abd al-Latif (1892-1948). Army officer of Dinka mother and a Nuba father.
>
> He founded the United Tribes Society and was arrested for nationalist agitation in 1922. In 1924 he formed the White Flag League, dedicated to drive the British from Sudan. Demonstrations followed in Khartoum in the summer and Ali'Abd al-Latif was arrested in July 1924. The demonstrations were suppressed in the autumn. When the Governor-General, Sir Lee Stack, was assassinated in Cairo by an Egyptian in November 1924, Egyptian troops were withdrawn from the entire Sudan. Ali'Abd al-Latif himself was sentenced to seven years of prison, and then they consigned him unfairly to a mental hospital in Egypt where he died.

Discuss in pairs
1. What were the consequences of the Closed District Ordinance?
2. List as many reasons as you can to explain why the Closed District Ordinance was implemented?

Discuss in class
1. Do you think the policy of separation was advantageous or disadvantageous for the South? Why/why not?
2. Why do you think so few women are prominent in Southern Sudanese history?

Education under the British

While the Sudan government invested little in Southern Sudan before 1920 the education policy after 1920 was meant to play an important role in differentiating the South from the North. Grants in aid were given to many schools in the South from 1926, and a language conference at Rejaf in 1928 decided that six indigenous languages should be used as medium of instruction in schools. Text books were prepared on the basis of this decision. English was promoted as the lingua franca, and Arabic was discouraged. The number of schools using indigenous languages as medium of instruction in the elementary schools increased from 4 in 1926 to 32 in 1930. Despite these efforts education in the South was not prioritized in the same way as in the North. The quality of teaching in the elementary school was mixed, the students attending the schools were very few despite the increase in the number of schools referred to above, and few secondary schools were established.

An intermediate school was started at Khor Atar in 1944, 20 miles upstream of the Nile Sobat confluence. The staff were British including the headmaster. The first graduates completed the four year course in 1947 and the school welcomed the first secondary students in 1948. However the government established a secondary school in Rumbek the same year and the students were transferred from Atar to Rumbek. The year 1948 thus meant the start of secondary education in the South.

Why was the education unsatisfactory in Southern Sudan?

One reason was that the government thought that they needed only a few educated Southerners for minor clerical posts. As they recruited most of them from the sons of soldiers, the government left the education to the Christian missionaries and the Muslim *khalwas* in towns. Therefore there was no common curriculum guiding the various missionary educators, no effective teacher training centres in the South and no financial support was forthcoming from the government for education of Southerners. In addition, there was fear of detribalisation, particularly among the pastoralists.

The missionaries and education. Positive and negative consequences

As mentioned earlier in this chapter government policies meant that the missionaries did not have a free hand in their work. The sphere system imposed in 1905 was most resented by the Catholic missionaries who were allotted the area of Bahr el-Ghazal in which to work. Islam was well established in Bahr-el-Ghazal. The Government was more supportive of the Anglican Church Missionary Society (CMS) in Southern Sudan than the Catholic church and this increased the tension between the Catholic missionaries and the British colonial government.

The missionaries established mission schools where people acquired education which they did not have before the missionaries came. Whereas the Roman Catholics had more resources and emphasized industrial and technical training, the Protestant churches emphasized literacy.

It is generally estimated that the population of the Southern provinces was between two and three million at this time. In the years 1928-46 it is realistically estimated that about 260,000 came into contact with some type of formal education. About 55,000 of these attended either elementary or secondary school. Teachers were however difficult to recruit partly because of limited financial resources, partly because of using English as medium of instruction. The limited financial resources first made it difficult to recruit Europeans, while the use of English as medium of instruction excluded Arab speaking teachers from North Sudan.

By 1930, the **Catholic Verona Fathers** (Comboni Fathers) had about 1,900 students in elementary schools and 2 post-elementary trade schools at Wau and Rejaf. 2 intermediate schools at Wau and Okaru. In the 1930's they set up two teacher training schools, one at Mupoi and the other at Torit.

In 1930, the Anglican Church Missionary Society (CMS) had about 600 students at the elementary level and a high school and intermediate school at Loka in the Yei region.

In 1930 the American United Presbyterian Mission (UPM) had elementary schools at Doleib Hill and Nassir.

The Comboni Fathers and Sisters in Bahr-el-Ghazal had bush schools and when students could read the catechism they were taught literacy in technical schools. There girls learned more religion, needlework, hygiene, domestic science, music, English and Arabic. The boys had technical lessons in carpentry, bricklaying, gardening, and some received a clerical training. The missionaries educated those Southerners who rose to positions of leadership after 1946 although their numbers were very few. They also gave a basic education to Sudanese who became part of the government administrative staff in Southern Sudan.

Missionary activities helped to bring slavery and the slave trade to an end. While their Muslim counterparts promoted the slave trade, missionaries condemned human trade. In this way the missionaries among others were instrumental in restoring the dignity to the South Sudanese.

Over the 50 years of Mission schools many ethnic groups in Southern Sudan came to value education. The missionary schools were thus important for the promotion of literacy skills, but they were of uneven quality. This suited the government who did not want a high standard of education in the South.

The missionaries were used by Government to limit educational attainment in the South. There was no clear understanding of how the missions were to implement their share of the government's Southern policy. The uneven quality of missionary education in Southern Sudan was criticised by the government during the decades of the Condominium when Cox became Director of Education in the 1930's. The missionaries were criticised for failure to organise education, the absence of qualified teachers and of effective teacher training, and for their commitment to evangelisation before education.

Although the government was critical of the education of the missionaries, it has to be noted that the government did not want a high standard in education there as they feared it would detribalise the students and create an educated class that could threaten the condominium. This policy of limiting educational attainment of Southerners is clearly spelt out at the conference of government officials and mission personnel which was convened in Malakal in 1941 to discuss the "Missions and Education Policy in Upper Nile Province." The policy of Native Administration in the 1920's tended in addition to discourage education among pastoralist people, because it was thought unwise to divorce the students from the customs of their own ethnic group.

In the late 1930's British officials discovered that this passive educational policy did not provide Sudanese staff who were trained for executive work and they were therefore not prepared for a future autonomous state. It was therefore urgent to improve the educational system to ensure the success of the policy of separation. A few grants-in- aid were made in 1939 to start teacher training centers by educationists, like the Verona Fathers and the Christian Missionary Society (CMS). Girls were however not encouraged to attend school. The education for girls was mostly concentrated on domestic accomplishments, and as a result girls and women's lives didn't change much in the condominium period.

Summary: In the 1920's the British administration implemented indirect rule in Sudan. They also enacted a policy of separation, where Southern Sudan was regarded as a closed district. The missionaries were running many schools, but education was not promoted in earnest in the South until the 1930s.

Questions

1. What made education in the South inadequate during the first decades of Condominium rule?
2. Name the main Christian missionary groups who came to Southern Sudan between 1850 and 1950 and explain their aims.
3. Imagine you are a Christian missionary in Southern Sudan in the early 1900's. You visit the local chief to persuade him to send his son to your school. The chief has many reservations. Dramatise the meeting that takes place between you.
4. What were the positive and negative consequences of the mission schools in the condominium period?

> **Discuss in class**
> 1. What were the reasons why the British administration changed their education policy to some extent in the late 1930's?

The consequences of British rule for the North-South and South-South relations in Sudan

The combination of the Closed District Ordinance, indirect rule and the lack of an offensive government educational policy increased the already existing political, economic and educational differences between the South and the North.

Religious diversity

The British policy towards the North and South differed greatly, especially in religious matters. While Native Administration encouraged indigenous religious diversity in the South, in the North the administration encouraged a greater homogeneity of Muslim practice by discouraging fanatical movements. At the same time, the basis for a broad cultural and social unity and a centralized administration provided throughout North Sudan by the Muslim regimes of Turko-Egyptian and Mahdiya was lacking in Southern Sudan.

Theoretically, the Native Administration allowed the development of the South along the lines peculiar to itself, influenced by British and Christian social, cultural ideals and safe from Muslim penetration. Christian missionary organizations played a major role in the administration's plan to de-arabize and de-Islamize the South, where Arabic language and even the wearing of Arabic attire were discouraged.

Fig. (12) Leonard Sharland (1904–1978) was a missionary amongst the Dinka people in the middle of the 20th century

The language policy from 1928 referred to above created a linguistic barrier to the north. Muslim mosques, schools and preachers were banned, to the extent that in Western Bahr el-Ghazal indigenous Muslim Arab-speaking groups were expelled to Kordofan and Darfur.

> **Question**
> What developments took place under the Condominium administration that widened the gap between the North and the South?

Economic diversity

While the South is the most fertile region in Sudan and with most of the national resources, it was and still is the least developed region. *Why is this the case?* As a result of a lack of development interests from the government of Sudan, no costly schemes for the development of the South and its people were implemented. On the contrary, from the beginning of the Condominium period, the central government participated in the exploitation of the South. Royalties collected on Southern Sudanese ivory sales and export went for instance to the central government, not to the regional government. In addition, while the Northern Sudanese could accumulate wealth through trade, in the South the trade was monopolized by Greek, Syrian, Armenian and Northern merchants. Southern Sudanese received therefore little benefits from the legal trade.

Even when the Closed District Ordinance regulated the Northern travelers, the Condominium government did not stimulate a Southern Sudanese commercial class to compete with the trading companies from the North. British officials blocked private development efforts because the indigenous population had supposedly no desire of improving their welfare. In addition, the infrastructure was badly developed and trading was costly. On the other hand, the British did introduce new crops in the 1930s, like cassava, due to droughts. Although cotton cash crop was not, as mentioned above, well received, farmers did grow ground nuts as a cash crop. During the Second World War Juba grew into a large town, and other towns started to grow based on old villages and zaribas. *Why did this happen?* As a result of relative peace, the population started to come back from the hills to their old villages. As a consequence diseases on animals were combated and people´s diseases were controlled. The population started to grow and there was an increasing urbanization.

At the end of World War II there was far greater difference in the development of the Northern and Southern part of the country than at the end of the Mahdi government. The lack of economic development of the Southern people, as compared with the riverain and urban Northerners, was a hindrance to the rapid integration of the two regions. The late 1940's integration policy which the central government adopted without much planning was not a good basis for a successful transition.

> **Questions**
> 1. How did the different economic development between the North and the South affect the relationship between the two parts of Sudan at the end of the condominium period?
> 2. To what extent do you think this economic disparity made the union of Sudan more difficult?
> 3. How has this policy affected the political, social and economic relations of the South and the North up to now?

Administration policy

With the policy of Native Administration in Southern Sudan, the British divided consciously the Southerners according to their existing or invented tribal and ethnic lines which internally hindered the South-South relations. In North Sudan on the other hand, the British Native Administration built on existing leaders from the Turko-Egyptian rule. Native Administration had therefore not the same negative effect in the North as in the South.

Also the policy of Native Administration in the South offered an opportunity for the native chiefs instead of educated people to assume high positions in the government. It was the native chiefs and not educated Southerners who were to determine the political issues of the region.

Summary: While Islam was encouraged by the British in the North, it was deeply discouraged in the South. While the British discouraged economic development in the South, some development programmes thrived in the North. While the British seem to have disrupted, to some extent, local authorities in the South, they built on local authorities in the North.

> **Questions**
> 1. What do you think were the consequences for the future of Southern Sudan that traditional chiefs instead of educated Sudanese were consulted about the future of the South?
> 2. How can ethnicity and "tribal" boundaries be a hindrance for an establishment of a more democratic system of administration?

The beginning of independence

The Graduates' General Congress

The Graduates' Congress was established in February 1938 by the Northern educated class with the intention of presenting a united front to the British administration in Sudan. The Condominium Government recognized the Congress on the condition that it would only be concerned with social matters.

The Congress proved, however, to play an important initial role in the independence movement, and in 1942, through a memorandum, they demanded the right of self-determination after the war. The Congress demanded that restrictions be lifted on trade and movement, that a standard syllabus for schools in the North and the South be established and that grants to missionary schools be ended for full government take over. These demands signaled a wish to integrate the South into the North of Sudan and end the separate development of the South which the Condominium Government had pursued. The attitudes of the Congress leaders to the South were, however, on the whole condescending. Al Azhari, the leading nationalist leader, is quoted as saying to the Congress: "The South is necessary for the economic development of the North."

The Civil Secretary, Sir Douglas Newbold, responded to the president of the Congress by reminding him that the Congress should confine itself to the internal and domestic affairs of Sudanese. However, the memorandum led to a split of the Congress into:

- Moderates who accepted the Government's policy of gradual transfer to self-government and self-determination and

- Radicals who refused to cooperate with the Condominium Government.

This split led to the formation of political parties. The main political parties were:

- **The Unionists:** The Ashigga (which means brothers of the same father and mother) Party emerged in 1943 from the radicals as the first Sudanese political party. It favoured a union with Egypt under the Egyptian crown. Their leader was Ismail al-Azhari.

- **The Independents:** The Umma (which means nation) Party emerged in 1945 from the moderates. The party called for complete independence and raised the slogan Sudan for Sudanese. It accepted cooperation with the Condominium Government to achieve self – government and self – determination. Their leader was Sayyid Abdel Rahman al-Mahdi

These political parties came under the patronage of the two influential religious sects in Sudan, because the educated Sudanese needed sectarian support to draw the masses to their sides:

- In 1944 the Ashigga Party gained the tacit support of the Khatmiyya religious order, headed by Sayyid Ali al-Mirghani.

- The Umma Party was under the patronage of the Ansar sect.

> **The Khatmiyya order** was founded by Sayid Mohammed Uthman al-Mirghani al-Khatim in the 19th century. He introduced the Arabic language and Islam to many isolated communities. The order collaborated with the Turko-Egyptian regime, and came into conflict with the Mahdi in the 1880s.
>
> The Khatmiyya order is concentrated in the northern and eastern parts of Sudan and has retained most of the old tribal loyalty.

The Ansar are supporters of the Mahdi. They rose with him in the 1880's, but had been the Mahdi's followers for years. They accepted him to be the expected Mahdi, chosen by God, who would fill the earth with justice and equity.

The Ansar is concentrated in the western and central parts of Sudan, and as the Khatmiyya order, they provide their followers with a religious and political organization.

From 1945 the Congress was dominated by unionist parties, especially the Ashigga.

Summary: The Graduate's General Congress was an important movement in the North that prepared the ground for independence. Sudanese political parties became attached to religious sects and developed sectarian politics.

Questions
1. What does the term Condominium Government mean and who were the rulers in the Government?
2. What was the Graduates' Congress' view of the South? Explain.
3. What were the main differences between the two parties of the nationalist movement?

Timeline
1898: The British-Egyptian reconquest of Sudan
1899: The Anglo-Egyptian Condominium rule
1909: The Pacification of Equatoria
1914: The Fall of the Ottoman Empire
1920: The Milner report who recommended indirect rule and Southern policy
1922: The Closed District Ordinance
1924: Ali Abdel Latif's insurrection attempt and Egyptian withdrawal from Sudan.

1927: The Nuer settlement
1928: The Rajaf language conference
1931, 1932, 1933: Drought and grasshopper swarms
1938: The Graduate's General Congress is established

Tasks

a) Write a story about your people's resistance against towards the British rule, either based on written sources like this chapter, or based on oral sources like interviews, legends or narratives.

b) Imagine that you are a young girl or boy in the late 1920's in Southern Sudan. Write a story about how you experience daily life.

c) Role-Play: Imagine you are a traditional chief and a British administrator comes to your compound and asks you to set up the chief's court, collect tax and provide a labour force for the Condominium Government. Dramatise that conversation and clarify what you will gain and lose in this arrangement.

d) Write short notes on the following periods during the Anglo-Egyptian rule in the South i) 1899-1920 ii) 1920-1945.

Group discussion

1. What were the reasons for the Anglo-Egyptian rule?
2. Why and how did Southern Sudanese resist the Anglo-Egyptian rule?
3. What would have happened to the political system in South Sudan if the British hadn't implemented Native Administration?
4. Southern Sudan would have been more united under the French colonial policy of total assimilation than the British's policy of separate development. Discuss.
5. How did the British view Southern Sudanese?

5
The Independence Struggle 1942 – 1958

Introduction

It is claimed that World War II opened the eyes of Africans because the West claimed to be fighting for liberty, fraternity and equality. All colonized peoples of the world including Sudanese started agitating more vigorously for independence after World War II. The fact should not be forgotten that the call for independence was stronger in Northern Sudan than in the South although the first anti-colonial uprising in 1923 was led by Abdal Latif who was himself a Southerner.

The years 1942–1958 were eventful years for both the North and the South. During this period the nationalist political activities in the North were developing at a rapid pace. This resulted in the achievement of self-government and self-determination when the Anglo – Egyptian Agreement was signed on 12th February 1953. The history of the South and North was closely linked during this period as the British abandoned their separatist policy and began to revise their Southern policy.

Phase Three: Change in the Condominium government's policy towards the South

As seen in chapter 4, the British had, during the Condominium, encouraged a separate development of the North and the South based on their social, cultural, linguistic and economic differences. This policy had resulted in lack of economic development of the South, with few if any development programs. Education in the South was primarily limited to primary education at missionary schools and as a result the Southerners were not well prepared for political performance and representation. The civil secretary's statement in 1930 mentioned above that the South should be developed according to 'African' rather than Arab traditions, and that the South possibly should belong to East African colonies in the future, underlined the lack of commitment from the side of the British Foreign Office to govern the South as part of Sudan, and this skepticism of a united Sudan was prevalent up until 1947.

> **Secret letter to the Governor-General's Council**
> "The eyes of Egypt and of the Northern Sudanese are on the South, and our Southern Policy (or lack of policy) has been heavily criticized both in Cairo and Omdurman... If we are to carry Northern enlightened opinion with us at all over our Southern Policy, it is imperative that we go faster on both education and material development." (Newbold, civil secretary of the condominium government 1944).

But at that time Britain changed their policy towards Southern Sudan completely (phase three). Educated Northerners from the Graduates' General Congress pressed on to abolish the Closed District Ordinance, to liberate trade and movements, and to unify the educational syllabi. Moreover the economic underdevelopment of the South was also troublesome for the government. The administration analyzed three alternatives for the South:

a) Integration of the South into the North

b) Integration of the South into East Africa

c) Integration of parts of the South with the North and the other parts with East Africa.

In the end the British administration chose the integration with the North. *Why?*

The pressure from the Graduates' General Congress mentioned above was one important reason.

At the same time the Sudan Administration Conference in 1946, with representatives from Northern Sudan and the condominium government, made clear recommendations for the unification of the North and South. Northern nationalists' and Egyptian insistence on a united Sudan compelled the Condominium Government to change its separatist policy. The Egyptians insisted on a united Sudan because of their vital interest in the Nile waters.

The Anglo-Egyptian treaty of 1936 had restored Egypt's sovereignty over Sudan. The rivalry between Egypt and Great Britain over Sudan was of long history and the British wanted to strengthen Sudanese administration against Egyptians pretensions.

Moreover, the separation between the North and South was increasingly difficult to administer. With the new development programs in the South, there was more need for Northern labour in the South. Schools were established and the Southern chiefs were required to provide a quota of boys for education. However, the decades of earlier neglect of Southern education meant that few Southerners were experienced in modern administration and commerce. The British recognized that for educational and economic reasons, the North and the South should be united.

Another reason for the change in British policy was that the East African colonies, according to some sources, did not seem to support the plan of annexing the South.

There were mixed reactions towards a reversal by the British administrators in the South. The educated Southern Sudanese were asked their opinion regarding the status of the South. Their responses were if not conflicting, somewhat mixed. The Southern Sudanese were nearly unanimous in rejecting incorporation into East Africa, and only a few rejected amalgamation with the North, but all rejected the idea of Southern Provinces being governed by a Northern Parliament. Some wanted Southern representatives in Khartoum while others wanted a separate Southern parliament. In presenting their answers, many Southern respondents cited distrust of Northerners based on historical experiences such as slavery, while others mentioned religious differences. Still, many British officials were skeptical to a hurried union without development in the South, and were concerned about the Arabs' intentions with Southern Sudan..

The change of British policy from separation of the South to the ultimate unity of Sudan meant that the British recognized the need to accelerate economic and educational development in the South to catch up with the North. Some of the British administrators in the South were, however, concerned about the Arabs' intentions with Southern Sudan. To consult the Southerners about the future status of the South and its role in the Legislative Assembly, the Juba Conference was convened in 1947.

Summary: Southerners responded differently to the change in the British policy towards the South, but they rejected almost unanimously the suggestion of integration with East Africa and they also rejected the idea of the Southern provinces being governed by a Northern parliament.

Work in pairs
1. Try to list the various Southern responses to the change in the British policy.

Summary: Southern Sudan experienced great changes in the 1940s. The British changed their policy of separation and encouraged education in the South. There was a growing urbanization and development of the economy.

Question
1. Why did the British change their policy towards Southern Sudan?

The Juba Conference 1947

In June 1947, Sir James Robertson, who had become civil secretary following the death of Newbold in 1944, called for a conference in Juba after the Sudan Administrative Conference recommended a closer association of the government with the Sudanese people. It was to seek the Southern Sudanese opinion on the future status of the South and its role in the Legislative Assembly, which meant a national parliament would be established in Khartoum. The conference was held in Juba, the capital of Equatoria on the 12th and 13th of June 1947.

The Juba Conference thus aimed at measuring 1) Southern reactions to the recommendations about the proposed unity between the North and South, 2) the representation of the South in the proposed legislative assembly, or parliament, 3) and the educational policy in the South. The seventeen delegates from the South were all selected by the British from among their employees; tribal chiefs, junior officials or police officers, among them, Philomon Majok, Clement Mboro, Buth Diu, Hassan Fertak, James Tambura, Chief Cir Rehan, Siricio Iro and Chief Lolik Lado. Some Northern members were Mohammed Saleh El Shingeiti, Ibrahim Badri and Habib Abdalla. The Governors of the Southern provinces also attended

The Juba Conference confirmed a major change of British policy which had been separation between the North and the South. The condominium government argued for a change for these reasons:
- Since 1945 economic and educational development had occurred in the South.
- It was recognized that Southern Sudan, because of its history and geographical position, should turn more to the Arab world rather than to East Africa.

This meant that the Closed Districts order had been abolished.

Despite the British claims that the situation in the South had changed somewhat since 1945, the Juba conference underlined how unprepared the Southerners were to take part in political discussions on a national level. Many of the Southern representatives did not have the needed educational background, and they did not have a consistent strategy to safeguard Southern interests during the conference.

There were mixed reactions towards a reversal by the British administrators in South. On day one of the Juba conference all the Southerners spoke against sending representatives to the Legislative

Assembly in Khartoum. But on the second day the Southerners had changed their minds and agreed to the idea of sending representatives to Khartoum.

One of the most prominent representatives from the South was Clement Mboro, whose changing statements from one day to the other underlined the lack of professionalism and amateurism of the Southerners at the conference.

> "I think we in the South are not sufficiently advanced to participate in the legislative assembly immediately, but we can attend as observers." Clement Mboro 12th of June 1947

> "We can go to Khartoum immediately to legislate together with the Northerners. It is best for us (Southerners) to go and legislate straight away in spite of our backwardness. Since we can speak for ourselves in the present conference, there is no reason why we cannot speak for ourselves in a Legislative Assembly. If any law is proposed which is not agreeable to the South we can stand up and object." Clement Mboro 13th of June 1947.

Fig. (1)   Clement Mboro

> **Clement Mboro**: Born 1919 in Mboro, west Wau, capital of Bahr el-Ghazal. His father was chief of the Nadgo tribe. He started his career as a clerk. Later he joined the school of administration of the Gordon Memorial College. Some of his posts were district commissioner, deputy-governor in Darfur and minister of interior in the transitional government following the 1964 October Revolution. Uncle Clement, as many Southerners used to call him, was a strong nationalist. He died in Kenya in 2006.

The Chairperson asked on the 13th of June why the Southern delegates had changed their minds from the previous day. James Tembura replied that Judge Shingeiti had convinced him that the only way to influence the future government of Sudan was to accept unity. They were also interested in having one education system, in introducing Arabic to Southern schools to enable Southern Sudanese to catch up with the North. The question of the unity of Sudan was, however, not decided upon, only postponed, nor was a separate administration for the South agreed upon

As a result of the Juba conference the Southerners were, due to their lack of consistent strategy, compelled to participate in the Legislative Assembly.

Following the Juba Conference, the Sudan Government allowed senior Northern officials to return to the South and Southerners were sent to study in the Gordon Memorial College in Khartoum instead of Makerere College in Uganda.

This was the first time Southern Sudanese had been asked their opinion during the time of the Condominium. The Southerners came together and Southern Sudan was identified as a region. This in turn resulted in the birth of nationalism in Southern Sudan.

Unrest in the South

Southern officials had established SOWC (Southern Officials Welfare Committee) in the late 1930s, and reformed it in 1947. They protested against different conditions between Northern and

Southern employees, the divide between Northern and Southern citizens, and unequal conditions in education. They asked for equal pay, equal treatment of Sudanese citizens and government schools in the South with the teaching of Arabic. The disparity of wages between Northern and Southern officials was however not addressed at the Juba conference, and in October there was a general strike in Juba. Due to this strike the condominium government promised to look into the working conditions of the Southerners.

Summary: In 1947 the British convened a conference in Juba where the conferees discussed how the South should be represented in the legislature. However, many of the Southern representatives did not have the needed educational background, and they did not have a consistent strategy to safeguard Southern interests during the conference. The result of the Juba conference was that the Southerners, due to their lack of consistent strategy, were compelled to participate in the Legislative Assembly.

Work in pairs
1. Give reasons why the Condominium Government changed the policy towards the South?
2. What was the Juba conference? Why was it important for the development of the South?

Discuss in class
1. In what way did the Southern representatives take care of the interests of the Southern region at the Juba conference?
2. Taking into account the fact that Southerners who were invited to the Juba conference were chiefs and administrators chosen by the colonial secretary, can they rightly be referred to as representatives of the South?

The Legislative Assembly

The Executive Council and Legislative Assembly ordinance were announced by the Governor – General, Sir Robert Howe, on 19 June 1948. The Executive Council replaced the Governor – General's Council, and consisted of twelve to eighteen members, at least half of whom had to be Sudanese. The Executive Council was responsible for executing government laws whereas the partially elected Legislative Assembly was responsible for proposing laws and consisted of thirteen Southerners and fifty two Northerners. The Governor-General retained his veto power on all issues.

The elections to the assembly took place on 15 November 1948 in the North and 14 % of the seats were allocated to the South.

The Southerners in the Legislative Assembly were:

Equatoria Province:
1. Andrea Gore,
2. Benjamin Loki,
3. Zakria Jambo,
4. Circio Iro
5. Buth Kaka.

Upper Nile Province:
1. Buth Diu,
2. Edward Adok,
3. ElHaj Mohammed Abdalla
4. Dual Deng.

Bahr el- Ghazal:
1. Abdalla Adam ElYas,
2. Chir Rayhan,
3. Khamis Mursal
4. Istanslaus Baya Sama.

Work in pairs
1. Explain the difference between the Executive Council and the Legislative Assembly.
2. Explain the functions of the Legislative Assembly.

Self-government

Fig. (2) Buth Diu

On discussions in the Legislative Assembly about 1) self-government/determination for Sudan and 2) a Federal Constitution for the whole of Sudan, the Southerners differed from their Northern counterparts. The Upper Nile MP Both Dieu represented the Southern viewpoint stating that self-government/self–determination for Sudan should be postponed until the South had reached the same degree of development as the North.

Buth Diu (d. c. 1972) came from Western Nuer. He had no formal education, but was one of the leaders of the Liberal Party in Sudan before and after independence in 1956. Although Buth Diu was in favour of a federal system for the South, he was not in favour of Southern secession- He was a District Commissioner in Fajak District and became a Member of Parliament and a Minister of Animal Resources.

The Southern members of the Legislative Assembly therefore voted against a motion tabled by the Umma Party members in December 1950 about granting Sudan self – government since Sudan, and particularly the South was not yet prepared for it. During the

Constitutional Amendment Commissions' deliberations Both Diew suggested a federal constitution within a united Sudan. He withdrew from the commission in protest of the Northern rejection of his proposal. However, the commission accepted the inclusion of special safeguards for the South in the draft constitution.

> **The Constitutional Amendment Commission** of March 1951
> The Commission consisted of 13 Sudanese members, of whom one was the Southerner Buth Diu and one British expert. The Commission recommended constitutional changes and prepared the Self-Government Statute.

> **Definition**
>
> A federal state is a type of sovereign state, where several partially self-governing regions are united by a central government. Certain issues such as foreign policy and the defence, is often the sole responsibility of the central government. The self-governing status of the regions is constitutionally well-established and cannot be changed by a unilateral decision of the central government.

The Self – Government Statute was enacted by the Legislative Assembly on 23 April 1952. This provided for an all Sudanese Council of Ministers responsible to an elected parliament. The Governor – General would retain special responsibility for the public service and external affairs, and could veto any legislation affecting the South.

On October 1952, the statute was approved by the British Government while the Egyptian Government had given up all rights by annulling the Condominium agreement and the Anglo-Egyptian treaty.

Summary: The Self-Government Statute was enacted by the Legislative Assembly and approved by the British Government. This was the first formal step to independence.

> **Pair work**
> 1. Why did the Southerners want self-determination to be postponed? Do you think it was a wise decision?

The new Anglo-Egyptian agreement

The monarchy in Egypt was overthrown on July 1952. The new Egyptian government recognized the Sudanese right of self-government and self-determination, and invited Sudanese political parties to Cairo. In Cairo agreements were signed with the Umma Party and the National Unionist Party (former Ashigga Party). Faced with the unity of Sudanese parties and Egypt, Britain had to accept a new Anglo-Egyptian agreement which was signed in February 1953.

Fig. (3) Northern Sudanese celebrate self-government (*The Book Guild Ltd*)

One of the most important issues in the negotiations about the new Anglo-Egyptian agreement was the position of the South and especially Article 100 where the Governor – General's special responsibilities and powers towards the South were defined. The unionist parties, the Umma Party and the Egyptian government insisted on the removal of this article. However, no Southern politician was invited to the discussions in Cairo. The reason given for not inviting the Southerners was that it was a meeting between Egyptian Government and the Sudanese political parties and since Southerners had no registered political parties, they were excluded. This may have been due to the fact that Southerners were not represented in Northern parties and, as mentioned, had no parties of their own although they were represented in the Legislative Assembly. This exclusion from the negotiations naturally embittered educated Southerners.

In the negotiation, British negotiators claimed that:
- The backwardness of the **Southern** Provinces justified this article.
- **Southerners** had more confidence in a British administration than in a Northern Sudanese one.

The Egyptian negotiators maintained:
- The inclusion in the Statute of such words as "**South**" and "**Southerners**" would undermine the unity of Sudan.
- The Governor General's retention of such responsibilities in the **South** might endanger their vital interests in the Nile waters.

The new Agreement, signed on 12 February 1953 kept Article 100 in the Statute, but the responsibilities of the Governor – General were worded differently. It stated that the Governor "*shall have a special responsibility to ensure fair and equitable treatment to all inhabitants of the various provinces of Sudan*". Article 5 in the Agreement stated that the British and Egyptian Governments would observe that the Governor – General's special powers in Article 100 of the Self – Government Statute would not be exercised in a way that would harm the unity of Sudan as one territory.

> **The 12th of February 1953 Anglo – Egyptian Agreement for Self – Government and Self – Determination for Sudan**
> Recognition of the Sudanese right to self-determination.
> A transitional period, during which sovereignty was to be kept in reserve until self-determination was achieved, but was not to exceed three years.
> The Governor General, who remained the supreme constitutional authority, was to exercise his powers with the assistance of a five member commission.
> An international electoral commission was to prepare for elections to a Sudanese parliament.

Summary: The New Anglo-Egyptian Agreement was established in 1953 establishing the steps towards self-determination. The Southerners were excluded from the negotiations. The most important decision for the Southerners was that the Governor-General lost the responsibilities in the South.

Work in pairs
1. Why do you think the Southerners were not represented in the discussions in Cairo about a new Anglo-Egyptian Agreement?
2. Explain, in your own words, the basic principles of the New Agreement.

Parliamentary elections

Fig. (4)   Polling station in Juba (*Cambridge University Press*)

During the election campaign in 1953 Northern politicians and journalists toured the South. The National Unionist Party (NUP) promised during the election campaign that all posts in the South would be filled by Southerners. This made Southern politicians such as Bullen Alier to join the NUP. He stood as a candidate in Bor and won in the constituency. NUP won 5 other Southern seats, but the other Northern parties did not win any seats in the South. The bulk of seats went to the newly established Southern Party. The following table shows the election results:

Party	Number of Seats
National Unionist Party (NUP)	50
Umma Party	23
Independents	12
The Southern Party/later the Liberal Party	10
The Socialist Republican Party	3

> **The Southern Party**
> - The First Southern Political Party, formed with British assistance in April 1953 before the elections
> - Selwyn Lloyd, the British Minister of State, had a core role in the formation of this party.
> - Shortly after the elections, the Southern Party became the Liberal Party under the leadership of Buth Diu and later Benjamin Loki (both former members of the Legislative Assembly).
> - It proposed federalism with a separate administrative status for the South.
> - In parliament it usually voted with the opposition party, the Umma.

The Sudanese parliament opened in January 1954 with Ismail Al-Azhari, the country's first prime minister, naming an all NUP cabinet. Al-Azhari named three Southerners in the cabinet, all with minor responsibilities.
- Bullen Alier,
- Santino Deng Teng (who had won Aweil East as an independent before joining the NUP)
- Dak Dei, the member for Central Nuer East.

The Independence Struggle 1942 – 1958

Fig. (5) Ismail al-Azhari (1901-1969): First Sudanese Prime Minister 1954 – 1956. A graduate of Gordon Memorial College, where he later became an able mathematics teacher. He was Secretary at the Graduates General Congress. He later became a leader of the Ashigga Party and a strong opponent of the Condominium Government. He supported unity between the North and the South

The Umma, the Federal Party and independent members formed the opposition block, and their leader was Muhammed Ahmed Mahjoub.

Under the terms of the Anglo-Egyptian Agreement, **a Sudanization Commission** was established in February 1954. The Commission's aim was to hand over the administration into Sudanese hands. When the Sudanization of the civil service happened, Southerners were very disappointed because only 6 of about 800 Sudanized posts went to Southerners despite NUPs promises before the election.

One of the reasons for this could be that most of the experienced Southern administrators had already been drawn into national politics. Others didn't fulfill the requirements of seniority, experience and qualifications. Less proficiency in Arabic may also have been a reason for bypassing the Southerners. Another reason might be that Southerners were not seriously considered for the posts due to a Northern bias. The Southern suspicions of Northern prejudices sparked great discontent in the South.

In October 1954, the Southern Party/the Liberal Party called a conference at Juba to discuss Sudanization and other grievances. Decisions were made to vote for independence of Sudan on the condition of a federal system for Sudan.

> **Questions**
> 1. Give some reasons why the Southerners were unhappy with the situation under the new Anglo-Egyptian agreement.
> 2. What does a federal system mean and why did the Southerners press for such a system?

Economic and social developments in the South 1942 – 1956

The largest development project undertaken in the South was the Zande Scheme in the Zande district of Western Equatoria. The Zande Scheme (financed by the central government and administered by an Equatoria Projects Board) had by 1952 improved communications and transport as well as established a power station and oil, soap and cloth mills. However, the Scheme never achieved its aim of complete social and economic stability of the Zande people. One reason was the low wages which necessitated forced labour and thus caused social unrest and a deteriorating relationships between the chiefs who supported the Scheme and the people. Another reason was that the British administrators did not entrust Southern Sudanese to be in charge of the Scheme because they were not thought to be qualified, and the Southerners didn't trust their Northern successors because the Northerners were considered to be the second colonialists.

Southern Sudan is potentially an agricultural country that could have supplied the whole Sudan with sugar, tea, coffee, tobacco etc. However, the government was not interested in losing their import duty revenue from the North if the South became dominant in agricultural production. Therefore they didn't invest much in the development of agriculture in the South.

Many communities in the South had communal land, where cattle owners and cultivators both used the land. Since the land was communal the land could not be sold, a fact which provided them with security in bad times. Ownership of cattle was also a buffer against crop failure, and secured marriages, settlement of conflicts and status. The size of the cattle herd depended on how many herders the family could provide. Over time the animal population grew and this eventually led to problems of overgrazing.

Large parts of Equatoria are unsuited for cattle raising because of the tse tse fly. An exception is the Toposa area where the men herd cattle while the women cultivate the soil. The Dinka and the Nuer were pastoral groups in Bahr el -Ghazal and Upper Nile. Their cattle produce good beef, but little milk. During this period the population in the South was gradually shifting towards sedentary agriculture and settling in larger villages and towns.

There was little development of infrastructure in Southern Sudan during this period. The most important means of transportation was still the steamers from Khartoum to Southern Sudan. Besides the river modes of transportation there were tracks and unpaved roads.

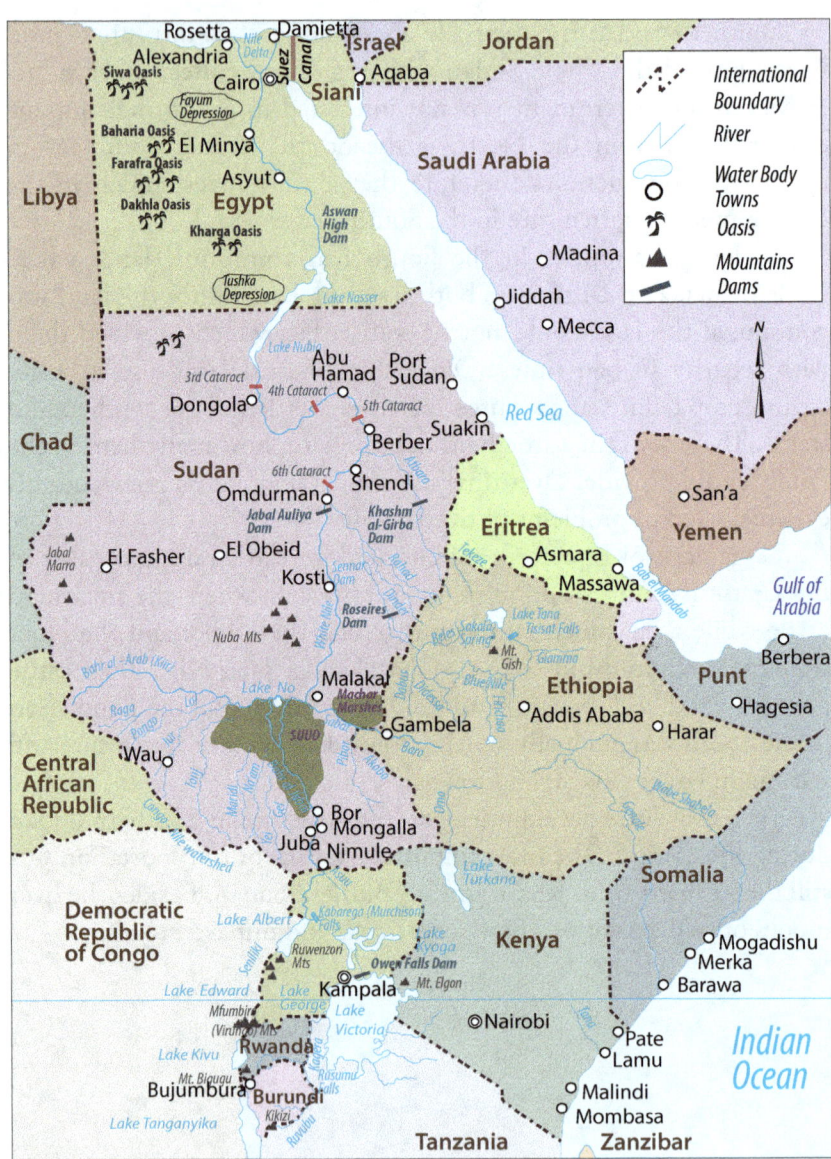

Fig. (6) The Nile Basin (*Cambridge University Press*)

Summary: The Zande scheme was the largest development project in the South. There was a growing urbanization, but most people had a rural way of life.

Pair work:
1. Why was the Zande Scheme not fully developed?
2. Why was cattle ownership seen as a security?

Discuss in class:
1. Why do you think the British administrators did not trust the Southern Sudanese to be in charge of the scheme?

Education

Girls' education

As we have noted in chapter four, education in the South during the condominium period was neglected, and in particular the education for girls. Catholic schools for girls among the Dinka commenced in the 1920´s in Kwajok, but didn't spread to other areas until the 1950´s. Post primary girls'education was restricted to teacher training. Dinka parents and other semi-nomadic groups were not very interested in sending their daughters to school. Most of the Dinka girls were only allowed to attend school up to 13 years of age so that they could marry. Education was further considered irrelevant and a liability, since educated girls were more inclined to resist some of the traditional cultural practices.. The missionaries tried to overcome Dinka parents´ resistance, but were not successful. However, a young girl, Sidonia Aman, resisted her parents' pressure to be married and decided to be a nun. She became a nun in 1941, worked as a hospital nurse, and then as a teacher. In the turbulent 1960´s she opened schools in Wau and in Aweil.

> ### Difficulties of going to school during the early years.
> In the condominium period, schools in the South were too few as there were many pupils who wanted to benefit. School administrations had to employ tough measures to screen the few pupils who were to be admitted. Schools were boarding schools where the pupils managed their own meals, so it was necessary to recruit older pupils. Hence, younger pupils no matter how bright they were had to repeat lower classes for many years. However, from 1956 when the Ministry of Education was able to provide food supplies to the schools, the policy was reversed in favour of younger pupils while the older pupils were sent home to get married. The process of determining age was quite brutal, as there were no birth certificates. Sometimes a yardstick was used to determine age, but at other times, pupils suspected to have already reached to puberty were taken to a room and inspected physically by the village school inspectors to determine whether indeed they were young or had reached puberty. This practice continued up to early 1960s, mainly in Equatoria.
>
> In the Bahr-el Ghazal and Upper Nile regions where most communities were cattle keepers, pupils were encouraged to bring a cow each so that their socialisation with cattle would remain uninterrupted even if they were getting classroom education.

The Ministry of Education in the Condominium Government was created in 1948 with the appointment of Abd al-Rahman Ali Taha, the Umma politician and able educationalist, as the first Sudanese minister of education (1949-1953). For the minister, the logic of the new Southern Policy of integration between the South and the North demanded an integrated, unified education system and the introduction of Arabic as the medium of instruction in the Southern schools. A pidgin Arabic was already the *lingua franca* in the South. Soon after taking office, he visited the South and spent six weeks there. During this period, he was able to visit all the state schools, as well as a large number of missionary schools. He met students in all the schools he visited. Upon his return, he presented a statement to the Legislative Assembly in which he mentioned:

- The unification of the educational policy in the North and South.
- The teaching of Arabic in the schools in the South.

The Minister stressed that the introduction of the Arabic language would not erase the local languages. The Southerners' mastery of Arabic would make them able to fill positions of responsibility in the administration of Sudan.

Catholic missionaries reacted negatively to these measures, but their recommendations were not followed by the Minister. Southern MPs were in minority in Parliament and could not stop the language policy. Others expressed their agreement with the new educational policy stating that it was to the benefit of the Southern population to learn Arabic, provided that this would not destroy the local languages.

A new five year education plan

A five year education plan (1951–1956) to expand education and improve its systems in the Southern districts was approved by the Legislative Assembly. Its main points were:
- The government had to undertake the bulk of the expansion by opening public schools.
- Missionary schools would continue under the supervision of the ministry which would give them financial support.
- Missionary schools should follow the curriculum established by the Ministry of Education.

The plan was based on several points:
- A more rapidly expanding government sector,
- A more intermediate and secondary provision,
- The unification of Northern and Southern education.

In order to secure the plan's success increased training of teachers, especially at intermediate level, was needed. With regard to secondary education, the five year plan called for tripling the intake at Rumbek, the first secondary school in the South, by 1956, but the opening of new secondary schools was neglected. This resulted in the lack of a modern educated class in Southern Sudan large enough to represent its people in the period of self-government and self–determination.

However, 50 new primary schools above the level of village schools were established between 1951 and 1955, and the number of pupils increased to 35,000. This marked a real revolution in primary education in the South.

In 1954, an international commission on secondary education had recommended that the government should be in charge of the missionary schools and that Arabic, not English, should be the language of instruction in the South. These recommendations were followed after independence, missionary schools were nationalized in 1957 and Arabic became the language of instruction in government schools.

Summary: Educational provision in the South increased dramatically from 1949 with the first Sudanese Minister of Education. Many government primary schools were opened and the number of pupils increased.

Class discussion
1. Why was it so difficult for Dinka girls to get an education? How is the situation for girls in various parts of the South now?
2. Is there a difference of lifestyle between women living in semi-nomadic societies compared to women living in societies based on agriculture?

Work in pairs
1. What happened to the missionary schools during Abd al-Rahman Ali Taha's office?
2. What were the main principles of the new five year education plan?
3. What could be the reasons why some Southerners wanted Arabic as medium of education and a unified education system?

The Torit mutiny, August 1955

Due to the massive influx of Northerners into the South to fill positions as administrators, top positions in the army and the police as well as teachers and traders, the Southerners felt betrayed and feared domination and colonization by the Northerners.

Some Southerners, who were worried about the Northern invasion, now turned to Egypt for help, preferring a union with Egypt to halt the Northern onslaught. Egypt was concerned about the water resources of the Nile and as the government started to move from enthusiasm for unity with Egypt to complete independence, Egypt found new allies in the South. Southern Sudan was also strategically important to Egypt because of its closeness to the sources of the Nile. Several Southern politicians began, with Egyptian backing, to openly call for federation with Egypt and for the postponement of the evacuation of foreign troops until Southern demands were met.

In July and August 1955, the political temperature in the South was raised by several unrelated events:

- Two Southern ministers left the cabinet (the Council of Ministers); one had resigned, and the other had been dismissed.
- The Liberal Party prepared for a conference to discuss the formation of a Southern bloc. The conference was held on 6-7 July 1955. The government arrested some of the participants.
- The Northerners had refused to discuss federalism with the Southerners before independence. However in 1955, Northern politicians convinced the Southern politicians to vote for independence. The Northerners said that federalism would be seriously considered if Sudan got independence.
- On 8 July 1955, striking Southern workers in the Zande Scheme were shot by Northern troops who tried to disperse them.

Summary: The Sudanization of government posts meant in reality that mostly Northerners were recruited. This naturally increased the Southerners' discontent. The situation became even more tense when Southern ministers left the cabinet and striking workers were shot in Zande.

> **Work in pairs**
> 1. Why was Egypt concerned about the South?
> 2. Why do you think the NUP changed their position in relation to Egypt? Try to give several reasons.
> 3. Give examples of Southern discontent and explain why Southerners were unhappy.

This general dissatisfaction in the South was most actively expressed in Equatoria where the main economic activity had been concentrated, and from where most recruits in the army and police were drawn. On 18th August 1955 the Southern Corps at Torit mutineed and the mutiny spread to all the major towns of Equatoria where northern officials and civilians were killed. The British refused to intervene and order was not restored until August 31st when Northern troops were flown into the South.

What were the reasons for the Torit Mutiny?

Soldiers in Sudan were recruited on a Corps system, where the soldiers served in their locality or region. British officers had been replaced by Northern officers and the Southern soldiers felt uneasy due to their replacement. On 18 August 1955 the Equatoria Corps of Sudan Defence Force (which became the Sudanese Army after independence) in Torit was scheduled for transfer to Khartoum and rumours spread that the Southern troops would be massacred upon arrival in Khartoum. Buth Diu and Siricio Irro got information about discussions by Northerners who colluded to transfer and disperse No. 2 Battalion in Torit and the two informed a sergeant called Saturnino about the intention of the Khartoum Government. The Southern corps in Torit were instructed to disobey the transfer to the North and the rejection of the transfer resulted to the revolution on 18th August 1955. The Equatoria Corps of Sudan Defence Force therefore refused orders. The mutiny was also due to Southern discontent with Northern attitudes. There was for instance a telegraph purported to have been sent to the Northern administrators in the South by the

Prime Minister Ismail el Azhari urging the Northerners to oppress the Southerners.

Other causes were, as already mentioned, the prevalent discontent with Sudanization of government posts and the massacre in Zandeland.

What were the consequences of the Torit mutiny?

The new Governor-General, Sir Alexander Knox Helm, declared a state of emergency and ordered mutineers to lay down their arms. Several hundred Northerners were killed during the mutiny including government officials, army officers, and merchants. Order was not fully restored until the arrival of Northern troops who executed many of the mutineers. Some of the mutineers escaped to remote areas and organized resistance to the government. Another result of the mutiny was the temporary transfer of Juba commercial schools and Rumbek secondary school to the North for security reasons.

The mutiny was not a well organized or coordinated movement. However, the mutinies were an expression of fear and anxiety about the future of Southern Sudan. The disorder mostly affected Equatoria, and the mutineers were mostly from the Equatoria province. The mutiny was, however, an omen of the next decades of bloody war.

Summary: The Torit mutiny came as a result of dissatisfaction with Northern attitudes as well as of rumours that the Southern troops to be relocated to Khartoum would be massacred on arrival.

Work in pairs
1. Why did the Equatoria Corps in Torit refuse to obey orders in 1955?
2. Why was the dissatisfaction with the development before independence expressed more in Equatoria than in other areas in the South?

The massacre in Abyei

The agro-pastoralist Ngok Dinka have lived in Abyei since the 18th century. The nomadic people Messiria used to graze their cattle through Abyei in the dry season, although they spent most of the year in Muglad. The Messiria lived therefore in the province of Kordofan, considered Northern territory, while the Ngok Dinka lived in Bahr el Ghazal, considered Southern teritory, at the establishment of Anglo-Egyptian Condominium. Records from this time state that the Ngok Dinka and Messiria had amicable relations. The British administration changed the borders in 1905 and relocated the nine Ngok Dinka chiefdoms to Kordofan. The Ngok Dinka and Messiria lived relatively peacefully until the massacre of 72 Ngok Dinka in the Messiria town of Babanusa in 1956, perhaps as a retaliation for the Torit mutiny.

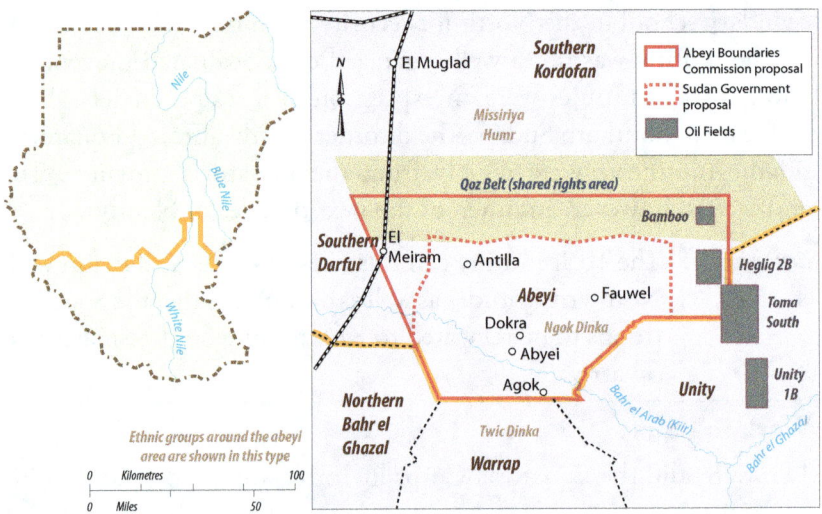

Fig. (7) The borders between the North and the South

Independence: The transfer of power

The Torit Mutiny had just reinforced the British desire of granting Sudan full independence because the British now felt that they had lost control and a meaningful position in Sudan. The British

The Independence Struggle 1942 – 1958

pressed for independence even before the parliament had agreed on a permanent constitution. This was a severe undermining of the Anglo – Egyptian Agreement, which had serious consequences for Sudan's further democratic development. The Northern politicians convinced the Southerners to vote for independence on the condition that the northern politicians would seriously consider a federal system of government after independence was given. Ismail Al-Azhari announced on 15 December 1955 the tabling of a motion concerning Sudanese independence.

- On 19 December the House of Representatives unanimously adopted a declaration of Sudanese Independence.

- A Transitional Constitution, under which the parliamentary regime would continue to govern, was enacted by the parliament on 31 December.

- The powers of the Governor-General were vested in a five- man supreme commission. Ciricio Iro (a Southerner) was a member of this commission.

- Sudan became a sovereign state on 1 January 1956. The Condominium flags were lowered and the Sudanese flag was raised. Both Britain and Egypt recognized the independence of Sudan

Fig. (8) Sudan's flag 1956-1970

Question
1. Why did Southern MPs vote for independence?

> **Work in pairs**
> 1. Who were the first three ministers from the South in the condominium government?
> 2. Why did the Northern politicians tour the South during the election campaign?

Summary: The events that led to the independence of Sudan 1946- 1956

1. 1946: The Sudan Administrative Conference recommends the unification of the North and the South. A change in policy towards the South.
2. 1947: The British called the Juba Conference
3. 1948: The Legislative Assembly was set up. This was the first step towards a National Parliament.
4. 1950: The Southern members in the Legislative Assembly votes against granting Sudan self-government
5. In 1952, the Legislative Assembly passed a Self-Government Statute. This was agreed by all the political groups in Sudan. In 1952, the monarchy was abolished in Egypt.
6. 1952: The Egyptians accept the Statute of self determination. The Egyptians invited Northern Sudanese political parties to Cairo where they signed agreements, but no Southerners invited.
7. October 1952: The British accept the Statute of self determination.
8. February 1953: The new Anglo-Egyptian agreement was signed in February
9. 1953: Formation of the first Southern Party which participated in the elections.
10. 1953: Elections. The NUP formed the government.
11. 1954: Ismail Al-Azhari was declared Sudan's first Prime Minister. The Southerners in the Cabinet had minor responsibilities (Bullen Alier, Santino Deng Teng and Dak Dei).

12. 1954: A Sudanization Commission was established in February to hand over the administration into Sudanese hands. Southerners were very disappointed because very few Sudanized posts were given to Southerners
13. 1955: Northerners promised to discuss federalism after independence with the Southerners
14. 1955: The Torit mutiny
15. 1955: On 19th December, the members of the House of Representatives (also the Southerners) approved a Declaration of Sudanese Independence.
16. January 1 1956: Independence: Sudan became an independent nation.

Post – Independent Sudan

Parliamentary period

Prime minister Al-Azhari was soon replaced by Abdalla Khalil, Secretary General of the Umma Party. The Khatmiyya and the Ansar sects feared the secular tendencies of Azhari and in June, twenty one members of the NUP formed the People's Democratic Party (PDP), with the support of Sayyid 'Ali al Mirghani,. On 5 July, Abdalla Khalil was elected Prime Minister in a coalition government of the Umma party and PDP while the NUP remained in opposition. The government was plagued with the historical sectarian rivalries between Sayid Abdel Rahman al-Mahdi and Sayyid 'Ali al-Mirghani.

Fig. (9) Sayyid 'Ali al-Mirghani (1879-1968) was the leader of the Khatmiyya religious sect and grandson of the founder. Sayyid Ali was a refugee in Egypt during the Mahdist rule. The rivalry between him and Sayyid Abdel Rahman al-Mahdi led him to support the unionist parties. However both of them met in December 1955 to fight the secular tendencies of Ismail al-Azhari.
(*Weidenfeld and Nicolson: London*)

During the 1956 parliamentary period the various elements of sovereignty were completed. The new republic was recognized by foreign governments, it became a member of the Arab League, and later of the United Nations. Sudan also printed its own pound. The first census was conducted in 1956. It estimated that forty per cent of Sudanese people were Arabs in the sense of cultural rather than racial identity, since Sudanese Arabs are a mixture of Arab, Nuba and black African ethnic groups. The total population of Sudan was 10.2 million with 7.4 million in the Northern provinces and 2.8 million in the Southern provinces. The Sudanese population was very mobile, and one million moved every year in search of better opportunities at the mechanized farms or to the towns.

> **Sayyid Abdel Rahman al-Mahdi** (1885-1959)was the leader of the Ansar religious sect. He was the son of Mohammed Ahmed al-Mahdi, leader of the Mahdist revolution. He collaborated financially with the British rulers. A strong opponent of the Egyptian claim of sovereignty over Sudan, he became the patron of the Umma Party who had the motto of "Sudan for Sudanese" and supported it with money. Rumours circulated that he was aspiring to kingship over Sudan with British support.

The government's economic policy concentrated on enlarging the country's agricultural capacity and improving communications. The concentration on cotton proved to be disastrous; the 1957 and 1958 cotton crops were poor and there was a falling price for cotton on the world market. The first years of independence did not witness any substantial socio–economic developments neither in the North nor in the South.

Parliamentary elections were held in March 1958. The new parliament consisted of 63 members from the Umma Party, 26 from PDP, and 40 from Southern Liberals. Again a coalition government between the Umma and the PDP was formed. Southern solidarity was torn away after the 1958 elections when tribal and personal rivalries took precedence over parliamentary politics.

Summary: Sudan became a sovereign state on January 1st, 1956, despite Southern politicians' reluctance. The parliamentary period was dominated by sectarian politics.

> **Discuss in pairs**
> 1. Outline briefly the changing power relations in post-independence Sudan. What does it mean that some parties feared Azhari's secular tendencies?
> 2. What was the count of Southerners in the first census?

Southern political parties and the federation controversy

The Southern Party, which was formed in 1953, had changed its name to Liberal Party, and co-opted membership from Eastern and Western Sudan. Some of the Southern party members joined Northern political parties. A Southern Union Party was formed in 1957 which shared the Liberal Party's demand of federation. Further demands were that Christianity should be the other official religion beside Islam, and that English should be the official language along with Arabic. The Southerners were apprehensive about a nationalist vision, shared by all Northern political parties, in which, through the spread of Islam and Arabic, the Southern peoples would be assimilated into a Sudanese, and Islamic identity. Southern fears increased as another issue besides the question of federation was hotly debated: should Sudan have a secular or an Islamic constitution?

What was the federation controversy about?

Most Southerners wanted federation because they feared the domination of a central Sudanese government in Khartoum. The Northerners' rejection of the demand from the South was due to their fear that a federal state would be the first step towards a separate South. Moreover the argument against federation was supported by a strong feeling in the North that the South had too few experienced leaders to govern the South. In addition also economic arguments were launched against a federal state: it would be too expensive to run a federal government in the South.

Only the Communist Party supported federation and regional autonomy for the South. This party had one member in the Parliament elected in 1954. Joseph Garang, a Southern graduate of the Faculty of Law, University of Khartoum, joined the Communist Party in 1955.

Fig. (10) The communist logo

The formation of a federal bloc

The rejection of federalism by the Northern parties strengthened the Southerners' suspicion against the Northerners, and made the Southerners organize more effectively in terms of political resistance. The Southerners in Parliament formed the Federal Block under the leadership of the Liberal MP Istanslaws Baya Sama, which tried to connect with movements in other neglected parts of Sudan. Between September – October 1957 it organized trips to eastern and western Sudan, the other marginalized areas. New Southern leaders emerged, among them the Catholic priest, Father Saturnino Lohure, who later succeeded Baya Sama in the leadership of this block. Undoubtedly federalism had strong support in the South and in other regions in Sudan as well, and this strong wind of federalism worried the ruling Northerners.

Fig. (11) Father Saturnino Lohure Hilangi was a Catholic priest who founded and led the first Southern Sudan struggle against the government. He was a member of the 1958 parliament. Saturnino Lohure was assassinated in Uganda in January 1967 by a Ugandan soldier on his way to his rebel bases in Southern Sudan. The remains of Fr. Lohure were reburied in Torit in January 2009.

Southern resentment was increased by the deliberations of the National Constitution Commission. This Commission was formed in late 1956 to prepare a permanent constitution for Sudan. Benjamin Luki and Buth Diu, members of the National Constitution Commission, withdrew from the commission on January 1957. They issued a statement that the Southern demand of federation for the South should be considered. On 16 June 1958 Southern members of Parliament handed in their resignations as the draft constitution did not include any reference to a federation.

By mid 1958, the position of the coalition government was fast declining. The government was unable to deal with the economic problems and Southern demands. The Umma party explored the possibility of a coalition with the NUP, and there were rumours of a possible NUP-PDP alliance, which if materialized, would remove the Umma from power. Before any of these plans could be fulfilled, the army, on the initative of the Umma Party, took power on the morning of 17 November 1958.

Summary: Southern politicians struggled hard for federation, but were not successful. The parliamentary period ended with a coup in 1958.

Work in pairs

1. Why were the Southerners worried about the changes in education policy?
2. What happened to the Southern Party after independence?
3. Explain the difference between separation and federation?

Discuss in class

1. What does "a secular state" mean? What is the opposite of a secular state?
2. Why were the Southerners worried about the discussion of whether Sudan should be a secular or an Islamic state?
3. Why did the Southerners want a federal state and why did the Northerners reject it?

Tasks

a) Imagine you are present at the Juba Conference in 1947 to represent the South. You are not pleased to hear it said that many of the Southern representatives do not have the needed educational background to take part in the political discussions. You speak to the members of the conference on the poor investments that have been made in education in the South by the condominium government. You share your vision for the future of education in the South and explain your views on the teaching of Arabic among your people. Relive that moment and give or write your speech.

b) Write a short essay about the role of Buth Diu in the history of Southern Sudan.
c) What is the relation of the South to the Nile Waters? List the other countries of the Nile Basin?
d) Summarise the situation in Abyei today
e) Explain the reasons for the Torit Mutiny.
f) Why did the British change their policy?
g) What was the result of Sudanisation?
h) Trace the Southern Sudanese struggle for independence between 1942 and 1958.

6
From Military Rule and Armed Resistance to the Addis Ababa Agreement of 1972

Introduction

This period is marked by the rise of military coups. The first one was General Ibrahim Abboud's rise to power on 17th November 1958 and his fall in October 1964. The military regime under General Ibrahim Abboud carried out a firm policy of Islamization and Arabization in the South, primarily through the education system. What had started after independence was accelerated during the military regime: the use of Arabic as medium of instruction. The Southern demands voiced before the military takeover were silenced and in 1958 and 1959 the government in Khartoum initiated repressive activities in the South by burning villages and arresting and torturing civilians. The repression resulted in increased opposition against the Khartoum government, and in the beginning of the 1960's Father Lohuro, Aggrey Jaden, Joseph Oduho and William Deng left for the bush and neighbouring countries. They formed the Sudan African Nationalist Union (SANU). It demanded full independence for the Southern Sudan territory. At the same time it started guerilla activities in the bush together with the mutineers from the Torit revolt. The guerilla movement changed its name to Anya Nya, a Ma´di word for poison. They attacked government posts and were counterattacked by the Sudan Armed Forces.

During Abboud's period the conversion to Islam was encouraged, and in 1964 all missionaries in the South were expelled. A systematic marginalization of educated Southerners took place. They were again being bypassed by Northern officials and they were excluded from key ministries. Only the insignificant ministries were allotted to Southerners.

A calm period until 1960 followed after the suppression of the Torit Mutiny. Some lone warriors waging guerrilla wars were the exceptions. Many of the former Torit soldiers went into exile in neighbouring countries and were later organized into armed struggle in 1962.

Abboud comes to power 1958

The new government following the 1958 election was a coalition of Umma and PDP parties. As mentioned earlier, the Mahdiyya and Khatimiyya Islamic sects united to exclude the secular NUP party from ruling Sudan. Although Umma and PDP were able to form a government led by Premier Abdalla Khalil, an ex-soldier, the coalition was soon torn apart by factionalism, foreign affairs, Southern Sudan policy and the unstable economy. The infighting among political parties and politicians, economic hardships following poor cotton harvests and Egypt's invasion of Halaib, a Red Sea port, only increased his problems. This forced Prime Minister Abdalla Khalil to invite General Ibrahim Abboud to take power in November 1958 until the situation of the country had returned to stability. General Ibrahim Abboud wasted no time in implementing his program of Arabization and Islamization.

Fig. (1)   General Ibrahim Abboud (1900-1983) (*www.sudan.net*)

> General Abboud was born at Mohammed- Gol, near Suakin. He went to Gordon Memorial College and Military College in Khartoum. During World War II he served in Eritrea, and rose to commander of the Sudan Defence Force after the war. He became the assistant commander in chief in 1954. Gen. Abboud led the new military government after the coup in 1958. His regime was overthrown in 1964. He lived several years in Britain, but died in Khartoum.

What was the objective of Abboud's programme of Arabization and Islamization?

The government wanted to foster national integration and unity through Arabization and Islamization of Southern Sudan. Islam and Arabic culture had united Northern Sudanese tribes and it was thought that the same policy could be replicated in Southern Sudan despite the fact that Islam and Arabic culture had not taken root in the region.

The military government's focus was education. Schools in the South which used to be run by Church missionary agencies, were nationalized by the government. New government schools were built and staffed by personnel from North Sudan. Six Intermediate Islamic Institutes were opened in Southern Sudan and one Islamic Secondary school was built. Moreover mosques were erected all over the South, and Sunday was replaced by Friday as the week day of rest. The status of the Arabic language was raised while English was downplayed. The administrators in Southern Sudan spent most of their working day promoting Islam and Arabic culture, with special efforts exerted to islamize chiefs and civil servants. Those who accepted conversion to Islam were rewarded as those who refused were punished, demoted or even dismissed from their jobs.

Southern response to Abboud's policy

At this point in time, all educated Southern Sudanese were a product of missionary schools and they strongly opposed the Northern policies. Southern Sudanese leaders saw Arabization and Islamization, and the shifting of the weekly day of rest from Sunday to Friday, as further evidence of the historical continuation of Southern domination by Northerners. The actions of the military government sparked off strikes from students and civil servants who insisted that Sunday should be respected as a day of worship and rest. Many schools were closed down, students and civil servants were jailed.

In spite of the forced Islamization the number of people converting to Christianity increased dramatically. The repressive actions produced a heightened spirit of resistance from politicians, civil servants, chiefs and students. Many started to run into exile and started organizing the resistance movement.

Work in pairs
1. What happened to the missionary schools after independence?
2. What were the major policies introduced during the military regime of General Ibrahim Abboud?
3. What was the Southern reaction to the repressive policy adopted by the military regime?

In December 1960, an alleged plot to carry out mass arrests of Southern politicians on Christmas Eve was discovered and a group of them fled the country to set up an organization in exile. As mentioned Father Saturnino Lohure, Aggrey Jaden, Joseph Oduho, William Deng (who was by then a District Commissioner in Kapoeta) fled Sudan. They later reappeared in Leopoldville (now Kinshasa) in Congo. In February 1962 they founded the Sudan African Closed Districts National Union (SACDNU). The Sudan Christian Association (SCA) was also formed. The headquarters of SACDNU was in Congo while that of SCA was in Uganda. Later SACDNU dropped "Closed District" and became Sudan African National Union [SANU].

Sudan African Closed District National Union SACDNU (1962)
President: Joseph Oduho
Vice President: Marco Rume
Secretary General: William Deng
Vice Deputy Secretary General: Aggrey Jaden
Patron: Father Saturnino Lohure

Fig. (2) Joseph Oduho (1927-1993) was born in Lobira village, Eastern Equatoria. He graduated from Bakht Al Ruda Teachers' Institute in 1950. As a teacher in Maridi, he was arrested after the Torit mutiny and sentenced to death. He was released after independence in 1956. He became the first president of SACDNU and SANU. After the signing of the Addis Ababa agreement, he was appointed as a minister in several Southern cabinets. In 1976 he was arrested, accused of conspiracy. In the second civil war, he joined the SPLA, but soon fell out and was executed by the SPLA.

The main activity of SACDNU/SANU was petitioning the United Nations, African leaders, Christian organizations and the Organization of African Unity as well as supplying information on events in Southern Sudan. Neither the UN nor the OAU, however, took note of Southern Sudanese protestations.

> **Excerpt from a letter by William Deng, N. Loro and Peter M. Biet of SANU to the African Liberation Committee, concerning mediation in the civil war. December 5th, 1963**
>
> The northerners having thus failed with their parties to convince the South by reasoning decided secretly to hand over the government to the Army in November 1958....general Abboud declared an indefinite State of Emergency directed against the South mainly and which has now lasted 5 years....All the forces of colonial domination that were held in check by parliament were now released and the General made a bid to fulfill the policy of forcible assimilation of the Southern Sudanese... We think that the policy of forcible assimilation cannot work in the 20th century where modern international ethics, the United Nations Charter which recognises the right of self-determination and the desire for world peace, have replaced the policy of the dark ages when might was always right.... Therefore, in order to save human lives and suffering under the present confusion in the Sudan, we, as the rightful representatives of the Sudan National Union (SANU) South Sudan and the entire population of four million hereby call upon the African Liberation Committee, the Organisation of African Unity (OAU)...to set up a neutral Commission to enquire into the North-South problem and to find a peaceful solution between the two races.

Abboud and the Christian missionary societies

In 1962 the Abboud military regime intensified its repression by producing the "Missionary Societies Act of 1962," aimed at regulating activities of Christian missionaries in Sudan. Although the Act was targeting foreign Christian missionaries, its scope was very wide. It included clauses which demanded that indigenous pastors should be registered and licensed by the regime's Ministry of Religious Affairs and Endowment. It even demanded that registered church workers should be paid by this ministry, but this move was rejected by the churches.

As a part of the repressive policy many schools, health services and relief services were closed by the regime in October 1962. This was followed by waves of strikes which were instigated by the political leaders in exile. Most of the students ran into exile, in the hope of joining a military struggle. They were assured by SANU propaganda that all the necessary arms were available, and ready for launching the armed struggle. However, the Sudanese school authorities tried to contain the situation and managed to convince many students to return to school.

> ***Summary:*** General Abboud took power in 1958. His policy was to Arabize and Islamize South Sudan, which was resisted by the. Southern politicians went in exile and started resistance movements.

Work in pairs
1. How did General Abboud come to power?
2. Why did General Abboud want to Arabize and Islamize South Sudan? Discuss the practical consequences of this policy?
3. Discuss the letter from SANU excerpted above. Explain in your own words what it says.

Discuss in class
1. Why were SACDNU and SCA established? What were their functions?

The beginning of the Southern Sudanese armed struggle

The revolutionary tide could not be stopped. November 1962 marked the unofficial beginning of the armed struggle when a group of former Torit soldiers, together with former policemen deserted and ran into exile. They organized themselves, and almost empty-handed, except for knives and sticks, attacked a border police station at Pamoju, near Kajokeji, on the Sudan–Uganda border on 16th November, killing a policeman, abducting another one, and gaining their first fire-arms. The armed struggle had started. Later the group withdrew towards the Congo border to carry out further preparation and training. The group was joined by some of the students and in May 1963, Lieutenant Joseph Lagu of Sudanese army joined the camp and gave the group a big boost.

> **Southern armed struggle**
>
> Officially SACDNU denounced violence, but by 1963 leaders such as Father Saturnino already wanted armed confrontation and came out with the Sudan Pan African Freedom Fighters (SPAFF) as the armed wing of SACDNU/SANU. The D-Day for the launch of SPAFF was fixed by Joseph Lagu on September 19, 1963. Later Joseph Lagu replaced the name SPAFF with Anya Nya. SANU's slogan was self-determination rather than secession due to the views of the international community, and the Organization of African Unity in particular, to keep the old colonial borders.

Fig. (3) Joseph Lagu

> Joseph Lagu was born on 21 November 1931, in Momokwe (northern region of Ma´diland). He is a Ma´di. On May 1960 he graduated from the military college in Omdurman, and, and became an officer in the Sudanese Army. He was the President of the High Executive Council (1978-1979). Lagu has played an important role in the freedom struggle of Southern Sudan, although his role, like most Southern politicians, is contested.

The D-Day in 1963 started with the attempted destruction of the Tore Bridge in the present Yei district at midnight with the hope of, among other things, attracting Sudan's Armed Forces out of Yei. But due to lack of experience the bridge was not destroyed. The bomb did, however, attract Sudanese Armed Forces out of Yei town for the first exchange of fire.

> **Definition**
> D-day is often used in military language and means the day of an attack or a military operation, especially when a very important military operation is going to take place.

As the Anya Nya intensified the armed struggle the Abboud regime desperate for survival, accused foreign missionaries of instigating and aiding Southerners to rebel. In May 1964 the regime expelled all foreign missionaries from the South, which only served to publicize the problem internationally. This was a huge blow for the Catholic Church, which hadn´t sudanized their clergy, because the celibacy vow was largely unacceptable within the Southern Sudanese culture. In 1964 they had only one Sudanese Bishop and 28 Sudanese priests in the South. The Anglican Church however, had educated and ordained 44 priests, and had begun to hand over property to Sudanese. Abboud's repression against the Church had, however, only just begun, and several priests, who were skilled spokesmen for the Southern cause, were killed.

Summary: The Southern resistance movement commenced their armed struggle in 1963. As a response Abboud expelled all foreign missionaries in 1964.

Discuss in pairs
1. How did the armed struggle begin? Why do you think SADNU began with violent resistance?
2. A Catholic priest was one of the most active in initiating the violent resistance. Comment upon the link between the Catholic Church and armed resistance.
3. What were the causes of the armed struggle?

Discuss in class
1. Was Southern armed resistance the only alternative in the conflict between the South and the North?

The overthrow of Abboud's regime

Meanwhile, the effect of the Southern armed struggle started to be felt in the North, especially in Khartoum. Students organized an uprising with trade unions in October 1964 which led to the overthrow of Abboud's regime. Through negotiations with the military and professional bodies who had taken over from the students, a peaceful transition to a civilian rule was agreed upon. In the same month a civilian care-taker government led by Sirr al-Khatim Khalifa came to power. Sirr al Khatim Khalifa had previously been an educationalist in Southern Sudan, and was respected by many Southern Sudanese people.

The October revolution in 1964

The beginning of the end of Abboud's regime was the appointment of a commission of enquiry to investigate the Southern problem. The commission invited the University of Khartoum to discuss the problem and the student's union concluded that a solution was impossible within a military regime. Despite the ban on further meetings by the Minister of Education, a meeting on 22 October resulted in the killing of one student. The mass funeral which followed quickly got out of control. The teachers and students established the Professional Front and called for a general strike. Moreover the leaders of the established, forbidden parties met and formed a United Front. The Army was also split, and Abboud had no choice but to resign.

Fig. (4)   Sirr Al-Khatim Al-Khalifa Al-Hassan (1919-2006).

> Al-Khalifa was born in Ed Dueim, and did his teacher training at Gordon Memorial College. From 1944 to 1946 he made further studies at Oxford University, Britain. He worked as a teacher until he was appointed Provincial Education Officer in Equatoria Province. After seven years he was promoted to become Assistant Director of Education for the Southern Provinces. He was nominated as prime minister of the transitional government in 1964. In 1966 he started his diplomatic career, and from 1973 he worked for president Nimeiri.

Just before the uprising in Khartoum that overthrew Abboud's regime, SANU held its first general assembly in Kampala, Uganda, during the month of August 1964. The assembly decided to change the leadership of the party, thus bringing Aggrey Jaden to replace Joseph Oduho as President and adding Philip Pedak as Vice President. This led William Deng to break ranks with his colleagues, and decided to lead a faction of SANU back to Sudan, thus dividing SANU into two, one outside Sudan known as Aggrey Jaden wing (SANU Outside), and the other inside Sudan known as William Deng wing (SANU Inside).

Fig. (5) Aggrey Jaden (1927-1985)

> He was a Pojulu from Loka Round in Western Equatoria. In 1952, he was the first Southerner to graduate from Gordon Memorial College in Khartoum. In 1953 he was appointed an Inspector in Darfur where he opposed the independence of Sudan without a serious consideration of the Southern question. He was then demoted to Manager Director and transferred to Malakal in 1956. Later he went into exile in Uganda where he participated in the establishment of SANU. After participating at the Round Table Conference in 1965 he moved to Kenya and had never again a major role in the resistance movement.

SANU welcomed the overthrow of the military dictatorship of Abboud and expressed a willingness to return home if:
- A general amnesty was declared
- SANU was recognized as a political party

Due to the new civilian government, political parties were allowed to be formed, and the Southern Sudanese intelligentsia in Khartoum came together to form a political party called the Southern Front. The Southern Front had members from all the southern regions, and many members also assisted Anya Nya. The new party was led by Clement Mboro who had been active in the 1947 Juba conference as mentioned in chapter five. The Southern Front was in reality SANU's representatives inside Sudan, and worked in close co-operation with SANU.

Clement Mboro was then appointed Minister of Interior in the care-taker government, the first time ever that a Southerner was appointed in that ministry. The second prominent Southerner was Ezborn Mundiri, who was appointed Minister of Transport. The caretaker government lasted from October 1964 to June 1965. During this period efforts were made to end the war in the South. Cease fire was declared, and many lines of communication were established between the caretaker government and SANU Outside. A round-table conference was convened to discuss the constitutional relationship between the North and the South. SANU Outside was invited to return to Sudan to take part in the conference, and outside SANU returned to Khartoum for the round table conference in early 1965.

Summary: Abboud's regime was overthrown by students and trade unions in 1964. A civil care-taker government was in charge until 1965. SANU was divided into SANU Outside and SANU Inside.

Discuss in pairs
1. Why was Abboud's regime overthrown?
2. What do you think was the consequences of the divisions in SANU? Give examples of other divisions within the resistance movements in Southern Sudan.
3. What was the relationship between SANU and the Southern Front?

The Round Table Conference

At the Round Table Conference in 1965, there were four parties representing Southern Sudan: Southern Front, Sudan African National Union Inside, Sudan African National Union Outside and the Liberal Party which had just been reborn. During the discussions, the Southern Sudanese did not present a united voice. The Southern Front and SANU asked for a referendum to establish the opinion of the Southern Sudanese, while the Liberal Party stood for autonomy and Southernization of the administration in the South. The Liberal Party asked for devolution and decentralization of the power because of the marked differences in race, language and culture. The conference led to more divisions inside SANU and split William Deng from the others. Deng remained the leader of SANU Inside and worked for a federation, while Joseph Oduhu and Aggrey Jaden went back to Uganda as leaders of SANU Outside and wanted self-determination and ultimately cessation.

Fig. (6) William Deng (1926 – 1968) was a Dinka from Tonj in Bahr el Ghazal. (*Ithaca Press*)

He graduated from Rumbek Secondary school in 1951. He became Assistant District Commissioner in Kapoeta. He was one of the founders of SANU where he became Secretary General. He was assassinated by government forces in 1968.

What were the reasons for Southern divisions?

One reason for the split in the movement, and further splits later was the strong personalities in the movement where 'everybody' wanted to be the leader. Another was the regional and ethnic affiliations. Leaders like Fr Saturino and Joseph Oduhu were Lotukas from Torit; Aggrey Jaden was a Bari from Juba, Joseph Lagu a Ma'di while William Deng was the first important Dinka leader from Tonj in Bahr-el-Gazal. Moreover the Southern Sudanese who went to start the guerrilla movement were not linked to any organized political parties, nor to a national consciousness uniting its different ethnic groups and imbuing its people with a sense of nationhood.

Excerpt from a position paper of the Southern Front at the March 1965 Round Table conference. March 18th 1965

I. THE ADMINISTRATION, POLICE AND PRISON SERVICE:
   1. a) Southernization of Administration, police and prison services and promotion of Southerners to fill all security positions in the South…
   2. As for the army, the Southern Front stands for a representative and proportional recruitment of Southerners in the army and the Armed Forces be mixed.

II. EDUCATION

   …The educational policy carried out in the South since 1954 was not designed to suit the conditions and desires of the African people of that part of the country, but instead was used as a means of assimilating them into Arab group through Arabization and Islamization. This policy has been the cause of stagnation and set-back in the educational advancement of the South. It has done irreparable damage to the South, and as a result, education and religion constitute major issues in the North-South conflict….

   1. The replanning and reshaping of the whole educational system
   2. The Southernization of all Administrative posts in the South in the Ministry of Education…
   4. a) All Headmasters and Headmistresses of Elementary and Intermediate Schools must be Southernized before the opening of of Schools in 1965 School Year.
      b) Immediate opening of Girls Secondary Schools in the South…
      c) Maridi Institute, Malakal Secondary School and Malakal Intermediate Technical School must be returned to the South
      d) The state must be secular…

> **IV. ECONOMIC DEVELOPMENT**
> ...No attempt was made to combat un-employment and to raise the standard of living of people....all foreign firms interested in the development of natural resources in the South were not permitted, while northern capitalists were permitted to monopolise and exploit the people. The Southern Front stands for the principle of welfare state and state control of major sectors of the economy...

The Northern parties were preoccupied with the forthcoming elections. They wouldn't give concessions to the South, but they downplayed their notion of Northern supremacy. They could at most grant Southern Sudan local self-rule which was similar to the suggestions of the Liberal Party. However, they did not accept a referendum about the future constitutional position of the South, because of fear of Southern secession. At the end, a twelve-person committee (six from south and six from north) was established to make a draft about the Southern problem. The committee recommended decentralization with regional autonomy. Since the recommendation contained ethnic pluralism which was against governmental policy at the time, it was rejected by the government. The Round-Table Conference was never reconvened.

Summary: The Round Table Conference was convened to end the Civil War. However, Southern parties were disunited and the Northern parties were afraid of Southern secession.

> **Work in pairs**
> 1. There were at least four different groups at the Round Table conference. What was the position of each group on the Southern Question?
> 2. List the demands of the Southern Front as stated in the excerpt above.
> 3. What do you think the Liberal Party meant by: "marked differences in race, language and culture"?
> 4. What was the Northern position?
>
> **Discuss in class**
> 1. "The Round Table conference could have succeeded with more unity among the Southern parties?" Discuss this statement.
> 2. In your opinion, what was the main reason for the SANU split?

Social and economic development

Gender

Women were quite active in the resistance against Abboud's regime. The first female martyr, Bakhita al-Hayfa, was shot during a demonstration against Abboud. Although women participated in the October revolution which led to Abboud's downfall, they did not gain high political positions in the 1960s.

Sudanese women organizations had since the 1940s worked to enhance women's rights. Women gained their right to vote in 1953, and were eligible in all elections. The Sudanese Women's Union published "Sawt al-Mara" in 1955, where they raised issues about equal pay for equal work, education, maternity leave and pensions. They were also concerned about rural women's health and education. In 1960, 7 % of the work force was women, and the first female judge was appointed in 1963. However, they were paid less than men. In 1969 women won legal rights to maternity leave, pensions and equal pay. Health, education and social service were expanded to the rural areas.

In the South, women had generally greater freedom of movement than their Arab sisters, but still they were restrained by marriage and labour divisions. The war had devastating consequences for them, as it disrupted agriculture, which was the women's responsibility. The great emphasis on livestock herding might have enhanced men's power over women.

Economic development

Most of the industrial development was enhanced in the Khartoum area during this period, but there was little development in the South because of the civil war.

An exception was the railway line to Wau which connected the town with Nyala in the west and Sennar in the centre. The Wau Fruit and Vegetable Canning factory was also built in 1967. The factory only produced 50 % of its potential, because of different problems. One was that local fruits and vegetables were of low quality. Another was that the delivery of imported tomato concentration was more popular and preferred by the people. The products were supplied to the army as rations during the war, but the factory didn't get any cash for it. As a result employment was limited and the workers were not qualified. In addition the factory didn't adapt very well to the free market after the war. The factory stopped producing in 1979.

Traditional agriculture still dominated Southern Sudan in the 1960's and the 1970. Very little of agricultural and livestock products got to the market.

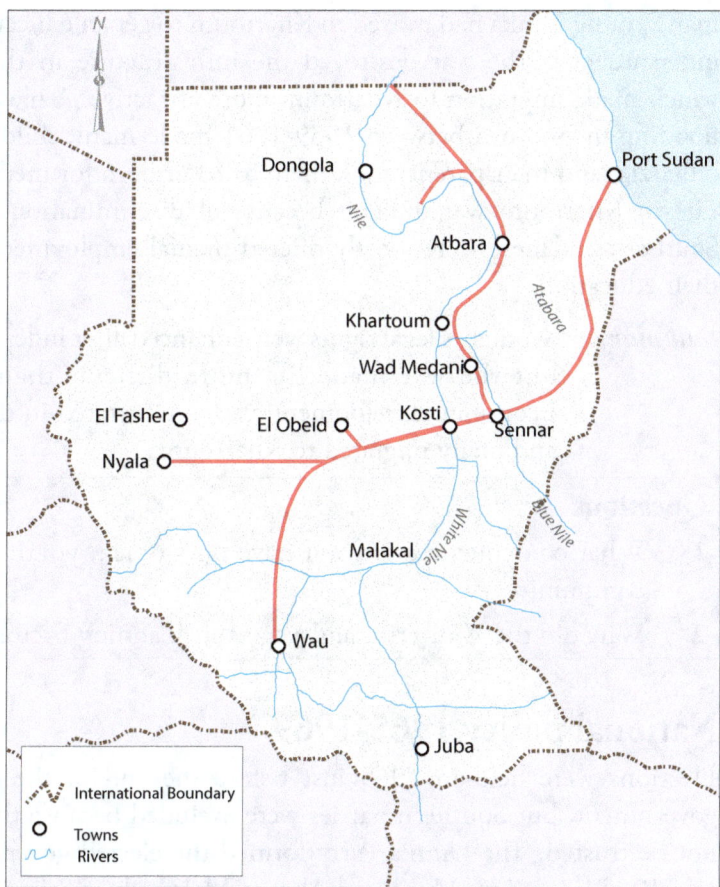

Fig. (7)   The railway system in Sudan (*The Macmillan Press Ltd*)

Social development

The expulsion of the missionaries and the closing of schools had interrupted young people´s education. Many of the community leaders were dead or in exile. The war had also destabilized indigenous leadership and village life in general. Many youth floated between the different towns.

Many rural Dinka had earlier avoided the towns because of the potential disruption of their family structure, religion etc. However, many young Dinka had moved to Khartoum to get an education after independence. The war destroyed the infrastructure in the South, which made migration to Khartoum more attractive. A massive Nile flooding in Bor area between 1959-1961 made many children ill of bilharzia, and their parents took them to Khartoum for medical care. Life in Khartoum was difficult because of discrimination, and the Southern Sudanese were mostly offered menial employment despite their education.

Summary: Women's legal rights were enhanced after independence, but the war made life more difficult than before. Economic development was concentrated in the North and many migrated to Khartoum.

Questions
1. What consequences did war have on women, youth and the community?
2. Why did the Wau Fruit and Vegetable Canning Factory fail?

National policy 1965-1969

Elections were held in 1965 just before the end of the caretaker government, but Southern parties were excluded because they could not be trusted. The Umma Party formed the elected government in July 1965 headed by Mohamed Ahmad Mahgoub as Prime Minister for a year. He was replaced by Sadiq El Mahdi in July 1966. The only Southern member of cabinet was Buth Diu who lacked popular support at that time. Soon after the formation of the new government in Khartoum, there were waves of massacres all over Southern Sudan. These massacres were carried out by the Sudanese Army and security forces. Among the towns affected by these waves of massacre were Juba, Wau, Bor, Yei, Torit, Malakal and Yambio. This led to more people running into exile, with some joining the political wing, while others swelled the ranks of the Anya Nya military struggle.

Fig. (8)   Sadiq al-Mahdi (1935-) was born in Omdurman.

> He is an Arab and great-grandson of the Mahdi. He graduated from Comboni College in Khartoum and then studied economics, philosopy and politics in Oxford.
>
> He was the leader of the Umma Party from 1964 and Prime Minister from 1966 to 1967, and from 1986 to 1989.
>
> He played a crucial role in the October Revolution. He was later arrested by both President Nimeiri and President al- Bashir.

Why did the Northern troops massacre civilian Southerners?

The policy of separating religion from the state had been valid until late 1940´s. After World War II, a branch of the Egyptian Muslim Brotherhood was introduced in Sudan. The Muslim Brotherhood wanted a theocratic society. Besides, the sectarianism of the Northern parties meant that people voted according to their religious affiliation. The result was that Islamization was a constant goal for all sectarian parties, like Umma and the united parties. In the 1950´s Islamization was presented as necessary for national unity, while in the 1960´s the parties openly professed an Islamic State. As Southerners believed that the Islamic state discriminates against non-Muslims, the Southerners, other regional politicians and Northern liberal party memebers opposed it.

Fig. (9)   The Muslim Brotherhood was founded in 1949.

> They have their support base among the students and educated people. Their goal is to institutionalize Islamic law in the entire country. It means a theocratic society in which a god, deity or religion is recognized as the state's supreme civil ruler. Their leader is Hasan al-Turabi. In 1965 the Muslim Brotherhood won 5 seats under the name of Islamic Charter Front (ICF). The Brotherhood persuaded the assembly to ban the Communist party on the grounds that it was atheist.

Parliamentary governments in this period were highly unstable with shifting coalitions dominated either by Umma or the Democratic Unionist Party (former NUP). Splits inside the parties and challenges from the regional parties, made the government more uncompromising regarding religion which was their only source of power. They were also pushed by the Islamic Charter Front, and an assimilation policy was the result. The government pursued therefore a military solution for the South. The all-Northern parliament resolved to give the security forces a free hand in solving "the Southern problem" in June 1965. As a result hundreds of civilians lost their lives. The Southern Front believed that the targets of the massacres were Southern intellectuals and chiefs who were suspected supporters of the Anya Nya rebel movement.

Press statement by Southern Sudanese Students at Khartoum university following the massacre of Southern Sudanese civilian population in Juba by the Sudanese Army. July 14th 1965

On 28.6.1965, the oppressive and savage policy of the new Arab government towards Southern Sudan, was declared by the Prime Minister, Mr. Mohammed Ahmed Mahgoub.... The policy aims at disarming the Any-Nya... The Arab army in the Southern Sudan was given a free hand and unlettered discretion to exterminate the negroid inhabitants of the Southern Sudan...The immediate result was cold-blooded unprovoked and brutal massacre of about 1.500 Southern Sudanese from 8th to 11th July, in the Town of Juba...We should like to make clear that the Juba massacre marks a decisive stage in our century-old struggle against Asiatic and European invasion, oppression, domination and exploitation...With the coming of the Umma- N.U.P. Coalition into power, a new wave of Mahdists terrorism and savagery has started in the Southern Sudan which culminated in the Juba massacre...The Arab forces in Juba, on no grounds, butchered defenseless, law-abiding Southerners-women, men, children; young and old –with automatic weapons for three days...Following the Juba blood-bath, another atrocity was carried out at Waw by blood-thirsty barbarous Arab forces wantonly murdered seventy Southern Sudanese...

At this calamitous and catastrophic juncture in our struggle against foreign domination, we sound a clarion call on the Southern People to face the Mahdist pestilence and Mahdist boot-licking stooges courageously...We have the conscience and conviction, but the conscience of the oppressor is guilty and stained. Our soil is soaked with blood of our dear brothers and sisters who have fallen, at the hands of the oppressor, for the freedom of the people of the Southern Sudan. The struggle must continue until we eradicate Arab colonialism in the Southern Sudan. Long live our struggle for political freedom.

The draft Islamic constitution

In 1968 a draft constitution was developed. Islam and Arabic were termed respectively the official religion and the official language. The draft established Shari'a as the source of criminal and civil law and the ban on all atheist ideologies. Regions would lose all self-determination and the discrimination of non-Muslims was institutionalized. The draft was based on ethnic nationalism, where minority groups' rights to their own language and religion were denied. As a consequence Southern MPs walked out of the Constitutional Committee.

> **Excerpt from a press statement by Southern Front after walkout at the constitutional committee talks, December 29th 1969**
>
> The walkout came when the representatives of the Northern parties on the constitutional committee rejected the second Southern amendment in a series of amendments to part One of the 1967 Draft Constitution, The Nature of the State."
>
> The two Southern Front objections are: first that the best suited constitution for the Sudan, judging from the religious and ethnic diversity in the country, ought to be secular and not religious (Islamic or otherwise) as the Northern representatives advocate. Secondly, the Southern Front contends that in earlier conferences and committees, the South and the North have agreed as a compromise on regional autonomy as the basis for the re-organisation of the country's administrative and constitutional system of government. Our position is this: We were party to the Round Table Conference and abide by the resolutions of that conference and the recommendations of the Twelve-Man Committee. We disagree and do not wish to be a party to an Islamic constitution and we think we are expressing the views of the Southerners of all religions. Our position on Islamic constitution applies also to a Christian constitution or any religious constitution. We respect Islam and other religions. But Islam being the religion of the majority in this country does not need the protection under the constitution. A secular constitution is what this country needs.

Summary: Democratic elections were held in 1965, but the consequence was an intensification of the war in the South. The New Draft Islamic Constitution was discussed in 1968. The Southerners rejected it and asked for a secular constitution.

Work in pairs
1. What were the reasons for the 1965 massacres in the South?
2. What was the religious goal of the Sudan government for the whole of Sudan?
3. Why did the Government fail to reach a peaceful agreement with the Southerners?
4. What is meant by a secular constitution? Why do you think the Southern Front wanted such a constitution?

Discuss in class
1. What was the role of Muslim Brotherhood?
2. The Southern Sudanese students in Khartoum issued a strong statement against the massacres in the South. How do they characterize the Northerners?

Southern factionalism

Taking advantage of the cease fire under the caretaker government Anya Nya soldiers were able to organize themselves better. Many Northern soldiers were losing their lives as a result of improved Anya Nya attacks, and as a consequence of the flow of arms into the South, courtesy of the crumbling Simba armed rebellion in the Congo. While escaping from the Congolese national army who were supported by white South African mercenaries, the Simba rebels fell into the hands of the Anya Nya fighters who disarmed them at the Sudan-Congo borders before sending them empty-handed to the Sudanese towns to take refuge.

Fig. (10) The Anya Nya flag.

In 1965 Jaden and Oduhu, after some disagreement, agreed to replace SANU Outside with the Azania Liberation Front (ALF) with Kampala as its location. The situation among the Southern resistance fighters in the mid 1960's was, however, very confusing. The two main military leaders Joseph Lagu and Emilio Tafeng fell out, and as a result should be exiled politicians were at times arrested by the Anya Nya. The organization of the armed groups followed ethnic lines, and the ethnically based and segregated armies were not easy to organize under one command.

Fig. (11) The Azania Liberation front flag (see page 334 for colour page)

In 1967 the ALF was replaced by the Southern Sudan Provisional Government (SSPG) with Jaden as the leader for a short period. He felt, however, wary as he was of what he termed the Dinka domination. Later, in 1969, the SSPG changed name to Nile Provincial Government while Joseph Lagu established Anya Nya National Organization.

Inside Sudan William Deng joined forces with Sadiq el Mahdi and the Umma Party in the 1968 elections, but was killed by elements of the Sudanese security near Tonj town in Bahr el Ghazal Province. That a 'moderate' Southern leader was assassinated by the Northerners was to many Southerners a bad omen for continued co-existence with the North.

The year 1969 was full of Southern infighting where Southern politicians went in and out of different movements, a fact which again caused confusion among ordinary Southerners. It was not until 1970 that Joseph Lagu managed to establish the Southern Sudan Liberation Front with a military and political wing. This establishment seemed to unite many of the factions referred to previously, and strengthened resistance against the Sudan Defence Forces (SDF) in the North. Undoubtedly the strength of the Southern Sudanese Liberation Front was one reason why the Addis Ababa Agreement became a reality.

Summary: The Southern resistance movements suffered many splits in the 1960's, and were not united until 1970 by Joseph Lagu.

Pair work

1. Try to list the various names of the Southern resistance movements after 1965. Why do you think the movement changed names so often?
2. What were the obstacles of the armed resistance movements?
3. What was the result of the armed struggle?

Discuss in class

1. Why was it so difficult for the Southerners to unite under one leader?

Support from abroad

Fig. (10) Idi Amin Dada Alemi (1924-2003) was a Ugandan politician and military officer. He was recruited into the British Army in 1946, and he was appointed Commander for the Army in 1966. Idi Amin became President in 1971 after a military coup. Being a Kakwa from Uganda with close affinities with Southern Sudanese, Amin helped the Anya Nya with military equipment, logistics and intelligence.

While Sudan on the one hand repressed the Southern demands for self-determination, it supported secessionist groups from other African countries. These countries on the other hand supported the Anya Nya and sheltered Southern refugees. One of these countries was Ethiopia which did not like Sudan´s support to Eritrean secessionists. In 1969 a training camp for Anya Nya was established in Ethiopia.

Sudan´s support to the Arabs after the Arab-Israeli war (1967) made also Israel more symphathetic towards the Southern Sudanese guerillas. Joseph Lagu wrote to the Prime Minister of Israel promising a second front against the Arabs. In return Israel supplied the Southern Sudanese guerillas regularly with arms and gave them access to military training. The arms and soldiers were chanelled to Anya Nya through Uganda.

One reason why Joseph Lagu managed to unite the various guerillas under his command was that he was the main beneficiary of army supplies from abroad.

> **Question**
> 1. In what ways did the policies of Sudan's neigbours affect the North-South conflict?

Nimeiri takes over in Khartoum

On May 25, 1969 Jaafar el Nimeiri seized power from the politicians, thus becoming the second army officer after Ibrahim Abboud to do so in the history of Sudan.

Fig. (11) Jaafar Nimeiri (1930-2009) was a Jali-Arab.

> Nimeiri graduated from Military College in Khartoum in 1952. He went to military training in Egypt in 1956. As a Colonel he led a successful coup in 1969. He became the leader of the Revolutionay Command Council and in 1971 he was elected president of Sudan. He was "re-elected" twice, but his regime became increasingly unpopular in the 1980's. He lost his power in 1985 when he was abroad, and went into exile in Egypt where he stayed for 14 years. He returned to Khartoum in 1999 and ran in the Presidential elections in 2000, but did poorly. He died in Khartoum in 2009.

Among the reasons Nimeiri gave for capturing power was the inability of Northern political parties to respond to the problem of Southern Sudan, and therefore the need to solve it, besides the rapidly deteriorating economy. He was supported by the illegal Communist Party, the only one that recognized the differences between the North and the South and advocated local autonomy for the Southern provinces within a united Sudan.

Fig. (12) Members of the Revolutionary Command Council, May 1969. Nimeiri in the middle (front). (*Ithaca Press*)

Nimeiri's statement of June 9th 1969 became the basis of making contacts with the Anya Nya in an effort to end the war. In that speech he promised to look at the grievances of the people of Southern Sudan. Nimeiri acknowledged the problems of Southern Sudan and their historical and social roots. For the first time in history, a Northern Sudanese publicly recognized and accepted the Southern Sudanese demand for political and cultural identity, i.e. recognition of unity in diversity. This change of attitude contributed to some extent in the success and acceptance of the later Addis Ababa Agreement.

But Nimeiri sent out contradictory signals. The Union between Egypt, Libya and Sudan established in 1969 was seen as the spearhead of Arab cultural unity. The government was also totally committed to the Arab cause against Israel. The Southern Sudanese accused Nimeiri's Government of leaning to the Arab world and paying mere lip service to Africa and African problems. Nimeiri hardened the Southern Sudanese opinion in an interview in Cairo; he was alleged to have said that the Southern Sudanese problem is not only a Sudanese problem, but an Arab one.

> **Petition from the Southern Sudanese political forces to Jaffar Nimeiri concerning the intention to join the Arab League. November 19th 1970**
>
> …The African population in this country has been viewing with concern the preponderant leaning of the Sudan towards the Arab world and mere paying lip service towards Africa and the African problems. Although it might be thought that the Tripartite Union is a step towards African unity, we think that it is contradicted by the very aims of the Union itself, which are:
>
> a) Spearheading the Arab cultural expansion into the heart of the Continent
>
> b) Providing a nucleus for an over-all Arab unity
>
> The elimination of Southerners as a minority group in the Sudan, as it was stated by the President in his press interview in Cairo, and that the Southern problem is not only a Sudanese problem but an over-all Arab one, has made us feel that the solution of the problem, in view of the status quo, is alarming…
>
> Hence, we the Southerners, the Students, the Youth Unions, the Workers, the Teachers, the Intellectuals and the Supporters of the Revolution, as citizens, we together raise our voice and say on the Tripartite Union, NO. But we should not be misunderstood. We do sympathise with the difficulties which the Arab nations are facing in their struggle against the imperialist in the Middle East…we support Sudan's stand on the side of the Arab states in the Middle East Problem, and the friendly ties it maintains with Arab nations.

> **Work in pairs**
> 1. Why were the Southerners warning against the intention to join the Arab League?
> 2. Why did the Southerners stress that they supported the friendly ties with the Arab nations?

In 1970 the Nimeiri government made quiet contacts with the Anya Nya military leaders who had established a more formidable leadership than the political leaders. Enock Garang, the editor of pro-Anya Nya news magazine called *Grass Curtain* and Lawrence Wol Wol were initially contacted by the Khartoum regime through third parties including the Geneva-based World Council of Churches and Nairobi based All Africa Conference of Churches. While these contacts were being made, an attempt to topple Nimeiri's regime was staged in July 1971 by some communists, led by Hashim El Atta.

Why did they stage a coup?

They reacted to Nimeiri's hostility and persecution towards his former allies, the communists. The abortive coup was crushed and the ring leaders, including Hashim El Atta and Joseph Garang, were executed.

The contacts with the rebels produced the first ever face to face meeting between the Sudanese government and the Anya Nya in Addis Ababa, Ethiopia early 1972. The Emperor of Ethiopia, Haille Sellasie was the patron of the meeting which was chaired by Canon Burges Carr from All Africa Conference of Churches. The Sudanese government delegation was led by Abel Alier, a Southerner, while the Anya Nya delegation was led by Ezborn Mundiri. This conference produced the Addis Ababa Agreement, granting Southern Sudan local autonomy with limited powers to run the South.

Fig. (13) Celebration of the Addis Ababa Agreement (*Ithaca Press*)

The Addis Ababa Agreement divided the Southern Sudan opinion. While a number of officers tried to disrupt the Agreement, the Southern Sudanese refugees in Uganda received the news with jubilation. In chapter seven, the Addis Ababa Agreement will be discussed fully.

Summary: Nimeiri seized power in 1969 and worked for an understanding with the Southern resistance movement. The result was the Addis Ababa Agreement.

Tasks

a) Arrange an interview with your grandparents about the first civil war. What was the cause of the civil war? What were the splits all about? What role did your grandparents play?

b) Arrange an interview with your grandmother about gender roles during first civil war:

c) One of the prominent members of SACDNU, Joseph Oduho, was later killed by SPLA. Try to find out from your teacher or from people in your community why Oduhu was killed.

Group task

a) What do you think are the reasons for the many troubles and conflicts within the various resistance movements in Southern Sudan? Visit some people whom you know were active in the resistance movement in the 1960's and ask them about the divisions in the resistance movement. Ask them about why this occurred.

Group Discussion

1. Give the main causes of the first civil war?
2. Why was the issue of Islamization so fundamental in the conflicts between the North and the South?
3. What factors led to the Addis Ababa Agreement?

Timeline

1958: The military coup by Abboud
1962: The formation of SACDNU
1962: The Missionary Societies Act
1963-1972: Armed struggle
1964: The overthrow of Abboud's regime
1965: The Round Table Conference
1965: The massacre of Southern Sudanese civilians
1969: The military coup by Nimeiri
1970: The Southern Sudan Liberation Front was united under Joseph Lagu
1972: The Addis Ababa Agreement

7
The Addis Ababa Agreement and the Southern Regional Governments 1972-1983

Introduction
The central issue of modern Southern Sudan has been the tension between African indigenous culture and imported Arab culture. During the period of the Southern Regional Government, both Northerners and Southerners tried to live peacefully, but the experiment was weakened due to the abrogation of the Addis Ababa Agreement leading to the division of the South into three regions and subsequent introduction of Shari' a law in 1983.

Background of the Addis Ababa Agreement
As we have seen from the previous chapters the policies pursued by the Sudan government in Khartoum resulted in wide- spread discontent and rebellion by different Southern Sudanese liberation movements. By 1969, when Nimeiri took over the government in Khartoum, the Anya Nya liberation movement managed to unite their military wings to form the Southern Sudan Liberation Army (SSLA) under the leadership of General Joseph Lagu Yanga. At the same time, Nimeiri and his new regime recognized that a new policy towards the South was needed because of the poor economy and political instability of the nation. The recommendations of the Round Table conference of 1965 and the Southern Front Party's proposals had also called for this new policy. Nimeiri acknowledged the cultural and historical diversity

between the North and the South and the need to develop economic and political structures in the South.

The unstable political climate in both the North and the South forced the Khartoum government to ask the Church to act as a broker in a peace agreement with the political wing of Southern Sudan Liberation Army (Anya Nya).

Who led the delegations to Addis Ababa?

Ironically two Southerners were heading the negotiations in Addis Ababa. Abel Alier led the Northern delegation and Ezboni Mundiri led the Southern delegation.

Fig. (1) Abel Alier Kwai (1933-) is a Dinka from Bor. He is a renowned lawyer and politician. He was a member of Nimeiri's cabinet from 1969-1972 (Minister of Supply and Internal Trade, Minister of Works, Minister for Southern Affairs and then Vice President of Sudan from 1971-1982). Abel Alier had a crucial role in the Addis Ababa negotiations and other negotiations between the North and the South. He was appointed the first president of the Provisional High Executive Council of Southern Sudan in 1972. Like Lagu Alier's role as a politician is contested.

The Southern delegation (Southern Sudan Liberation Movement-SSLM) was very small, and lacked substantial expertise in economic matters. When the delegations were to form economic, political and security sub-committees the SSLM was not able to establish an economic sub-committee. This lack of economic expertise had huge consequences for the economic outcome of the negotiations. A political sub-committee as well as a sub-committee on security was established. This proved productive in terms of quickly reaching consensus on a future regional government. The security sub-committee reached agreement on ending the fighting and integrating the guerilla forces into the Sudanese forces.

Differing goals and understandings of regional autonomy at the Addis Ababa talks

The North had one condition for the negotiations, namely that the unity of the country was not being contested. This precondition disappointed many Southern politicians in exile who were unhappy about abandoning the ultimate goal of independence. Moreover, the South and the North differed in their understandings of what 'regional autonomy' meant. To the South 'regional autonomy' meant federation with a full federal structure also in the North. The Southern argument was that without a regional system the central government would in reality be a Northern government, and not a government for all regions. The North rejected this and the negotiations centered on defining the powers of the central and the regional governments. Not unexpectedly the Southerners wanted as much power as possible to the regional government.

The African National Front was one of the southern factions that didn't actively participate in the negotiations of Addis Ababa agreement, but had sent a clear message to negotiators on how the proceedings could move.

Excerpt from a statement of the African National Front (ANF) on the negotiations in Addis Ababa. February 26th 1972

The African National Front stands in favour of the following procedures:

a) The talks ought to be held between the North and the Southern true Representatives i.e. those mandated and not opportunists and adventurists acting in complicity with the Arabs and their Agents, being they Southern Sudanese or foreigners wearing clothes of humanitarian organisations.

b) The talks ought to take place without any pre-condition like the Arabs imposition of Local Autonomy.

c) The talks ought to take place under the auspicies of impartial organisations like the UN or the OAU.

d) The Arabs must know that the fraud that they are now committing in Addis Ababa will never help in defeating the Southern Sudan.

Gordon Muortat Mayen, President of the African National Front (ANF).

Fig. (2) Gordon Muortat-Mayen (1922-2008) was a Dinka from Karagok village, south east of Rumbek.

> In 1951 he was among the first Southern Sudanese to graduate from Sudan Police College and became a police inspector.
>
> In 1964 G. Muortat-Mayen became one of the founders of Southern Front (SF), and headed the Southern Front delegation at the Round Table Conference. He was appointed Minster of Works & Mineral Resources in the transitional government of Sirr El Khatim El Khalifa.
>
> In February 1967 he left the country and joined the Anya Nya national liberation movement. Later he had high positions in several of the resistance movements. In 1971 he was elected President of African National Front. This organisation was superseded by the Addis Ababa Agreement, and Gordon Muortat-Mayen became the leader of the Kinshasa Group that denounced the Addis Ababa Agreement as a sell-out and fraudulent.

Summary: After 17 years of war, the North and the South negotiated a peace agreement, despite disagreements among Southerners and differences between Northern and Southern positions.

Discuss in pairs:
1. Two Southerners headed the delegations from the North and the South. How do you think this impacted on the negotiations?
2. What was the most contested issue in the negotiations?
3. Why did the African National Front not attend the negotiations? List their complaints.
4. Explain the Northern and Southern positions in the negotiations.

The Addis Ababa Agreement

The agreement was signed in Addis Ababa on 27th February 1972. The agreement granted Southern Sudan Regional Autonomy. The agreement also stated the following:

> "The Provinces of Bahr El Ghazal, Equatoria and Upper Nile (as defined in Article 3.[iii]) shall constitute a self-governing Region within the Democratic Republic of the Sudan and be known as the Southern Region" (see appendix 1 : The Addis Ababa Agreement).

Geographically the Southern Sudan Autonomous Region was the three provinces mentioned above and in accordance with the boundaries drawn on January 1, 1956. Abyei was another area that was culturally and geographically part of the Southern Region that could be included after a referendum or a plebiscite.

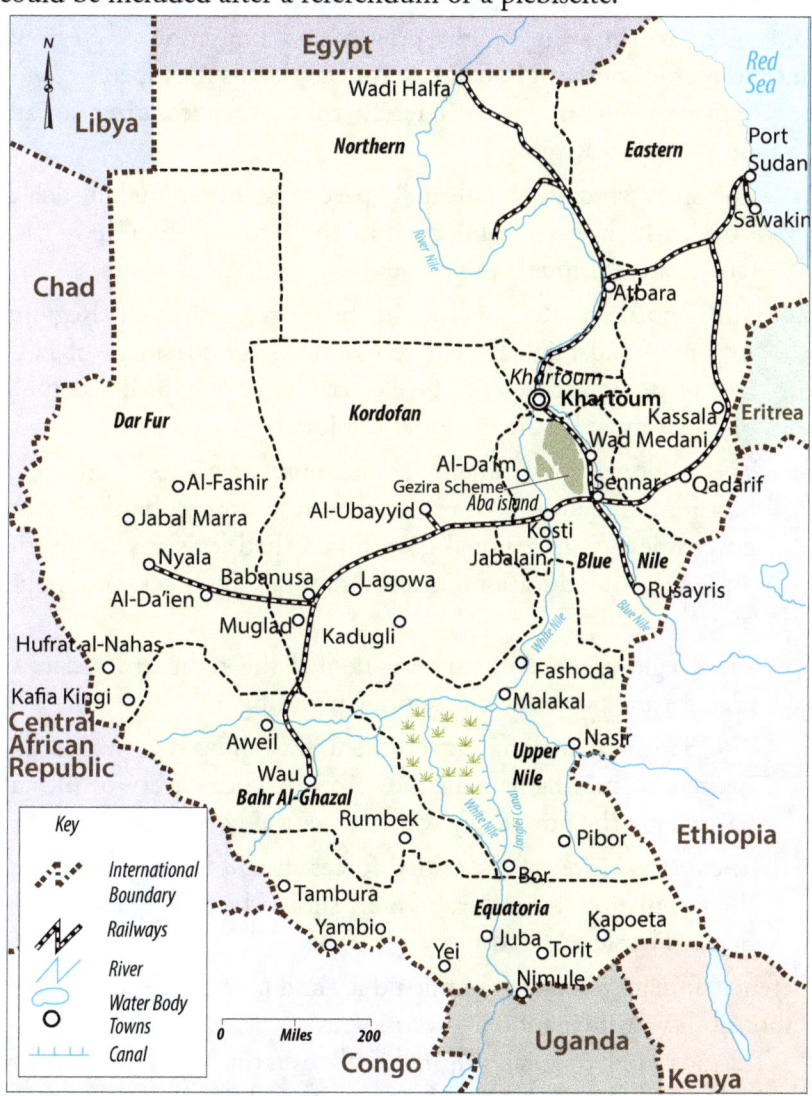

Fig. (3)   Sudan and its regions (*Indiana University Press*)

> **Definition**
> A referendum or plebiscite is a direct vote where the entire electorate is asked to either accept or reject a specific proposal.

In summary there were six issues decided by the Addis Ababa Agreement which spell out the powers and limitation of Regional Autonomy for Southern Sudan (see further details in Appendix 1):

1. Southern Sudan was, as referred to above, recognized as one Autonomous Region.
2. The areas which were culturally part of Southern Sudan such as Abyei, which was administered by the North were to have their fate decided through a referendum.
3. The Southern Region should be governed by a Regional Assembly and High Executive Council. The President of High Executive Council was to be elected by the Regional Assembly, but appointed by the National President.
4. The regional government could raise revenues from local taxation, and additional revenues were promised by the central government. The regional government had legislative authority on issues of education, health, natural resources and police matters.
5. The regional government was denied the right to legislate or exercise any power over economic planning.
6. The Southern regional government was allowed to legislate in matters of mining, but in the case of the discovery of oil and natural gas the powers lay with the central government.
7. The composition of the armed forces should be proportional to the population. Anya Nya fighters should be integrated into the Sudan People's Armed Forces.

Defence, foreign policy, economic policy and planning were to be the responsibility of the national government.

The most controversial issue in the talks was the fate of the Southern guerilla forces, the Anya Nya forces. The SSLM, by proposing to divide the country into two regions, suggested two regional armies, as well as a third national army which would be supplied by the regions. This proposal was unacceptable to the government. In the talks that followed the SSLM delegates asserted that the Southern soldiers should stay in the South to protect Southern civilians from the Northern army. The government was afraid that a Southern army of former guerillas was a potential secessionist threat. In the end it was accepted that the Southern garrison would have an equal number of Northern and Southern troops. It was not clear if the two armies were to be integrated within 5 years and there was no clarity on the status of the army after that time.

> On the Addis Ababa Agreement: "I believed I had done my part in bringing both sides together, in formulating key policies that brought about the settlement, in getting involved with the talks and helping to work out a mutually acceptable settlement."
> (Abel Alier)

Fig. (4) From the right: Joseph Lagu, Zein Abdel and Abel Alier (*Indiana University Press*)

Another controversial or contested issue in the new Constitution was the strong powers of the national presidency. Many Northerners were not happy with this arrangement, while many Southern leaders were eager to see the Addis Ababa Agreement implemented and supported the powers of the presidency. They perceived President Nimeiri as a strong defender of the Agreement, and of Southern interests. As mentioned in chapter six, however, Nimeiri's attitude to the South was dubious or ambiguous at best.

The Addis Ababa Agreement was ratified in March 1972. Amendments to the agreement could only be made after a referendum in the South.

Summary: The Addis Ababa Agreement was signed in 1972. The agreement laid the foundation of Regional Autonomy in Southern Sudan.

> **Discuss in pairs**
> 1. In your opinion, which were the weak parts of the agreement and which were the strong parts? Explain your reasons in some detail.

Reactions to the agreement

The Agreement was welcomed by many people in the South because of war fatigue. However, many of the Anya Nya fighters, politicians and the enlightened population in the South were not happy with the speed at which the Agreement (and some of its articles) was negotiated.

> "We tried to oppose it. But realising that it was not going to be successful and opportune because the masses of the people in Southern Sudan were not prepared to support our move to continue with the war we stopped the opposition. We thought that it was going to be a futile opposition because the South, the springboard of our opposition, was not prepared to back us. We realised that the people badly needed peace and not war. We thus suspended our activities and knowing the character of the Agreement after close analysis, we accepted to be absorbed into the Sudan Army. Of course we were aware that contradiction and conflict that brought the situation would continue and could be exacerbated during the course of time. We calculated that the clique in Khartoum would erode the government in Juba because its basis of the Agreement was first to absorb the Anya Nya into the National Army, second to integrate it after absorption and third to destroy it. So you have the process of achieving a cheap victory over the Anya Nya Forces." (Dr. John Garang).

In North Sudan, the Agreement was also received with mixed feelings. Although many welcomed the agreement, others called it a sell-out to the South and swore to destroy it at the first opportunity. The Northern politicians, whom Nimeiri had overthrown, believed that the Agreement granted too many concessions to the South and would result in separation claims. The Muslim Brotherhood and others, who favoured an Islamic state, saw the agreement and the 1973 Constitution into which the Agreement was incorporated as an impediment to their kind of Islamic state. Others wanted to overthrow the Nimeiri regime, but saw the support gained from the South as being a hindrance for the overthrow of his regime. This proved right when Nimeiri, with Southern help, survived two Muslim coup attempts between 1975 and 1976.

> **Definition**
> An Islamic state is a state that has adopted Islam, specifically Shari´a exclusively as its foundations for political institutions and has implemented the Islamic ruling system *khilafah*. Shari' a guarantees certain rights to non-Muslims.

Summary: The Addis Ababa Agreement was met with mixed feelings both in the North and in the South.

> **Work in pairs:**
> 1. What were the different arguments against the Agreement by the Northerners?
> 2. Can Garang's opinions in the interview explain why he took up arms 11 years later?
> 3. Explain why many Northerners and Southerners were dissatisfied with the Addis Ababa Peace Agreement?

The politics of the Southern regional governments

The circumstances surrounding the negotiations and the conclusion of the Addis Ababa Peace Agreement were seen by many as a repetition of the 1947 Juba Conference. According to some observers the Southerners were in both instances caught unprepared for the deal. They could not fully understand its implications and were to regret it long afterwards.

The Southern leaders were troubled by internal rivalry from the outset. This rivalry was exploited by President Nimeiri when he appointed Abel Alier as President of the Provisional High Executive Council and promoted General Joseph Lagu to Major General in the Sudan Army without consulting the SSLM or the two leaders. The two politicians experienced this event totally differently, and it was the beginning of a long-lasting rivalry.

> "The SSLM delegation wanted Joseph Lagu in the Sudan Army in his Anya Nya rank as Major General: He himself (Lagu) wanted it this way. He wanted to be in the army to oversee his troops taking their position in the Sudan army, the police and prison forces. Joseph Lagu was duly appointed Major General." (Abel Alier).

> In Addis Ababa I was promised the post of Vice President of the Republic, and I was completely devastated by the fact that I only was given the Major General post. I felt bamboozled by Nimeiri. (The author's formulation, but Lagu's point of view as disclosed to Arop Madut-Arop in 2002).

Yosa Wawa interviewed Lagu in 1994 in his West London home. This is what Lagu told Wawa: "According to Lagu he and his close associates had expected that he was going to be head of the first Regional Government. On coming to Khartoum Nimeiri asked Alier to form the Regional Governement and said his role was to integrate the Anya Nya into the Sudan Armed Forces, an idea that he thought was bright."

It is not entirely clear, however, who promised Lagu the post as Vice President. After what happened Lagu is reported to have been bitter. This bitterness seems to have been long lasting and had negative consequences for the development in the South even though some scholars say that the rivalry between Lagu and Alier started much later. Lagu was of the opinion that since he had won autonomy for Southern Sudan on the battlefield and at Addis Ababa, he should also influence the nomination of the President of the High Executive Council. Two camps in the South developed, and the differences in opinion between the camps can be seen as an important reason why the Addis Ababa Agreement was eventually dismantled. Although Lagu felt cheated, he helped to implement the agreement. President Nimeiri's interference in the case of Alier and Lagu was no exception, rather the rule in how the central government interfered with issues relating to the Southern Regional Government up to the abrogation of the Addis Ababa Agreement.

Summary: The implementation of the Addis Ababa Agreement was plagued with political rivalry from the first moment.

Questions
1. Try to explain why the two politicians Alier and Lagu presented the events referred to above so differently? Try to find out what Alier's and Lagu's roles were in the struggle prior to the Agreement.
2. What consequences do you think the divisions among the Southern leaders had for the success of the Southern regional governments?

The first regional governments 1972 – 1978

This period can be divided into two: the transition period of 18 months and the 4 year ordinary period.

The transition period 1972-73

The new provisional government took up its responsibilities in Juba on 25th April 1972. There were several tasks to be completed during this period. Abel Alier, who was the interim president, focused on several issues. The first was repatriation, resettlement and rehabilitation of refugees/returnees and internally displaced people. This was carried out from April 1972 to May 1974.

It was one of the biggest repatriations ever undertaken by United Nations High Commission for Refugees {UNHCR}. In 1972 and 1973 more than a million people returned to their homes, 500,000 from refugee camps in neighbouring countries, and 550,700 from internal displacement in other parts of Sudan. Even though many refugees were still in the neighbouring countries, the work of the Repatriation, Relief, Resettlement and Rehabilitation Commission (RRRRC) was prematurely stopped on 30th June 1974 and the commission was liquidated thus bringing an end to the repatriation process. The remaining refugees had to find their way back by themselves and a good number of Southern Sudanese ended up settling in the neighbouring countries, especially in Uganda and Kenya.

Fig. (5)   Internally displaced persons from Southern Sudan

Another task was to set up the regional system of government. Manpower had to be recruited and trained; departmental structures had to be established, offices and accommodation spaces had to be provided for. Basic budgets had to be drawn up for the ministries and departments to start functioning, but the government lacked sufficient funds, transport and communication facilities.

It was a formidable task to find space for the 40,000 returnee school children at various levels on the educational ladder from primary to secondary schools. This led to more secondary schools being opened to accommodate more learners. The children came from different backgrounds and had different languages of instructions. Those from Ethiopia used Amharic, those from Congo, Central Africa and Chad used French and those from East Africa used English. Yet those from rural areas used their mother tongues. Eventually as schools were established with the support of international agencies, refresher courses were run for the teachers to improve the quality of teaching and learning in the schools.

Fig. (6) School in the countryside (*Ithaca Press*)

The most difficult issue in the implementation of the cease-fire was the security arrangements. The integration of 6,000 Anya Nya fighters in the army was complicated by distrust after 17 years of fighting. The gradual integration of the Anya Nya in the army was met with rejection leading to the Akobo incident where the former Anya Nya staged a mutiny in 1973-1974. Other higher officers deserted from the army and many of these guerrilla fighters were to play an important role when the fighting resumed in the 1980's.

Others were suspicious of the Northern army and did not want to mingle with soldiers from the North. Still others were dissatisfied with the low ranks they were given in the army. The dissatisfaction and suspicion among the former guerrilla fighters led to open conflict in many instances, but not to large mutinies. Some Anya Nya forces were also recruited to the police and prisons services. The excess number was recruited to roads works and farms, while others were simply laid off.

> "We also accepted to be absorbed (into the army) because we knew that the North would dishonour the Agreement, and the South would be ready for the war. Then we would be ready to launch a genuine movement, the people's revolution." (John Garang, 1987)

Another important task was to prepare the way for the first general election to take place in November 1973. Voters' registration was carried out in the middle of 1973. As part of the registration, a national census was also conducted. The elections were carried out despite the poor voter registration process.

Moreover it was important to build confidence among the different groups of citizens in the region - northerners and southerners, returnees, IDP's and different ethnic groups to form new relationships based on equality of citizenship and mutual respect. Bitterness and distrust generated by many years of conflict had to be consciously replaced by a spirit of reconciliation and forgiveness.

> "During that period, bitterness, hatred and distrust were widespread and endemic along the North-South divide. Sudan was a sick and divided country scorned and ignored by the family of nations." (Abel Alier)

In October 1973 the election process started and the results were released at the end of November. Abel Alier was now elected to the position of President of the High Executive Council.

Summary: The transitional government had to repatriate refugees, set up the regional government, provide schools for returned refugees and internally displaced people, integrate Anya Nya soldiers in the regular army and prepare elections. Abel Alier was elected the president of the High Executive Council.

Question

1. In your opinion, what were the major challenges for the new regional government?

The first elected regional government 1974-78

As referred to above the October 1973 election gave Abel Alier the mandate to form the first elected Southern Regional Government that lasted up to December 1977. Despite poor financial means and interference from the Central Government, the first Regional Assembly managed to implement some basic development schemes in the areas of education, agriculture & forestry, health, roads and communications through the support of international partners and NGO's.

Fig. (7) The Southern regional cabinet 1973 (*Ithaca Press*)

This period also witnessed a major rift and political rivalry among the Southern Sudan leaders who were dissatisfied with the Abel Alier government. One reason was Abel Alier's dismissal of four ministers in 1974. Moreover, the arrests of Benjamin Bol, Joseph Oduhu and Clement Mboro, which followed these dismissals, heightened tensions.

The opposition against Alier was particularly strong among Equatorians. Many Equatorians were suspicious of the disproportionately high number of the Dinka in senior civil service positions. The Dinka, however, argued that they had been discriminated against in colonial times. The British had discouraged their education because they believed it would interfere with their 'tribal' lives. As a result their number in civil service had been unrepresentatively low and their increased number in civil service was according to the Dinka a natural result of their education outside Southern Sudan.

Many Southerners were also dissatisfied with the failing of the Central Government to fulfil their economic obligations, and that former Anya Nya soldiers weren't given their share of the higher posts. One of the greatest disappointments of the Southerners was how President Nimeiri changed his policies and attitude to the South after the Addis Ababa Agreement. He was now regarded as a Northern Sudanese Arab Muslim only working for the interests of North Sudan, showing little if any interest in the development of the South.

Nimeiri seemed to view Alier as becoming too pro-South, and to perceive the South as an uncontrollable region, also because of the animosity between the two camps referred to above (Alier and Lagu). Both Nimeiri and Sadiq al-Mahdi seemed to think that a weakened Southern region was advantageous.

The opposition against Abel Alier rallied around his former 'opponent', Joseph Lagu. President Nimeiri took this opportunity to support Lagu's political ambitions as a means of dividing and ruling the South with ease., Abel Alier was coerced by Nimeiri to withdraw, and Joseph Lagu, without any candidate opposing him, was unanimously elected President of the High Executive Council in 1978. At the swearing ceremony, General Lagu was ordered by Nimeiri to retire from the army which he did.

> "It was significant that Lagu should be ordered not to wear in uniform, which at the time gave an appearance of military prestige to a constitutional office holder. El Bagir, Abu El Gasim and Omar El Tayeb all wore military uniform, years after their formal retirement. Lagu's position was unique and that in itself raised irritating questions" (Abel Alier)

Summary: The first elected regional government was headed by Abel Alier, and this government implemented some basic development schemes. The period was also dominated by personal and regional differences.

Question
1. Why do you think the Southern politicians accepted the interference by Nimeiri?

Work in pairs:
1. Discuss the regional differences in the first regional government.

The second regional government 1978 – 1980

Lagu's election in 1978 was supposed to balance the ethnic issue and to speed up the development in the South. Unfortunately Joseph Lagu did not succeed on either issue.

Lagu was soon forced by President Nimeiri to reduce his cabinet in the High Executive Council. This meant that a number of people had to be dropped from the Council. It alienated many of those who had elected him, among them some Dinka. Some members of his cabinet were accused of corruption and his government was accused of unconstitutional use of power both in the legislative and judicial system. Tribal rivalry also increased when Lagu welcomed educated Equatorians who returned to the South following the fall of former President Idi Amin in Uganda. The Equatorians were serving in various government positions in Amin's Uganda. who sought exile in Southern Sudan. Soon Lagu was accused of a corruption scandal that made opposition politicians like Clement Mboro, Bona Malwal, and Abel Alier and others to ask for Lagu's dismissal late in 1979. President Nimeiri used this excuse to unconstitutionally dissolve the Southern Sudan Regional Assembly in Juba and to get rid of Lagu.

> **Group task (3 or 4 students together)**
> 1. Try to find out in your community from elders and other members of the community how they view the two leaders, Abel Alier and Joseph Lagu. Try to explain why there are different stories to the same event.
>
> **Question**
> 1. Do you know of any tribal rivalry in your community? If yes, what consequences does it have for your daily life?

The third regional government 1980 – 1981 and the abrogation of the Addis Ababa Agreement in 1983

The elections to the Third Regional Assembly were concluded by the end of May 1980 and brought Abel Alier back to the position of President of High Executive Council (PHEC). Unfortunately 'tribal' rivalries were a core issue in Alier's third presidency. Many Equatorians were suspicious of the fact that 50% of the cabinet members were Dinka. Many ministerial posts were given to former SANU opponents and members of the Southern Front, a move which was interpreted as 1) an intention to win over the majority of his former opponents and 2) an intention of Dinka domination. Abel Alier's administration was blamed for nepotism.

The Question of dividing Southern Sudan

One of the major issues of contention was the issue of division or union in the South. The Equatorians and Lagu in particular wanted the South to be divided into three regions. Lagu lobbied in Khartoum and in the South for decentralization or re-division. His argument was that the backwardness of Southern Sudan was due to the unmanageable size of the region and the remoteness of Juba, the regional capital. Many Southerners genuinely believed that decentralization would develop all regions more equally. Moreover, decentralization was a chance to get rid of what they thought was Dinka domination in the regional government. The two other regions, Bahr el-Ghazal and Upper Nile, reacted strongly against the decentralization policies and wanted to crush the Equatorian opposition. According to Lagu, this group renamed the decentralization "re-division." They felt that Equatoria was unpatriotic and should therefore be subdued. Moreover, they thought that a re-division would weaken a strong South, exactly what the central government wanted. They were also suspicious of Northern advocates for re-division as they had been the fiercest opponents to the Addis Ababa Agreement.

When Abel Alier's government became more active in economic politics, Nimeiri felt threatened and allied himself with Northern and Southern supporters of decentralization of the South. He supported Lagu's campaign for decentralization in order to weaken the South. Nimeiri dismissed Alier's government in October 1981 and called for a referendum.

A provisional government headed by General Gismalla Abdalla Rassass, Commander of the Sudan Military College was installed in the office. Rassaas was a personal friend of Lagu, but had neither experience nor knowledge of the South. Like a good soldier Rassas took up his new appointment and included in his cabinet many high ranking army officers. It was alleged that some of these officers who were still young joined Rassas' cabinet on condition that they were to rejoin the army after the end of the interim period. To their dismay, they were retired soon after serving in Rassas' gpvernment. This made many observers think that Nimeiri simply wanted to get rid of these people from the army. The reaction for and against was strong, and in a new move, in February 1982, Nimeiri postponed the issue of division, dissolved both Regional and National Assemblies and announced new elections in April 1982.

The elections to the National Assembly in January 1982 resulted in a majority of Southern opponents of decentralization. The internal opposition from the Southerners made Nimeiri reconsider the decentralization policy. However, the regional elections in April 1982 resulted in the election of the engineer Joseph James Tombura as the President of the High Executve Council. He was supportive of the decentralization policy. Tombura sought to devolve some of the powers to the provinces, which he lobbied for in Khartoum. Following the April election Nimeiri issued a decree for regionalization (decentralization) of the South into three regions of Bahr El Ghazal, Equatoria and Upper Nile while several of the opponents of decentralization were arrested.

In 1983 President Nimeiri decreed unconstitutionally the division of Southern Sudan into three regions (Bahr-el-Gazal, Upper Nile and Equatoria). The regionalists (favouring decentralization) had thought that Southern Regional Autonomy would remain intact for the three provinces of Southern Sudan in line with the Addis Ababa Agreement. This did not happen. On the contrary the powers of the regions were reduced considerably. The Southern Regional Government had powers to raise taxes of their own,but the taxes from new regions were remitted to the North and redistributed by the Central government. This arrangement was particularly frustrating to a then rich region like Equatoria. The regions were also clearly disappointed by the fact that President Nimeiri appointed the governors of the three provinces while the President of the former Southern Region was elected. Soon after the dividing the South into three regions Nimeiri declared Shari'a laws in September 1983. The decree of Shar'a law consolidated resistance against the Khartoum regime.

Summary: Abel Alier's third presidency was dominated by the question of re-division/decentralization. In 1983 Southern Sudan lost its regional autonomy.

> **Discuss in class**
> 1. Try to explain the terms re-division and decentralization.
> 2. Explain the difference in views between the unionists and the re-divisionists in the South. In what way do you think the two positions were based on geographical location and ethnicity?
> 3. Why, in your opinion, was the Addis Ababa Agreement dismantled?

Conflicting issues from the Addis Ababa Agreement to the second civil war

The crisis over oil

Since independence 1956, the Northern politicians and the various Khartoum governments have not been concerned with political and socio-economic development of the South. When the Regional Government was established after the Addis Ababa Agreement, natural resource exploration became a constant demand from Southern Sudan. When finally in November 1974 the oil companies, Chevron and Total, received concessions to conduct oil exploration in the South, without Southern consultation, the Northern political leaders feared that the new found riches would threaten the unity of the country and strengthen those who wanted separation. In 1978 oil was discovered in Bentiu. The Central Government attempted to downplay the amount of oil that had been discovered. The discovery of oil made the Addis Ababa Agreement even less digestible to the North, as the Agreement stated clearly that the regional government had the right to tax the profits from the export of mineral resources from the region. Southern Sudanese demanded to be included in the membership of Petroleum board, but to no avail.

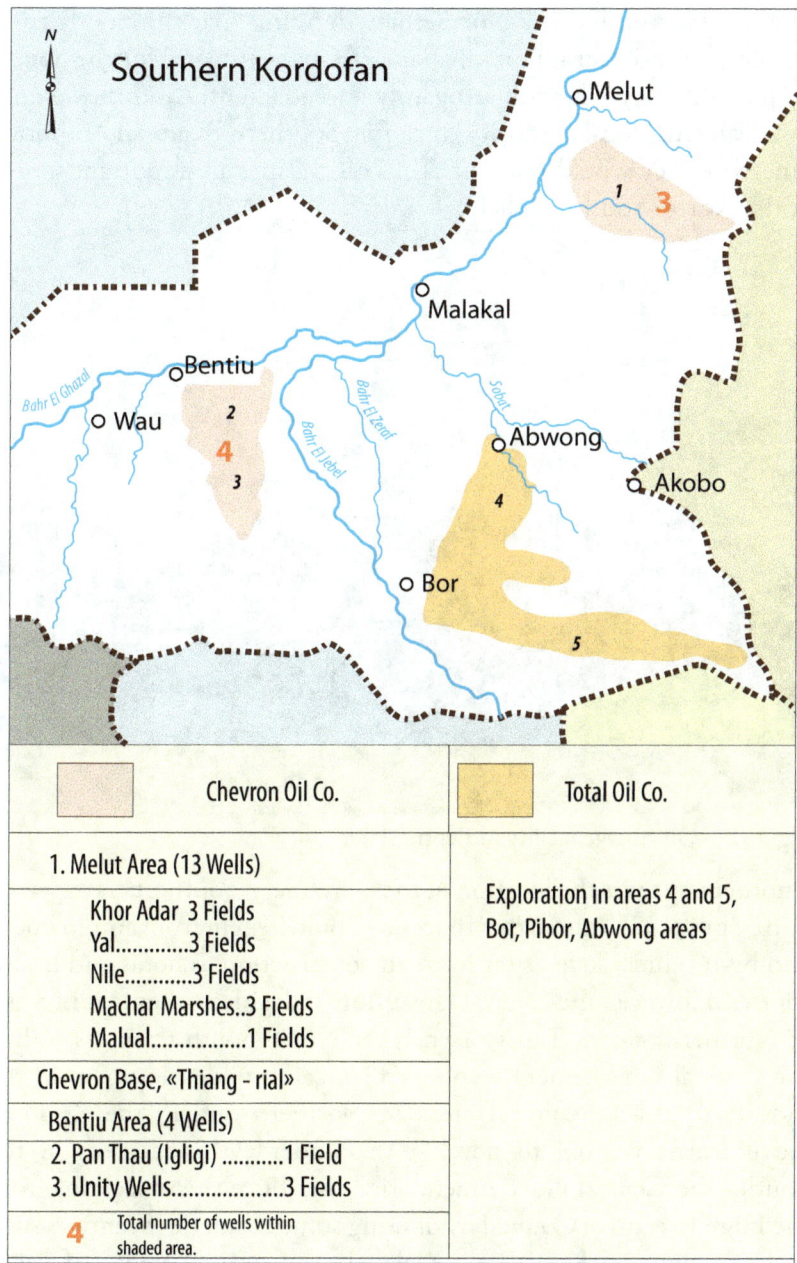

Fig. (8) Oil map of Southern Sudan in the 70s (*Ithaca Press*)

The oil issue united the Northerners deciding that the Southerners should have no decision in oil affairs. To make it worse for the South, the oil company Chevron arrogantly and adamantly said they would not deal with "local authority" meaning Southern Regional Authority, otherwise they would pull out. Thus oil became an important source of the North–South conflict.

Fig. (9) Oil storage facility in Bentiu state.

Another issue was the location of the oil refinery. Southerners expected it to be built in Bentiu so that the South could benefit from employment and by-products such as tar for road construction, schools and health centres. However, the Central Government decided to build it in Kosti in Northern Sudan. This worsened the North-South relations. While the Central Government wanted to concentrate development in the industrial and agricultural areas of Northern Sudan, the Regional Government wanted to develop the underdeveloped areas in the South. The Central Government tried to reduce the objections from the High Executive Council by offering some cosmetic incentives such as upgrading the Kosti-Rank-Malakal road, improvement of water and health services for the Bentiu Council, provision of self-propelled badges to transport oil products, and the creation of a development authority for Bentiu Council, but none of the promises was fulfilled by neither Chevron nor the Khartoum Government.

Even before the Addis Ababa Agreement could find foot in Southern Sudan, Nimeiri formed a committee chaired by Clement Mboro to engage the Southern Sudanese opinion about the Government's intention to create six provinces in Southern Sudan from the then Bahr el Ghazal, Equatoria and Upper Nile. It was the argued that the creation would take services nearer to the people with the resultant development. Opponents of the idea argued that it was not the creation of new provinces but provision of development funds that was central to development. As it was in Nimeiri's time, his will was always done.

In the early 1980s, Joseph Lagu came out with pamphlet calling for the creation of three regions. One of the main ideas behind the call for the creation of the new region was the fight against, as he put it then, Dinka domination. His proposal was opposed by the Abel Alier camp. The call for division of the Southern Sudan into three regions was promoted under the *Kokora* (a Bari, Kakwa, Kuku, Mundari, Pojulu) word for division. Interestingly enough, the idea of Dinka domination or Kokora found support among some Dinka in Bahr el Ghazal and the non-Dinka in Upper Nile. Thus, using Southern Sudanese themselves, Nimeiri was able to dismantle the Addis Ababa Agreement and the Southern Sudan Regional Government.

Discuss in pairs
1. Why did the Northerners exclude the Southerners in decisions concerning oil issues?
2. In your opinion, has the exploitation of oil led to development or underdevelopment of Sudan? State the reason for your answer.

Borders

The Addis Ababa Agreement provided for the possibility of transferring some areas in the North to the South. Some of the areas had been part of the Southern provinces before the independence and should be automatically retransferred. Other areas were deemed culturally similar to the South and were subject to a referendum for the possible transfer to the South. None of this happened.

The border question was very delicate. Some Arab cattle herders in Kordofan were concerned about their access to water if the disputed territory of Abyei should be transferred to the South. In reaction to this, armed gangs attacked Dinka villages with the intention of driving them into Bahr al-Ghazal in the late 1970's and early 1980's.

The border issues were further complicated when oil was discovered. In 1980 the Central Government attempted to transfer the rich agricultural and pasture lands and oil-rich areas, from the South to Southern Darfur, Southern Kordofan and White Nile Provinces. This was followed by the decision to build the oil refinery in Kosti. Popular demonstrations and protest from the Regional Assembly and the High Executive Council made Nimeiri appoint an Investigation Committee under Judge Khalafalla Rasheed. The committee recommended the retention of boundaries fixed on 1st January 1956 as stipulated by the Addis Ababa Agreement. Tactically, the President accepted the recommendation. To date a number of boundary issues remain unresolved between the South and the North.

Fig. (10) Political map of Sudan. (*www.theodora.com/maps*)

Summary: The borders were another contested issue, as they were not clearly agreed upon at the Addis Ababa Agreement.

> **Discuss in class**
> 1. Why did the border issues become more complicated after the discovery of oil in the South?

Economic development

To the great disappointment of people in the South there was little economic development in Southern Sudan. The Regional Government received annually only about 20% of the allocated grant for Southern development. The Central Government was more interested in large scale projects within the golden triangle in the Blue Nile State, e.g. Gezira and to some extent in Western Sudan rather than in Southern Sudan. The Khartoum government and many Northern officials directly or indirectly were opposed to Southern autonomy and therefore diverted the limited resources meant for development schemes in Southern Sudan to the North. Planned development projects such as the Mongala Agro Industry Scheme, the Aweil Rice Scheme, the Nzara Agro-Industrial Complex and others were allowed to die away, and funds and equipment were diverted to schemes in the North.

In response to this, Bona Malwal, the Minister of Industry and Mining in Alier's government, used his Western and Arab contacts to raise funding for the development in the South. There were several internationally financed programmes for small and large scale projects in the Southern Region between 1972 and 1983, focusing on the improvement of infrastructure and services, as well as the overall economic productivity of Southern Sudan.

One problem was, however, that there was little practical coordination of projects undertaken by various international agencies, and the regional government did not take a leading role in planning the various development schemes. Some progress was made in the development of schemes like coffee in the Yei area, tea in Upper Talanga and forestry products in Katire, Yei, and other parts of Southern Sudan. Infrastructural development was however slow and just a few murram roads were made in Southern Sudan. These included roads and bridges financed by the Dutch (375 miles Nimule-Juba-Kongor); the Federal Republic of Germany (600 miles Juba-Yambio-Wau); by EEC-USAID (500 miles Kenya border- Kapoeta-Juba).

Fig. (11) Bona Malwal

Bona Malwal (1935 –) is a Dinka Tuic from the same area of North Bahr el Ghazal as Salva Kiir. He was a founding member of the Southern Front. He served as a Regional Minister of the government of Alier and as a Minister of Information in the Nimeiri government before he was forced out due to the Shari'a laws and the break with the South. Living in exile in England for most of the 1980's and 1990's, he reconciled with the Bashir government in the late 1990's, returning to Khartoum. He is the founder and editor of the Vigilant, Sudanow, Sudan Times and the Sudan Democratic Gazette. He has now retired from politics.

Summary: The financial support from the National Government to Southern Sudan was meagre, but some private funded development schemes took place in this period.

> **Discuss in pairs**
> 1. List some of the development projects in the South in this period. Do you know of any development projects in your area and who are in charge of them?

Women

In the South, women organized themselves under the Sudan's Women Union. The local groups of the Union arranged many activities, like needlework, nurseries and training in handicraft. Only urban women could engage in these activities since there were no centres in the countryside. The Women's Self-Help Development Committee was another organization which trained and assisted in the financing of self-help groups that engaged in handicrafts and vegetable gardens to create an income. The organization's head office was in Yei, and it supervised many groups in the whole of Equatoria province. The Institute for Integrated Rural Development was established in Amadi, Western Equatoria in 1977. Women and girls were trained in childcare, nutrition and agricultural activities.

The women in the South also made important contributions during the civil war. Some fought on the front lines while others travelled with the guerilla groups, carrying supplies and providing medical support. While some women served willingly, others were forced into the war activities against their will. There was also a lot of sexual abuse for example, rape and forced prostitution, by all parties in the war.

In 1980-1981 only 25% of the students in school were girls and 90 % of the women were illiterate. Their relative powerlessness was reflected in the marriage arrangements. When a young woman married, the husband had pay a dowry for her. The marriage was seen as a transaction between the husband and his family and the wife's family. The woman was therefore dependent on support from her family if she wanted a divorce. In that case, her family was required to pay back the dowry. The women did not generally own property or administer their own income. There were and still are, however, different dowry arrangements from one ethnic group to another.

> **Questions**
> 1. What do you think is the most important reason for women's relatively low status in the South?
> 2. Name one woman's organization and tell about its activities.

National politics

In the 1970's Sudan was seen as the future bread-basket of the Arab world and the government consequently invested large amounts of money in mechanized farming. However, mismanagement and corruption replaced the "bread-basket" dream to a nightmare of drought, famine and huge foreign debt. The failure in economic policy as well as the proposal by the International Monetary Fund to cut in public expenditure and eliminate subsidies, which Nimeiri agreed to, made the government very unpopular in the North.

Nimeiri relied on shifting alliances during his presidency. From the signing of the Addis Ababa agreement and onwards he was strongly supported by the South. However, after two coup attempts Nimeiri wanted to have his enemies closer and broaden his Northern support. He brought former Prime Minister and leader of the Umma party, Sadiq al-Mahdi, home from exile and released Hassan al-Turabi, leader of Muslim Brothers, from prison. He soon fell out with his new ally, Sadiq al Mahdi, but Hassan al-Turabi became Minister of Justice. Southerners were worried about this policy of "National Reconciliation" in the North and how it would influence the Addis Ababa Agreement. They had every reason to worry as Hassan Turabi always stood for the Islamization of the Sudan. He had been alleged to have said that since Southern Sudanese had no culture, Islam could always fill that void.

Nimeiri created also strong alliances with the United States. The US was worried about the development in the Marxist Ethiopia and was hostile towards Libya. As a counterweight the US chose Sudan, which may have been one of the reasons that Nimeiri was confident about resuming a new war in Southern Sudan.

Summary: Nimeiri's economic policy proved to be a failure, and he shifted his alliance partners during his presidency as a means to hold on to power.

Questions
1. Why do you think Nimeiri wanted to reconcile with the Islamite leaders?
2. To what extent did this influence North-South relations?

Shari'a law

By 1980 Nimeiri's position was constantly under threat. With the intention of neutralizing his opponents, Nimeiri gave Islam a prominent place in Sudan's political and economic life. He abandoned military dress and used the jallabiya when appearing in public. He presented himself as an Islamic, and not a military or socialist, leader. Hassan al-Turabi used his central role to determine the legal change in Sudan to Shar'a law.

Fig. (12)   Turabi, Hassan Abdallah (1930-) is a Beari-Arab.

> He graduated from Law School at the University of Khartoum in 1958. He pursued further studies at the London University and at a university in Paris.. Later he became Secretary-General of Muslim Brotherhood/Islamic Charter Front between 1964 and 1965. He became General Attorney and Minister of Justice in 1979. He has been imprisoned several times by different regimes.

In September 1983, in a move to consolidate his new political alliance, Nimeiri announced the imposition of Shari´a provisions in the criminal code as well as the family code. The new criminal provisions applied in principle to all Sudanese, Northerners and Southerners, Christians or Muslims. However, they failed to be fully applied in the South and never beyond the major towns.

> **Definition**
> Shari´a is the body of formally established Islamic Law. It is based primarily on commandments found in the Quran. In theory it governs religious matters, but also political, economic, civil, criminal, ethnical, social and domestic affairs in Muslim countries and communities.

In a dramatic move Nimeiri illustrated his new political course by standing on the banks of the Nile and publicly pouring spirits and other alcoholic drinks into the river. Southerners, Christians and moderate Muslims were disturbed by the law, which allowed for the amputation of limbs for theft and violent crime. It soon became clear that these penalties were being applied mostly against Southerners and Western Christians.

With this step, which gained him some temporary support within the radical Islamist camp in the North, Nimeiri finally lost all credibility and support in the South. The implementation of the Shari´a Law was a major blow to the Addis Ababa Agreement and the Constitution of 1973, and was therefore a trigger to the Second Civil War led by the Sudan People's Liberation Movement /Army. Since

1983 the removal of the September Laws was one of the contentious issues in the North-South relations.

Summary: Shari'a law was implemented in 1983 and caused much bitterness in the South.

Discuss in pairs
1. Why was the implementation of the Shari'a law so critical for the North-South relations?
2. Try to find out what happened in Juba when Nimeiri announced the Shari'a law.

The failure of the Southern regional government and the outbreak of the second civil war

Below is a summary of the main factors that accelerated and led to the destruction of the Southern Regional Government.

1. The conflict with the central government over the Southern region's borders. The failure of the Southern Regional Government to co-ordinate the development of the region's resources and more especially their failure to deliver to the South the benefits to be accrued through the exploitation of South's oil and other minerals.
2. Discontent within the South over the fate of the Anya Nya guerrillas who were absorbed into the national army.
3. Division between the Southern politicians allowed corruption and nepotism to flourish.
4. In the North, Nimeiri brought back his Islamist opponents (the Umma and the Muslim Brothers) through national reconciliation in order to guarantee political stability. The conditions which the Islamists imposed for national reconciliation was the reform of the Law based on Islamic principles.

Time line

1972: The Addis Ababa Agreement
1972-1977: The First presidency of Abel Alier
1977: The "National Reconciliation" between Nimeiri and Islamite leaders

1978: Oil discovery in Bentiu
1978-1979: The Presidency of Joseph Lagu
1979-1980: The Presidency of Peter Gatkuoth
1980-1981: The Second Presidency of Abel Alier
1981-1982: The Military provisional government
1982-1983: The Presidency of Joseph Tombura
1983: The Decree of division of Southern Sudan
1983: The introduction of the Shari'a Law
1983: The Second Civil War

Tasks

a) Interview your parents or grandparents about the Addis Ababa Agreement and the causes of the Second Civil War.

b) Imagine you are a Northern student during the peace period between 1972 and 1983. Tell about some of your experiences in those years.

Imagine you are a Southern student during the peace period between 1972 and 1983. Describe your life in those years.

c) Work in groups of 2 or 3. Trace Nimeiri's development and try to explain his shifting attitudes to the South. Write an essay and give it to your teacher.

d) The students should organize in groups of 4. Dramatize one of the conflicts in the Southern Regional Assembly for the rest of the class.

Group discussion
1. What was the most important issue that triggered the Second Civil War?
2. How could the Southerners have reduced the possibility of Second Civil War?

8
The Second Civil War, 1983-2005

Introduction

The developments following the Addis Ababa Agreement of 1972 resulting in the formation of the regional government in Juba were not without problems. Some of the disputed issues were related to:
1. Lack of economic development in the South.
2. The discovery of oil reserves in Southern Sudan and Nimeiri's attempt to redraw the provincial borders (1980) by cutting off oil rich areas in Bentiu with the intention of annexing it to the North (Southern Kordofan Province).
3. The construction of the oil refinery in Kosti instead of Bentiu (1980)
4. The position of former Anya Nya soldiers who were dissatisfied with the Addis Ababa Agreement
5. Nimeiri's policy of Shari'a law,
6. The abrogation of the Addis Ababa Agreement and the division of Southern Sudan into three weak regions.

Not only was Nimeiri's policy of administrative decentralization aimed to dilute and undermine the authority of the Southern Region, but it was also designed to intensify divisions among the people of the South. One example was the administrative division of the Shilluk Kingdom into two administrative areas Jonglei and Upper Nile provinces, resulting in armed dispute between the Shilluk and the Dinka of Atar.

This discontent soon led to the formation of many underground insurrection movements, each mobilising the people of Southern Sudan for the resumption of another liberation war. The most notable of these underground movements was that of the Anya Nya Absorbed Forces with junior officers like Francis Ngor Machiek, Salva Kiir Mayardit and Chagai Atem. By 1981, some of the Anya Nya I forces which were opposed to the Addis Ababa Agreement formed Anya Nya 2 and were fighting for the total liberation of Southern Sudan. The key leaders of this movement included Lt. Samuel Gai Tut and Major William Abdallah Chuol.

The founding of the SPLA/M and its aims

Perhaps as part of his plan of weakening the Southern Sudanese unity or perhaps as a warning to Anya Nya 2, Jaafar Nimeiri ordered in January 1983 the transfer of Battalion 105 based in Bor to Northern Sudan. The soldiers refused to move, partly because of the Addis Ababa Agreement that stated that southern soldiers should only serve in the South. John Garang, head of the Staff College in Omdurman, went to Bor allegedly to mediate in the conflict. The Sudanese Army attacked Bor in May 1983, which resulted in further mutinies and desertions in the South. By July 1983, 2500 soldiers were in military camps in Ethiopia along the Sudan border in a swampy place called Bilpham. It was to Bilpham that thousands of Southern Sudanese students, peasants, civil servants, police, prison officers and game and army units flocked to join the rebel training centres. Another 500 remained in the field in Bahr-el-Ghazal and in addition there were Anya Nya 2 troops in military action inside the South.

The formation of the SPLM /SPLA and the leadership question

Before the formation of the SPLM/A, Akuot Atem had already delared himself Chairman of the Movement. He appointed Samuel Gai Tut as Minister of Defense, Joseph Oduho as Minister of Foreign Affairs;

Martin Majier as Minister of Legal Affairs and Justice and Dr. John Garang as Chief of Staff.

In preparation to meet the Ethiopian authorities, Akuot Atem wrote a manifesto of the Movement that stated that the Movement's aim was to fight for the total liberation of Southern Sudan. This proposal was rejected by the Ethiopian authorities because it was believed to violate the Organisation of African Unity (OAU) charters. It was also against Ethiopian interests to back a separate Southern Sudan as Nimeiri was backing a secessionist movement for Eritrea. Ethiopia was ready to assist the South, but not on the secessionist ticket. Ethiopia wanted to get rid of Nimeiri, but since it had a separatist problem in its own backyard, Ethiopia did not want to support a secessionist movement in the neighbouring country.

The Southern leadership headed by Akuot Atem came back to the refugee camp of Itang dumfounded and unable to comprehend what the Ethiopian chief of Staff, Mesfin, wanted them to do as a precondition for soliciting support. Joseph Oduho appealed to Dr. Garang to write a position paper that would be acceptable to the Ethiopian authorities. Dr Garang accepted and wrote the paper that later became the SPLM Manifesto. The position paper proclaimed the ***creation of a socialist, united and secular Sudan.***

The Aims and Objectives of the SPLM Manifesto were as follows

- to evolve a Sudanese identity reflective of the Sudan's multi-ethnic and multi-cultural character.
- to build unity of the country on the totality of the components that make up Sudan's historical and contemporary diversities, and separating religion from the state.
- to restructure power in the center and decentralization of power by redefining the relationship between Khartoum and the regions and devolving more powers to the regions.

- to foster democratic governance in which equality, freedom, economic and social justice and respect for human rights are not mere slogans but concrete realities.
- to promote environmental and even sustainable development.

Garang was elected leader of Sudanese Peoples Liberation Movement

When the SPLM Manifesto was presented to Chairman Mengistu it was accepted and the Sudanese were asked to launch their movement. Thus the name of the movement became the Sudan People's Liberation Movement (SPLM). John Garang, the Chief of Staff of the Movement, was asked to remain behind in Addis Ababa in order to work out logistics requirements before the official launch. The chairman of the movement, Akuot Atem, suspicious of the Ethiopians' request to keep Garang behind to solicit logistics requirement, told his supporters that Ethiopia was attempting to impose John Garang on them as the leader of the movement. Akuot Atem ordered his supporters to move back to Sudan where they would launch the People's Revolution for the Liberation of Southern Sudan. Thus all his followers moved to Bilpam Camp to join Gordon Koang's soldiers who were with Samuel Gai Tut.

After an intensive debate both about leadership and policy issues John Garang de Mabior was elected in Itang in August 1983, as Chairman of SPLM and Commander in Chief of the SPLA. What tipped in his favour was the Ethiopian support for Garang for his alleged fight for a united Sudan. Moreover Garang was younger and better educated than his rivals.

South-South battles: Anya Nya 2 vs. SPLA

The rivalry between Garang and Akuot Atem was not based on ethnicity since both were Twic Dinka from Kongor district. Throughout 1984 the rivalry between the two factions continued, and Akuot Atem as well as Gai Tut continued with their independent military activities in Waat and Kongor. In late 1984 both were killed, and William Abdallah Cuol took command of the two combined forces. Under Cuol's command a new Anya Nya 2 appeared on the scene with the tacit support of the Nimeiri government who hoped to establish a Nuer army to defeat the so-called Dinka SPLA. Cuol did not, however, enjoy the support of all Nuer, and thus he even fought against the Nuer elements in SPLA. The fightings between Anya Nya 2 and SPLA were ferocious, and many civilians were killed in various battles. The government policy of backing tribal militias which began under Nimeiri continued till the signing of the Comprehensive Peace Agreement (CPA), and was a strategic move to make the world believe that the civil war was really a war between various Southern factions only. The creation of militias forced SPLA to fight on two fronts, the government forces and militia groups, transforming the war from not only a North –South, but also a South-South war.

Fig. (1) Dr. John Garang (1945-2005) was the first Southern Sudanese to hold the position of 1st Vice President of the Republic of Sudan since independence. Dr. John Garang was the leader of the rebel Sudan People's Liberation Movement/Army. A member of the Dinka ethnic group, he was born into a poor family in Wagkulei village, near Bor in the Upper Nile region of Sudan in the present Jonglei State.

The first civil war ended with the Addis Ababa agreement in 1972 and Garang, like many other Anya Nya fighters, was absorbed into the Sudanese military force. For eleven years, he was a career soldier and rose from the rank of captain to Lt. Colonel after taking the Infantry Officers' Advanced Course at Fort Benning, Georgia. During this period he took four years academic leave and received a master's degree in agricultural economics and later a Ph.D.

In 1983, Dr. Garang in a pretext of going to bring back his family to Juba, joined the Bor mutiny. The mutiny was by Southern soldiers of Battalions 105 and 104 who were alleged to be resisting being transferred to posts in the North. He played a leading role in the founding of Sudan People's Liberation Movement/Army (SPLM/A), which was opposed to military rule and Islamic dominance of the country. From 1983 to 2005, he led the Sudan People's Liberation Army during the Second Sudanese Civil War, and following a peace agreement he briefly served as First Vice President of Sudan from January 2005 until he died in July 2005 in a helicopter accident.

"From June to November 1983, we engaged in an extensive and intensive debate concerning the direction of the newly formed Movement. Ardent separatists, reactionaries and opportunists gave us a very hard time. People like Akuot Atem, Gai Tut, Gabriel Gany, Abdalla Chuol and others stood for the forces of reaction. They wanted a movement similar to Anya Nya 1, a movement connected with international reaction and calling for a separate and independent Southern Sudan. It took us six months of bitter struggle to resolve the correct direction of the Movement. The principles proclaimed in our revolutionary Manifesto prevailed. The forces of reaction and separatism were defeated." (John Garang)

Summary: The Bor Mutiny marked the start of the Second Civil War. The foundation of SPLM/A was plagued by internal rivalry, but John Garang became the leader.

> **Work in pairs**
> 1. What led to the formation of the SPLM/A?
> 2. What was the difference between the positions of Dr. John Garang and Akuot Atem?

The liberation war

Almost immediately after the naming of Garang as the Chairman of SPLM and Commander in Chief of the SPLA the following were appointed members of the top leadership of the Movement called the **Politico-Military High Command (PMHC):**

1. Colonel Dr John Garang de Mabior, Chairman and Commander in Chief of SPLA.
2. Major Kerubino Kuanyin Bol was promoted to Lt. Colonel and appointed Deputy Chairman and Deputy Commander In Chief so as to bring him nearer to Colonel John Garang in the military hierarchy.
3. Major William Nyuon Bany was promoted to Lt. Colonel and appointed Chief of General Staff of the SPLA.
4. Captain Salva Kiir Mayardit was promoted to the rank of Major and appointed Deputy Chief of Staff for Security and Military Operations.
5. Nyachigag Nyachiluk was given a military rank of Major and appointed alternate Member of Politico-Military High Command.

Having launched the Sudan Peoples' Liberation Movement/Army the next step was the recruitment, training and arming of soldiers. Between 1983 and 1984 the SPLA depended almost entirely on its arms and ammunition brought from the uprisings, and arms captured on battle grounds from the Sudanese army. These were supplemented with military supplies from the Ethiopian regime. After some time, Libya became a strong and committed arms supplier of the SPLA.

Having acquired sufficient logistics and trained guerrilla forces, the SPLA started their military campaign from November 1983. This led to the closure of the Compagnie Centrale Internationale (CCI) that was digging the Jonglei Canal. By 1985, the SPLA had managed to assemble a formidable force capable of confronting the Sudanese Army with conventional weapons. The recruitment to the SPLA differed from region to region. In the Equatoria region SPLA was viewed as a Dinka organization and the recruitment from Equatoria was considerably less than from other regions.

> **Child soldiers**
>
> From 1983 to 1987 children, farmers and herders rushed to the SPLA's recruitment camps, where they got military training. Almost no one was turned down, and the result was a large number of child soldiers. Training was rigorous and conditions in the training camps were severe and harsh to say the least. The camps were especially hard for the children, with disease, poor hygiene and few caretakers. Nevertheless, most of the volunteers persevered till the end of the training sessions when they were deployed.
>
> Not all child soldiers were volunteers. The 1991 Country Reports on Human Rights Practices stated that SPLA had forcibly abducted at least 10,000 boys. The SPLA practice was the following: to abduct the children, to isolate them from their families and to train them militarily before they recruited them into the Army. SPLA abducted children as young as seven years old and took them into their ranks from the age of eleven. The battalions of child soldiers were called the "Red Army", and had a hard time during battles, because they were not good soldiers. Many died in the battles or in the camps because of the bad conditions.

Nimeiri's reactions to the mounting insurgency

President Nimeiri and his generals in Khartoum ordered all the national material and human resources to be used to crush the SPLM/A. He declared the Sudan Armed Forces the *"**Army of God**."* The Sudan

Army responded by pledging their unconditional loyalty to Nimeiri. The national media coverage was devoted towards discrediting the SPLM/A. On its part, the SPLM/A established a radio station to counter the Nimeiri propaganda.

As mentioned Nimeiri started a policy of establishing and arming **tribal militias** in the South (in Upper Nile, Equatoria and Bahr el Ghazal) to counteract the SPLA achievements. At the same time Nimeiri tried to start peace negotiations with the SPLM/A, with the help of two big business enterprises, the Saudi Adnan Kadshoogi and the British Tinny Rowland. Nimeiri offered a peace package based on the 1972 Addis Ababa Agreement. Garang was offered the position of Vice President of Sudan and to administer Southern Sudan as he saw fit. In response Garang assured the nation that the SPLA would never betray the Sudanese people by negotiating with their oppressor.

Slavery

As already mentioned, the Sudan government supported militias as part of their offensive against the Sudanese People's Liberation Army. The most devastating militia was Murahalin that operated in Kordofan and Northern Bahr el-Ghazal, where they attacked the Ngok, Abiem, Malual and Twik Dinka. The raiding was partly a result of the drought in the early 1980's, but also due to the loss of land use rights because of the flourishing of mechanized farms. The Murahalin raided cattle, women and children. The women and children were traded or kept in slavery.

Slavery was reported to have re-emerged in Southern Sudan in 1983. Over 50,000 Southern Sudanese had become enslaved from 1983 to 2000. 5% were brought to Chad, while the rest supplied the farms in southern Darfur and western Kordofan.

Displaced people by famine or oil exploitation were easy victims of slavery. Since displaced southerners in the North do not have the same rights or the same political status as the Northerners because they are not Muslims, they are often excluded from public services, and stigmatized as Southern rebels or infidels (non-believers).

Fig. (2) A group of children freed from slavery. (*University of Pennsylvania Press*)

Summary: By 1985, the SPLA had a formidable force to confront the Sudan Army even though the recruitment differed from region to region. Nimeiri armed tribal militias, which meant that the SPLA had to fight on several fronts.

Work in pairs
1. Explain in your own words what a liberation war is?
2. Why do you think the SPLA recruited child soldiers?
3. What were the main reasons for the slave trade during the Second Civil War?

The overthrow of Nimeiri

On 6th April 1985, President Nimeiri was overthrown in a popular uprising led by the National Alliance for National Salvation (NANS). NANS was a coalition of trade unions and professional organisations including the Umma Party and Sudan Communist Party. The causes of the uprising were the war in the South with its human and financial costs, political repression in Khartoum and a collapsing economy.

The army came in to fill the vacuum after Nimeiri by forming a Transitional Military Council (TMC) under the chairmanship of Sowar Al Dhahab who was to administer the country. The TMC did not, however, abolish the Shari'a Law, contrary to the demands of the SPLM/A.

However, in solidarity with the masses, the SPLA unilaterally declared a seven day cease-fire within which the Movement asked the TMC generals to hand over power to the NANS. On its part the TMC established a civilian cabinet on April 25 1985, but the army was largely in control. Garang was suspicious of the new leadership and did not see a strong break with the Nimeiri policy. Al Dhahab's recognition of the Shari'a as the foundation of Sudan's legal system confirmed Garang's position. The SPLM demanded that a constitutional conference be convened that would include all parties before they would take part in elections. However, the TMC passed election laws on October 10th 1985 without regard to the SPLM/A position.

> Garang on SPLM's position to the OAU summit July 18th 1985:
>
> The Central Problems in the Sudanese war are the dominance of One Nationality; the Sectarian and Religious Bigotry that dominated the Sudanese political scene since Independence; and the unequal development in the country…unless the Nationality Question is solved correctly, the Religious bigotry is destroyed and a balanced development for all the regions of Sudan is struck, war is the only inevitable option in Sudan.

The Koka Dam Declaration

Contacts were established between the SPLM and the National Alliance (NANS) in late 1985 and early 1986, and SPLM agreed to meet NANS and chart out the future of the country. The National Alliance included the Umma party as well as secular, revolutionary and progressive forces, but neither the Democratic Unionist Party (DUP)

nor the Muslim Brothers, the National Islamic Front, participated. On 19th March 1986, NANS and SPLM met at a small town outside Addis Ababa called Koka Dam. At the end of the meeting the parties committed themselves to:
1. A peaceful resolution of the Sudanese conflict
2. The establishment of parliamentary democracy and the convening of a national constitutional conference
3. The reinstatement of the 1964 consititution
4. The abolition of the Shari'a Laws
5. The abrogation of the Military Pacts with other foreign countries (Libya and Egypt) which impinged on national sovereignty

The Koka Dam Declaration was not implemented by the new coalition government

National elections were carried out on April 12 in 1986 without SPLM's participation. No elections were held in the Southern constituencies because of the war. The elections resulted in the election of Prime Minister Sadiq al Mahdi who formed a coalition government of the Umma Party with the DUP and other minor parties. The coalition government under Sadiq al Mahdhi did not implement the Koka Dam Declaration even though the Umma party had taken part in the Koka Dam discussions. Sadiq al Mahdi seemed to have one postion in opposition and another when in power. After Nimeiri's fall many Southern parties were revived and new ones were registered, but their relative significance was difficult to measure since no comprehensive elections in the South were held in this period. All Southern parties were supportive of the Koka Dam Declaration and that the SPLM/A should be included in negotiations about the fate of Sudan in the future. But since the Koka Dam was not implemented by Sadiq al Mahdi the war continued.

When Sadiq became Prime Minister in 1986 the North seemed to be in a stronger position than the SPLM/A because of support from Libya and the Gulf states. Muammar Gaddafi of Lybia, one of the first supporters of SPLM/A, stopped supporting the movement after the overthrow of Nimeiri. Sadiq al Mahdi could even count on US military assistance. This support from foreign actors seemed to harden Sadiq's position against the South and his unwillingness to deal seriously with the SPLM/A. The support to militia groups increased under Sadiq and particularly Murahalin raids in 1986-87 caused many human rights violations. Cattle were raided in Dinka areas, Dinka villages were burnt and women and children were killed or abducted to the North where they kept or sold as slaves.

The Sudanese People's Liberation Army acquires a wider base

By 1989 the SPLA had become stronger, not the least because of the close cooperation between Anya Nya 2 and the SPLA. The SPLA managed therefore to defend the civilians from Murahalin and government forces., But the civilian losses due to militia attacks were severe in this period.

Fig. (3)   Orphans after a slave raid in Gok Machar (*University of Pennsylvania Press*)

The SPLA relationship with the civilian population in the South was problematic up to 1987 and particularly in Equatoria because the SPLA attacked the civilian population whom they thought was hostile to the SPLA. After 1987 the SPLA seemed to understand that this tactic alienated large population groups in the South, and the guerilla army tried to improve their relationship by disciplining the SPLA soldiers and by trying to avoid harassing civilians. The increased popularity of the SPLA after 1987 also made recruitment from non-Dinka areas in the South easier and the image of SPLA as a Dinka army was slowly vanishing.

Sadiq al Mahdi's popularity as Prime Minister was decreasing after the first two years of his premiership, particularly because he had not been able to solve the pressing problems Sudan was facing.

The Sudanese Peace Initiative

The DUP, the junior partner of Sadiq's Umma led government was dropped from the coalition government in favour of the Muslim Brothers and NIF. This forced the DUP leader to enter into serious negotiations with the SPLM in November 1988. The two leaders, John Garang and the DUP leader, Muhammed Uthman al –Mirghani, went to Addis Ababa and signed the Sudanese Peace Initiative which was a modified version of the Koka Dam declaration. The initiative aimed to bring about peace to Sudan through the

1. Cessation of hostilities
2. Lifting the State of Emergency that had been in force since 1983
3. Suspension of the Shari'a Laws
4. The holding of a National Constitutional Conference to decide the country's future.
5. Abrogation of the military defence pacts with foreign countries

Mirghani was received as a hero on his return to Khartoum clearly signalling that the Northerners wanted the war to end as soon as possible.

Sadiq's reaction to this declaration on intent between the DUP/SPLM was negative, but Umma and the NIF coalition were pressured by the public to accept the DUP/SPLM Peace Initiative as a basis for peaceful settlement of Sudan's problem.

At the same time, the army went a step further by giving the Prime Minister an ultimatum in a 21-point memorandum which is summarized in the following points:

1. Reorganise a genuinely broad-based government
2. Make a drastic re-appraisal of Sudan's foreign policy
3. Supply the army with modern weaponry to fight the SPLA
4. End hostilities in Southern Sudan.

The prime minister's acceptance to implement the DUP/SPLM Peace Initiative in April 1989 made the NIF resign from the coalition government. The NIF could not accept any agreement that would modify their goal of an Islamic state. The result of this was that the Umma had to go back to the DUP to form another coalition government. Sid Ahmed Hussein (DUP) became Deputy Prime Minister and was appointed to lead a Ministerial Government delegation to negotiate with the SPLM about the details of the Sudanese Peace Initiative. The Government delegation returned to Khartoum with positive results and the Cabinet endorsed the Initiative. The date for the National Constitutional Conference was set to September 18 1989. With the peace settlement close to being implemented, a group of committed Muslim officers in the army supported by the NIF and led by Brigadier Omar Hassan Ahmad al Bashir took over the government in a bloodless coup.

Summary: Nimeiri was overthrown in 1985. SPLM and NANS met at Koka Dam for peace negotiations. The new government did not endorse the Koka Dam Agreement. The Sadiq government was ousted by Bashir in 1989.

> **Questions**
> 1. Explain the main points of the Koka Dam declaration.
> 2. Why was the Koka Dam Agreement not implemented?
> 3. What were the consequences of Sudanese Peace Initiative?
> 4. What features were common among Northern Sudanese political parties towards Southern Sudan?

The NIF military coup

The National Islamic Front (NIF) has had a long history and policy of promoting itself as the principal carrier of Arab-Muslim nationalism and protector of orthodox Islam and Arab interests in Sudan. The NIF policy caused discontent in Sudan in general and in the South in particular and impacted negatively on Sudanese politics, socio-economic as well as religious and cultural life. Freedom of speech and a certain tolerance towards dissenters had traditionally been a part of Sudanese culture. Now the intelligence services arrested intellectuals, university professors, journalists and human-rights activists. Political prisoners were tortured or killed in detention centres. The result was a massive emigration of the brightest Sudanese to Arab countries, Europe and North America. The Islamists dominated the judiciary, the government, the parliament, the military and institutions of higher education and repressed the media and trade unions. The Shari'a laws were more comprehensive than the September laws of 1983. Non-Muslims were discriminated against, and priests and Christian relief organizations were harassed.

After the NIF coup, a 15-man military junta known as The Revolution Command Council (RCC) was formed. The RCC created a more organized militia, the Popular Defence Force (PDF) than the militias started byNimeiri and continued by Sadiq el Mahdi's regime The NIF formed the National Congress Party (NCP) and this new party included some non-Muslim members; mainly some Southern Sudanese politicians.The government abandoned the Sudanese Peace

Initiative, and the SPLM concept of the New Sudan which meant freedom from racism, sectarianism and underdevelopment. The NCP and the SPLA were back on the battle fields.

Fig. (4) Omar al Bashir (1943-) was born in Shendi.

He is a Bedari-Arab and has a working class background. He has been Prime Minister, Commander-in-chief, Minister of Defence, Chairman of the Revolutionary Command Council for National Salvation and President of Sudan. He has studied at Wadi Saidina Military Academy and Sudanese College of Commanders, and also in Malaysia, the US and Pakistan. He was a military counselor to the United Arab Emirates until 1997, and had since higher official positions in the Sudan Army. In July 2008, the prosecutor of the International Criminal Court (ICC) accused al-Bashir of war crimes, i.e. crimes against humanity and genocide in Darfur. The court issued an arrest warrant for al-Bashir on March 4 2009.

Women

The NCP regime pursued a discriminatory policy towards women. Female employees were dismissed and requested to dress in Islamic style. The ideal Muslim woman was a housewife and a mother. Sudanese women were not allowed to travel abroad without a male relative.

In Southern Sudan conditions for women became worse because of the war. Traditionally women had no right to choose their husbands and control their body. Often they were married young, which had negative effects on their education and their health. During the war only 6% of the pupils in primary schools were girls and less than 2 per cent graduated from primary school. The number of girls was even less in secondary school. Early marriages also had detrimental effects on the health of girls.

The civil war changed women's lives. Traditionally women did most of the farm work; they planted, and were responsible for weeding, harvesting and crop processing. However, during the war the women's workload increased heavily since most of the men were soldiers or refugees, Moreover the activities of fuel gathering and water-fetching became very dangerous because the women could run into the SPLA or national army forces in the bush or by the river. Many did not survive such encounters.

One consequence of the increased workload was that many women quit breast feeding at an early age. This meant in many cases that the interval between pregnancies became shorter, since sexual contact during breast feeding was/ is taboo. Another consequence of the war was that children ended up malnourished. The lack of medical services in rural as well as in urban areas made this situation even worse. Moreover, many of the roads in the South were heavily mined endangering lives.

The disintegration of many families due to war meant that discipline in the home became difficult, and many children ran away from home, especially when there wasn't enough food. Many women tried to solve the desperate economic situation by migrating to the towns in the South or in the North, but often to no avail. However, some church groups evolved in urban areas where women were engaged in income-generating activities. Most of the women's organizations established before the war ceased to exist, and the war situation also impacted negatively on the women's possibilities for education. Many women took a more active part in the war, and their experiences were similar to the experiences women had during the Anya Nya 1.

Summary: The NCP regime transformed Sudan into their version of an Islamic State. Women's lives in Southern Sudan changed dramatically for the worse during second civil war.

Work in pairs
1. Try to explain the NCP policy while in government.
2. Describe briefly how the lives of women were affected by the civil war in North and in Southern Sudan.

Conflicts among Southern Sudanese

Since its formation in 1983, the SPLM/A can be said to be one of the most successful organized rebel movements in the world. Politically, it won itself many friends in Africa, Europe and the Americas. Despite these military and political successes, the SPLM/A faced a lot of challenges as we have referred to above. Poverty, the divide and rule strategies employed by the successive regimes in Khartoum and the yearning for power among individuals generated conflicts amongst Southern Sudanese and had a negative impact on the SPLA war efforts.

The guerilla struggle in the first civil war was hampered by factional and tribal divisions as well as confusion over political objectives. The leadership of the Sudanese Peoples' Liberation Movement/ Army learned the lessons of the first civil war. The SPLA tried to prevent factionalism by suppressing internal dissenters and on attacking military rivals. The SPLA had an internal security branch that purged the movement of dissenters, suspected government agents and political rivals. As a result some were killed and others, like Kerubino Kuanyin and Arok Thon Arok were arrested and detained and arrested for a long time. However, the causes of dissent were not removed. The centralization of the Army was limited, and local commanders were quite autonomous and acted the way they saw fit. The establishment of an effective civilian administration was severely neglected, and the SPLM leadership was accused of dictatorship because it did not convene national convention meetings as people had expected, and not until 1994.

Around 1990, many started to question the overall strategy of the movement, but there was no forum to discuss these questions openly, besides talking to John Garang. This made Lam Akol and Riek Machar question the lack of democratization and accountability in the movement, and made plans to replace Garang as a leader. The plans became more realistic when the SPLA's greatest supporter, the Ethiopian leader Mengistu, fell in 1991. In 1991 this dissent flared up resulting in the break-up of the SPLM into two factions, the Nasir and the Torit factions.

Fig. (5)   Dr. Riek Machar Teny Dhurgon (1952 –) joined the Sudan People's Liberation Movement/Army (SPLM/A) in 1984.

He split from (SPLM/A) in 1991 with Dr. Lam Akol and Gordon Kong Chuol to form SPLM/A-Nasir Faction (1991–1993), later SPLA-United (1993–94). He accepted in 2011 responsibility for the Bor massacre. Machar signed the Khartoum Peace Agreement in 1997. Thereafter the name of his movement changed to South Sudan Independent Movement (SSIM). The military wing was South Sudan Defense Force (SSDF) (1997–2002). The Agreement meant that Machar and his team joined the Islamists in Khartoum. The Khartoum Peace Agreement offered the South self-determination on paper and made Machar the Assistant to the President of the Republic of Sudan and the President of the Southern Sudan Coordinating Council (August 7, 1997 - January 31, 2000). Machar became soon disillusioned with the broken promises of the Khartoum government and in January 2000, Machar went back to the bush. He joined Garang's SPLA/M in 2002. After the death of Garang Machar became vice-president of Southern Sudan. Machar became Vice President in South Sudan after independence in 2011, but was sacked by President Kiir in July 2013. Machar was in December 2013 and in the beginning of 2014 heavily involved in a violent power struggle with President Salva Kiir.

The impact of Mengistu´s departure from Ethiopia on the SPLA

Due to Mengistu's fall and the loss of support from Ethiopia the SPLA had to act fast to relocate its forces and the refugees into Sudan in the midst of Sudan Air Force plane bombardments. The SPLA lost their protected bases and their secure supply lines as well as their radio station. The hostile Ethiopian government handed over all security files on the SPLA, and the SPLA was afraid that the Khartoum government would be allowed to use Ethiopian territory to attack the SPLA.

Under these new circumstances Riek Machar and Lam Akol as commanders of Upper Nile felt marginalized because of the concentration of SPLA soldiers in Equatoria, the closeness to hostile Ethiopia and the reinforcements of government troops in Malakal.

Fig. (6)   Areas under SPLA control and administration 1989 (*Ithaca Press*)

The two commanders became in charge of a huge refugee camp at Nasir, and made contacts with humanitarian agencies. The USA had been increasingly critical of John Garang and his alliances with Mengistu, and the Nasir commanders felt they had the US government support to overthrow Garang. They had also made contacts with the Government-appointed Governor of Upper Nile, and had been promised military support against Garang. Other SPLA commanders, apart from Gordon Kuong Col, were reluctant to support a violent overthrow of Garang in such a critical time for the SPLA. They felt that a violent change in leadership when the SPLA was so weakened was a mistaken and counterproductive strategy.

The 'coup and overthrow' of John Garang was announced on the SPLA radio network on 28 August 1991. Lam Akol and Riak Machar denounced Garang as a dictator, outlined their policy by underlining the need for greater democracy within the SPLM/A, and proclaiming their respect for human rights and a halt to the recruitment of child soldiers. They also stressed that the political goal of SPLM/A was the independence of Southern Sudan. The coup was however poorly prepared (both commanders had spent their energies in securing outside support), and it was only the Nuer districts, which were already under the command of the Upper Nile region, which supported the coup. The attempted coup resulted into the split of the SPLM into the Torit and Nasir factions, but the Nasir faction did not receive support from other parts of the SPLA as it had expected.

Unlike the Torit faction led by John Garang, the Nasir faction of Riek Machar and Lam Akol claimed to be fighting for the total liberation of Southern Sudan. Despite claiming to fight for the liberation of Southern Sudan, the Nasir faction received military assistance from the NCP Khartoum regime to fight the SPLM/A. Many Southerners concluded that Lam and Riak were about to align themselves with the Khartoum government, given the fact that they were accepting arms from Khartoum.

The war between the Nasir and Torit factions led to huge civilian losses.

The Bor Massacre

On November 15, 1991 forces led by Riek Machar of the Nasir faction and Nuer civilians attacked greater Bor (three months after the coup) and killed more than 2,000 people and wounded several thousand more during a period of two months. More than 100,000 people left the area due to the massacre. Famine followed in its wake and 250,000 people are reported to have died during the famine. Machar's forces looted and burnt villages and raided cattle. Riek Machar called the massacre "propaganda"" at the time, but in 2011 he admitted that he ordered the massacre and the former vice president (forced out of office in August 2013) apologized for the misdeeds. His motive for the massacre was probably to hurt the Dinka in order to diminish the Dinka domination in the SPLM leadership. The Nasir faction's stress on human rights was therefore seriously questioned.

Motivated by power or money, many other SPLA splinter groups emerged all over Southern Sudan in addition to the Nasir faction. These groups included the following:

1. *The SPLA-Unity Group* led by William Nyuon Bany. His forces consisted mostly of Nuers and a few Equatorians. Nyuon was assassinated by the Southern Sudan Independence Movement/Army forces (Machar's faction) in Eastern Upper Nile in 1995.
2. *The SPLA Bahr el Ghazal Group* led by Kerubino Kuanyin Bol. He fled from the SPLM/A prison in Buma. Kerobino's forces went to Western Upper Nile where he aligned himself with Anya Nya 2 under Paulino Matip. With the support of Anya-Nya 2 he crossed over to Gogrial town where he killed many civilian at Wunrok. Kerubino defected and rejoined the SPLM/A several times before being killed by the Sudan Armed Forces in Bentiu in 1998.
3. *The SPLA Bor Group*: This splinter group was led by Arok Thon Arok who was at the time of defection a Deputy Chief of Staff in SPLA. Arok's headquarters was in Bor town which was by then a Sudan Government controlled garrison town. Omer El Bashir promoted him to the rank of Brigadier General but he died in a plane crash in Nasir town on 12th February 1998.

4. *The Equatoria Defence Force* led by Dr. Theophilos Ochang with its command post in Torit town. At one moment Theophilos was alleged to have joined hands with the Lord's Resistance Army (LRA) of Uganda to wage a concerted war against SPLM/A. As the Comprehensive Peace Agreement was about to be signed, Theophilos renegotiated his way to SPLM/A in 2004.
5. *The Southern Sudan Freedom Fighters Front*: This faction was formed by Dr. Richard K. Mula. It had a short life because its leader re-joined the SPLM/A.
6. *The Southern Sudan Patriotic Liberation Front*: After spending many years in prison, Alfred Lado Gore came out to form this movement. He was mainly based in Kampala conducting a diplomatic war. SSPLF had no links with Al Bashir government and did not actively engage with the SPLA militarily.

Southerners help Bashir to fight the SPLA

Given the split in the SPLA which clearly weakened the SPLM/A Torit faction, the government of Omer al Bashir was able to launch the February 1992 military offensive code named "Hemlat Seif al Obuur" (the dry season campaign). This offensive aimed at wiping out SPLM/A once and for all in Southern Sudan. Like previous governments in Khartoum, Al Bashir managed to recruit, train and arm various ethnic groups in Southern Sudan to fight the SPLM/A. These groups included the Fertit and the Murahalin in Northern Bahr el Ghazal, the Toposa in Eastern Equatoria, the Murle militia in Jonglei, the Mundari militia in Central Equatoria, the Tang-inya militia in Upper Nile and the Nuer militia in Unity state. When the Nasir Faction of the SPLM/A which had claimed to be fighting for the total independence of the South became weak, it joined Bashir and helped to fight the SPLM/A Torit faction.

Soon the government army captured Faholla town followed by Shambe Port and Yirol Town. By the end of April 1992, most of the major towns in Upper Nile Region were either in the hands of the Nasir Faction or effectively under the government control.

With most of the major towns in Upper Nile and Bahr el -Ghazal brought under the government control, the next target was to capture

Equatoria regions. With the help of Toposa tribal militia, Kapoeta was captured with heavy losses to the SPLA Torit faction. In June 1992 after a string of battles between Juba and Torit, the SPLM/A Torit faction tactically evacuated Torit town leaving it to the enemy. In Chukudum clashes between the SPLA and local Didinga groups were quite frequent with the last fighting taking place probably in 1999. With the pressure from all sides, SPLA had to eventually relocate towards the Kenya and Uganda borders, and for the next three years it became a true border war. The war brought untold suffering to ordinary people of Southern Sudan resulting in the International Community campaigning to find an end to this protracted war (see more on the consequences of war in the next subchapter).

The Nasir faction and the Peace Charter of 1995

The problem which the Nasir faction soon faced was that while it was fighting for the independence of Southern Sudan, it was getting military help from the Khartoum government. Lam Akol and Riak Machar soon lost their credibility as a viable option to Garang's faction which ultimately led to their movement's downfall. What added to their problems was the signing of the Peace Charter with President Bashir in 1995. The Peace Charter underlined the unity of Sudan and Shari'a as the basis of legislation in the country. At the same time it promised that a referendum would be held at the end of an unspecified period where the South was to decide its political future. The Charter also implied security arrangements which meant that Machar had the obligation to transfer his forces to the government. It became apparent, however, that in the following year (1996) Machar did not have full control over his forces and did not even manage to convince all of the Nuer of this endeavour. The Peace Charter remained an agreement on paper that could not be implemented.

By 1996 the SPLM/A Torit faction had gained momentum and came on the offensive again, opening military fronts and waging wars in the North, in the Blue Nile, Kasala and Kordofan areas. In January 1997 the SPLA took the two towns Kurimuk and Quaissan in Northern Sudan near the Ethiopian border, and made substantial progress towards Juba in the next months. SPLA's success was at least partly due to the cooperation between southern and northern opposition groups, under the name of NDA (National Democratic Alliance). Still there were conflicts between various groups in the South.

International and local pressure on the SPLM/A

In the 1990's the SPLM/A was pressurized by foreign actors like the USA to sit at the negotiation table with the Khartoum government, and in 1997 the IGAD negotiations were reopened. The SPLM insisted that the basis for the negotiations had to be a secular nation state, a demand which was rejected outright by the Bashir government. However, the war between Eritrea and Ethiopia effectively blocked any further initative from IGAD in the late 1990's. (The various peace intiatives will be dealt with in more detail in the next chapter.)

Inside Southern Sudan people started to discuss Garang's political goal of a united Sudan, and many seemed to opt for a separate South, mainly because of all the broken promises from the North. People were also weary of the split in the movement which had led to so much misery and the loss of so many lives among the civilian population. Increasingly there was a demand for a change of direction in leadership, and more focus on a civil administration in the South, thus paying more attention to the needs of the civilian population. Around 2002 Garang seemed to respond to these demands. The Nasir and the Torit factions united under the leadership of Garang. The reconciliation between Garang and Machar in 2002 seemed to indicate that the main actors listened to the calls from the grass roots. Garang announced the establishment of a comprehensive NDA army as well as an improvement of civilian administration in the SPLA–controlled areas. But the war went on because none of the fighting parties were able to get the upper hand until the Comprehensive Peace Agreement was signed on January 9 2005.

It is worth noting at this stage that the civil war between the Bashir government and the SPLA/M was one of several civil wars or internal struggles in Sudan: there were conflicts within Islam, in Darfur, in eastern Sudan, as well as in Southern Blue Nile, but space does not allow us to dig more deeply into these other armed strifes in Sudan.

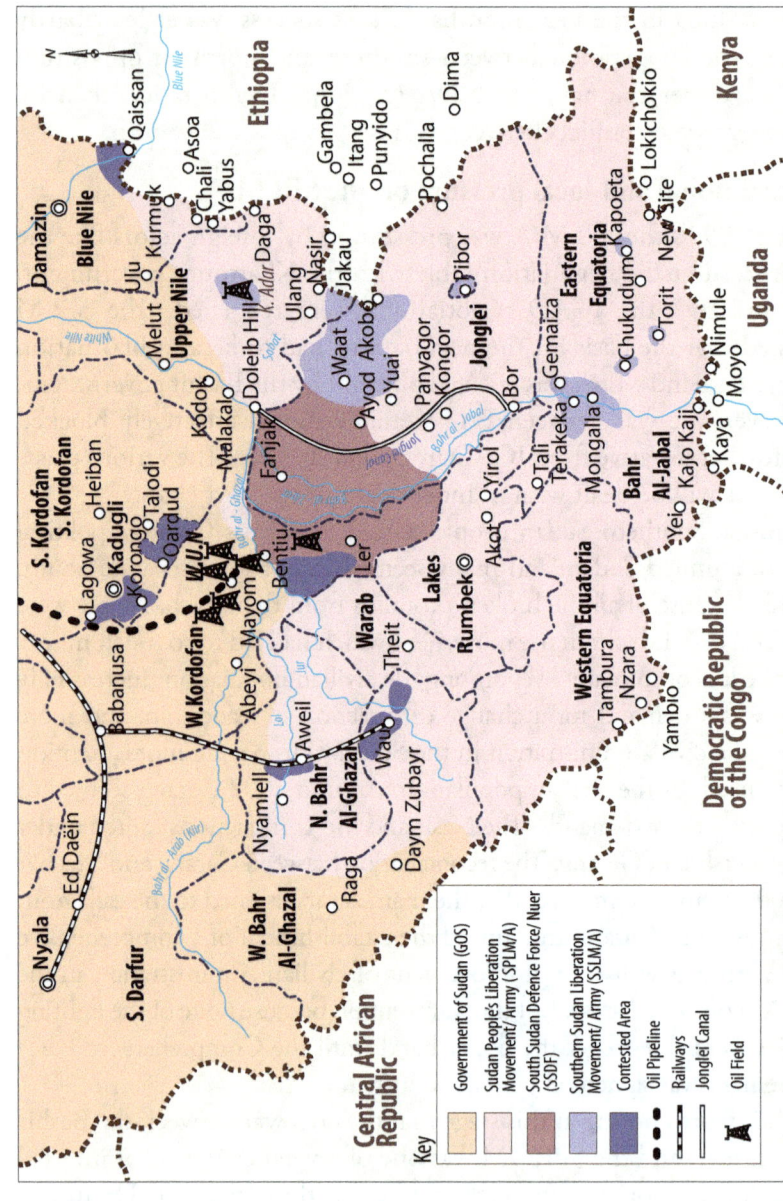

Fig. (7) Positions of the warring parties in 2002. (*Cambridge University Press*)

Summary: In 1991 the SPLM/A split into the Torit and the Nasir faction. Several other splits followed, and weakened for some time the South's resistance to the Northern regime. In 2002 the Nasir and Torit factions united under the leadership of John Garang.

Work in pairs
1. Try to explain what militias are. Name some of the militias which have been active in the South.
2. Why did the Sudan government use militias to fight the SPLA?
3. Discuss the internal problems that the SPLM/A faced. Try to explain why there were so many splinter groups in the South. How did these splits affect the fight against the North?

The consequences of war

The lives of the people in the South were more or less completely conditioned by a civil war which, as we have seen, lasted with certain intermissions since 1955. More than two million people died between 1989 to 2005 and the human suffering among those who survived can hardly be fathomed. The war resulted in a vast migration of various ethnic groups both inside the Southern territory and also to the areas around Khartoum and beyond Sudan to neighbouring countries, like Kenya, Uganda and Chad. Thousands more found their ways to the USA, Europe and Australia. Most Southern Sudanese were united in their persuit of total freedom from Northern domination. Even those who sought refuge in Khartoum and other Northen cities/villages were boumd together in their wish to have the Khartoum government defeated and the South freed.

Obviously the glue that bound people together across the ethnic divisions in many of the multi-ethnic communities in the South during the war was resistance against the Arabs.

> **Discuss in pairs:**
> What does a multi-ethnic community mean? What was the glue that bound the various groups in the South together?

A Southern identity

During the intensified migration of the civil war, cross-ethnic relations between groups were reinforced, and a Southern identity was created. It was an unambiguous African identity with strong elements of Christianity and secularism.

During the war the animosity in the South against the Arabs was pervasive and seemed more or less inherited from one generation to the next and cut across ethnic affiliation. The Southern identity was due to oppression over decades (and even centuries) and was firmly confirmed by the Antonovs (bomber planes) and other brutalities of the NCP regime during the civil war.

The war was thus not merely a war of resistance against Islam, but ethnic resistance against the dominance of the Northerner and their frequent claim of racial and cultural superiority to the Black Africans.

> **Discuss in class**
> 1. Why do you think the war was fought? Do you think the reasons above were the only reasons why the war was fought?
> 2. What is meant by a Southern identity? In what way do you think a Southern identity was strengthended during the war?

Interviews with Southerners during the war (Breidlid, 2006 and 2010) underlined the Southern identity: "Many of us learned good things from other ethnic groups. We are more a nation than before." Another informant added: "Another prominent factor that minimizes traditional education to its death are multi-culturalism or mixed ethnicity." One informant stated that cultures that disunite people should be discarded "because they promote ethnic segregation." The positive impact of more ethnic integration was underlined by another informant: "The war has already created a unity of the oppressed people of the Sudan."

The war created, unfortunately enough, a spirit of defiance against the Arabs which was wideseprad across age groups in the South young or old, women and men, educated and non-educated. Even among the pupils who had lost their parents and other relatives in the war defiance was undisputed. As one pupil stated:

> I lost my father and many relatives. I lost also my sisters and brothers, all killed by the war.
>
> The Jalabas (Arabs) brought the war to us. They want to oppress us so that we remain their slaves.

And another:

> Despite all the difficulties, the war should only stop when the Jalabas withdraw and leave us alone in our country. Let the sufferings end with us so that the future generations live in peace.

The anti-Arab sentiment was all-pervasive. One informant's response was typical:

> The Arabs despise African culture and see the Africans as inferior to them. Most of our people see the Arabs of the Sudan as killers, slave traders and greedy people.

Another informant confirmed a fairly stereotypical view of the Arabs:

> Arabs want to take over our land for themselves and want to take all the resources for themselves. The Arabs kill our people. Traders of the Arabs take our materials cheaply and insult us by calling and treating us as slaves.

The devastating consequences of the war for the population in the liberated areas voiced by one informant came across as quite typical:

> The war has ruined my life in all aspects and not only my education. It cut me off from the outside world for over 12 years staying in the bush and made me not progress with my education after secondary school.

Another informant stated:

> The war separated me from my husband since 1991 who up to now is in Khartoum. I lost a lot of or all of my personal things including my educational documents and certificates. My books were all destroyed.

My brother was killed at the battlefront during the war. Many of my other relatives were also killed.

Fig. (8)   Displaced people (*Routledge*)

A school boy told his story:

> We are very poor. We are hungry at school every day. Many of us have lost our mothers. It is because of the war. It is because of the Arabs.

In a country where war had been the life-long companion of everybody under 50 (with certain intermissions) the singling out of war as the overarching reason for their despondency was not unexpected and certainly was influenced by the SPLA radio.

Most people supported the war against the North. There were, however, different opinions about the activities of the resistance movement, the SPLA, often linked to ethnic affiliation. The divergent opinions on SPLA did not relate to the liberation army's ultimate goal of freeing the South from the Arabs, but were related to the overall public objectives by Dr. John Garang (leader of the SPLA) of a united, secular Sudan. Many informants wanted an independent Southern Sudan, and many voiced their scepticism to what many perceived as domination of a certain ethnic group, and the tactics and behaviour of the SPLA on Southern territory.

The various ethnic groups which had migrated to Yei during the war exposed a common attitude towards the enemy. At the same time there was competition and conflict between various ethnic groups. In Yei the conflict between half-nomadic cattle people (the Dinka) and the resident farmers (the Luo speaking population) was based on a conflict of territory: the Luo speakers needed territory for agricultural production whereas the Dinka needed land for grazing purposes. There was also ethnic conflict in other areas due to migration e.g. between the Didinga and the Dinka.

Summary: The resistance and compact front against the Arabs were thus both solid and volatile at the same time. It is too early to say if ethnic conflict will be the end product of the war, or if the pressure of war and the common enemy made a Southern identity a more permanent category that will survive the tensions of ethnic conflict.

Discuss in class
1. Even though the front against the Arabs in the South was enormous people had different opinions about the SPLM/A. Try to explain what the different opinions about the SPLM/A were all about?
2. What kind of problems did the massive migration during the war cause?

Displaced persons in and around Khartoum during the war

The numbers of displaced persons who actually lived in and around Khartoum during the war were uncertain, but figures ranging from 1.5 to 1.8 million indicate the vastness of the problem. In any case, the total number of displaced persons in Sudan represented 25 per cent of the world's internally displaced persons, putting the Sudan "at the top of the list of countries" containing a displaced population. While the early migrants to the capital fled the drought in Western

Sudan in the mid-1980s, the Southerners who fled the terrors of war arrived at the beginning of the 1990s, reaching a peak around 1994-95.

While some of the migrant merchants and civil servants were not subject to impoverishment, the majority of those displaced from the South living in and around Khartoum were forced to live there due to the war and were to a large extent terribly marginalised and impoverished.

As a result of the very profound cultural and religious rift between the South and the North, the migrants from the South were not welcomed by the Islamic authorities as they poured into Khartoum. They were accused in Arabic-language newspaper of bringing disease, alcohol and prostitution to the city. Women who brewed local beer for survival were often flogged and imprisoned. The government considered the Southern refugees as fifth column for the SPLA and discouraged relief work in their camps. Since they had not crossed an international border, they did not have legal right to protection from international agencies.

The situation of the internally displaced persons was very difficult socially and economically, but also religiously and culturally. They felt alienated, and this alienation took many shapes, from the government's deliberate eradication of their housing areas (many areas were simply bulldozed down) to more sophisticated structural and cultural impositions.

While the migrants in Khartoum were Sudanese citizens and in principle held the same rights and duties as the native population in the capital (the Constitution states that "Everyone born of a Sudanese mother or father has the inalienable right to Sudanese nationality, its duties and obligations" (Article 22)), the reality was quite different. The Southern, Christian migrants were in many ways looked upon and treated as immigrants whose rights depended on the somewhat unpredictable support of the Islamic government.

> **Discuss in pairs**
> 1. How were the migrants received on their arrival to Khartoum?
> 2. What does fifth column means?

The construction of a Southern identity in and around the capital

The brief narrative below gives a glimpse into one of the displaced camps. The camp for internally displaced persons (IDPs) has here been given another name to avoid problems:

- The history of Windhoek IDP camp dates back to the late eighties when southerners, after fleeing from the disasters of the renewed war in the South, arrived empty-handed in Khartoum. Windhoek is located on a sandy plain on the outskirts of Khartoum. It took us around 40 minutes to reach there in a minibus provided by the NGO that helped us. We travelled the last stretch on sandy desert ground and "jumped" across a railway line because there was no proper road.

- The huge camp with many roads, walled compounds, small shops, clinics, schools and churches gives in many ways the image of a traditional Southern village. But here, the round tukuls with coned grass or with thatched roofs are replaced by rectangular houses constructed by the dwellers themselves. Walls and roofs are built in local material – sun dried bricks – and smeared with mud. After heavy raining, the walls and roof often collapse with fatal results. Within the village, donkeys are used for transport and for water supply. There are no water pumps in the camp and when it is raining heavily the area is flooded due to the hard, sandy surface. A teacher told us that house building is very expensive. It is a big problem that the land or plot is not measured and registered to the owner of the house. Sometimes, the government decides to bring bulldozers and tear everything down. This happened in a different camp during Christmas. People here from various parts of the South fear that the same may happen in this camp. There is no registration system in Windhoek. It is as if these people do not exist…

> **Individual work**
>
> Write in your own words how a displaced camp is described (see above).

In the displaced camps there were ethnic groups from various parts of the South. It can be contended that the various ethnic groups groups in and around Khartoum shaped another, Southern identity for political and pragmatic reasons which was due to the fact that they lived in the same locations in and around Khartoum.

The common Southern identity in the North was primarily linked to religion (various branches of Christianity) and cultural identity. This identity was also based on symbolic solidarity and was provided by a mythology of the past characterised by a common experience of oppression, slavery and the longest lasting civil war in Africa.

> **Discuss in class**
>
> How is a Southern identity in the Khartoum characterized? Is this identity similar to the identity created in the South during the civil war?

The following is based on research conducted by Breidlid (2006) during the war.

The existence of a common Southern identity was confirmed by our informants: "I look at myself as an Acholi, Christian and Southern Sudanese."

Another informant confirmed this impression:

The war has disrupted everything. Certain things – economic power – have been disrupted. Here, there are different people from different backgrounds. No more cattle, no more agriculture. Before, if you crossed to a different area, you would be killed (he talked about previous hostilities between groups and villages in the South). Now, here, they have to live together...

Even marriage practices are changing: "...it was not easy for people from different tribes to get married before. A Dinka had to marry a Dinka. But now the situation is changing."

While internal ethnic conflicts within the various Southern groups existed, the statements above seem to be representative of a fairly comprehensive process among the Southern ethnic groups which may be called a common Southern identity. The civil war thus had a major impact on inter-ethnic relations which possibly would not have taken place in a peaceful South. While it is true that such cultural hybridzation was resisted among certain pockets of these groups, the younger generation especially with little experience from the South had fewer qualms about this trend. Moreover, a Southern identity that cut across ethnical interests was seen by most Southern political leaders as instrumental and strategically necessary in the interactions with the Islamic regime.

In short, the common Southern identity overrode Dinka or Lotuka, Ma'di and Acholi particularities and was directed against its counterpart, i.e. Islamism. This Southern identity was, however, contextually and politically determined and quite fragile, not the least in the South due to strife over hegemony and power.

The relationship between the Southerners (with their Southern identity) and the 'native' population in Khartoum was one of strife and conflict, but also one of pragmatic, necessary co-existence. The Southern migrants had physically invaded the city of the native population in Khartoum, whereas the Southerners had experienced a violent intrusion on Southern territory. There was a sense of intrusion on both sides of the ethnic divide.

Discuss in pairs
Do you think it is easier for the younger generation to accept a common Southern identity than the older generation?

Education in the SPLM/A-controlled areas: Reinforcing Southern resistance

Education in the South

After all the years of civil war most infrastructures were demolished and social institutions dismantled in the South. Schools were destroyed, and many qualified teachers were killed or abducted. Some became guerilla fighters or went into exile. The civil war was the main reason why two generations in the South were without schooling. It was in fact the people who lived in the refugee camps outside Southern Sudan, in Kenya and Uganda, who received the best education. But also inside Southern Sudan local community groups and organisations came together to re-open primary schools in their villages and towns. In addition many International Non-Governmental Organizations (INGOs) supported primary schools across Southern Sudan.

In the final stages of the war only 12% of all the pupils in Southern Sudan in grades 1-8 were in the top four grades, and 88% were in grades 1-4. Almost 40% of all pupils were in grade 1. A further 22% were in grade 2. The problem of retention was thus enormous (UNICEF 2002).

The SPLM/A Education Secretariat

Despite the low education figures referred to above the impact of education in the resistance struggle should not be overlooked. In Southern Sudan the implementation of the education programme was left in the hands of the Secretariat of Education of the SPLM. Even though Sudan formally and constitutionally was one country the civil war virtually split the country in two where the SPLA controlled vast areas in the South. In terms of education this split created two separate education systems.. While the Government of Sudan advocated an Islamic educational system, the SPLA/M implemented an educational system which was clearly secular.

The Secretariat of Education functioned as the *de facto* Ministry of Education. It worked hard to improve the education system in the areas under its control. This work included production of various educational documents. These documents included a policy document on education, a strategic educational master plan and a document on learning opportunities, syllabi, textbooks and other support materials, teacher education and training, coordination of NGO's to support schools and other educational activities. The Secretariat followed and adopted the principle Education for All (EFA) .

Undoubtedly SPLM/A education plans for the liberated areas of New Sudan were very ambitious, but faced many problems:

- The curricula used in schools stemmed from Ethiopia, Kenya or Uganda.
- There was no Examination Secretariat/centre in the South and it was better for the learners to do the Ugandan or Kenyan examinations to enable them to continue beyond the education levels being offered in the South..
- While the Education Policy of the Movement states that English is the medium of instruction children in some areas used Arabic and those near Ethiopia used Amharic. In the Nuba Mountains the actual policy was to replace Arabic with English despite the role of Arabic as a *lingua franca* in the region.
- Indigenous languages advocated by the education policy could not be taught systemetically because of lack of books and qualified teachers. Therefore much teaching was not suited to the culture and environment, and experienced teachers among the informants claimed that the standard of education had declined drastically.
- The Secretariat followed the recommendations of EFA and aimed at education for all children by 2015. The intention with the education system in the South was to foster some sort of commonality and identity across the ethnic borders in the South.

> **Question**
> Try to explain why the education situation was better for people living in refugee camps outside the country than for those remaining in Southern Sudan.

Education on the ground

One of the reasons why youths in the South readily took up arms against the government during the civil war was the feeling that they were being denied educational opportunities. Young volunteers joined the SPLM/A because they strongly disliked how the whole school system had been managed from Khartoum. The frustration of Southern Sudanese youngsters who felt that they had been virtually left out of the educational machinery was not difficult to understand given the enormous infra-structural, pedagogical and motivational challenges. This was also confirmed by one informant: "Denial of education is one of the main causes of the war."

Due to the dismal situation in the South it was a miracle that schools functioned at all and that some pupils learned the basic skills which in fact they did. The volatile situation was underlined by one informant:

> The war made our teachers to be volunteers and no salary is paid to them and we all suffer with them. There are hardly any text books and even chalk for the blackboard is hard to find.

As another pupil in the 7th grade in Yei stated:

> I lost my father in the war. And my mother has disappeared. I live with distant relatives who don't treat me well. Every day I walk two hours to school. I am always hungry at school because I only eat at night. To pay for the school fees I dig pit latrines, but the demand is not big.

He continued:

> I want to go secondary school and then become a doctor. I have straight A's in all the subjects (confirmed by the teacher). But the fees are higher in secondary school, and nobody can help me pay.

There was a spirit of defiant resistance among the pupils and some teachers, insisting on education against high odds in order to help their own people: "I want to become a nurse in order to help my own people." And another: "My dream is to become a teacher so that the children will be educated and make a better future in the South." And a teacher:" Life is very difficult. I teach without getting any government remuneration. But I can't stay away from school and let the pupils remain uneducated."

Even though the learning objective in the local schools was essentially very basic: to make children read, write and learn some arithmetic, schooling in Southern Sudan nevertheless was more than a mere instructional institution. Education as a tool in the resistance struggle was mentioned both by reference to past experiences and to the contemporary situation:

> If we are not to be fooled as our leaders with no education were in the past, our people must be educated on the same level as the Arabs.

And another:

> History is important because it makes us understand why we are oppressed

> Education is very important because we want the citizens to know why they are fighting a liberation war.

Discuss in class
1. Which period in history do you think the pupil refers to when he/she states that we are not to be fooled as our leaders with no education were in the past?

Also SPLM/A reiterated the importance of education in the resistance struggle:

> In the movement we regard education as number one among our priorities. It is the backbone of development. Some people think we can liberate this country by only using the gun. We need different ways and strategies to liberate the people of Sudan – education is one of them that can develop the people.

(All quotes from Breidid, 2006.)

During the war education in the liberated areas helped to build the communities under SPLA control, and distanced itself from the education system supported by the Government of Sudan.

The education system in the South was therefore a matter of serious concern to the government in Khartoum because it reinforced the resistance in the South also because major parts of the South were outside the Government of Sudan's sphere of educational influence.

Work in pairs

1. Describe the education situation in the liberated areas during the war. Who was responsible for this system and in what ways was this system different from the education system in the North?
2. What were the major challenges in the education system of the South?

Task for groups of pupils (3/4)

Visit people in your community who either fought in the war or knew close relatives who fought, and ask them why the war was fought. Write down what you found out and present in class.

Time table

1983: The mutiny in Bor
1983: The foundation of the SPLM/A
1985: The overthrow of Nimeiri
1986: The Koka Dam Declaration
1989: The military coup
1991: The SPLA split in Torit and Nasir factions
1991: The Bor massacre
1992: Hemlat Seif al Obuur (the Khartoum offensive)
1995: The Peace Charter between Machar and Khartoum
1996: The SPLA- Torit offensive
2002: Reconciliation between Machar and Garang

9
The Meaning of the CPA

Introduction

As we have seen from the previous chapters, the civil war in Sudan between the North and the South lasted, with certain intermissions (e.g., the cease-fire between 1972 and 1983) from 1955 to 2005. The cease-fire achieved in 1972 came to an end when Sudan President Jaafar al-Nimeiri issued a decree in 1983 to incorporate Shari'a law into the penal code. In this context Army Colonel Dr. John Garang de Mabior from Southern Sudan went underground and established the SPLM/A. After the Northerner Sadiq al-Mahdi won elections with his Umma party in 1986, the new Sudanese government had agreed in principle to cancel Nimeiri's decree and initiated peace negotiations with the SPLA. However, the hopes of a negotiated peace were smashed when the Islamist military regime led by General Omar al-Bashir came to power following a coup in 1989.

The Comprehensive Peace Agreement (CPA) of January 9, 2005, between the National Congress party (NCP) and the SPLM/A defined a 6-year period after which a referendum was to be held in Southern Sudan to determine whether Sudan would remain a single country or be divided into two. In the interim, the two parties were to find solutions to a range of hotly disputed political issues from the distribution of the oil revenues to border demarcations, from the issue of Abyei to the profile of the education systems.

Before the CPA there had been several attempts by various external actors, including neighboring states and international organizations, as well as the parties themselves, to bring the civil war to an end. The signing of the CPA on January 9, 2005 was the end result of a protracted process under sustained pressure from the international community, including the UN Security Council.

Peace negotiations: International attempts to bring peace between the South and the North

Conscious of the human sufferings in Southern Sudan, the international community became alarmed and efforts to bring the conflict and therefore human sufferings to an end were sought. Below some important peace initiatives are mentioned briefly.

The Carter Foundation (1989)

In December 1989 the former US President Jimmy Carter sponsored peace talks between the NCP Regime and the SPLM/A in Nairobi. The SPLM/A asked for the adoption of the Koka Dam Declaration as the basis of these talks. The Bashir Government rejected the request, and accused Jimmy Carter of being biased for having suggested a three months' cease fire with the suspension of the Shari'a Laws.

The Herman Cohen Blue Print For Peace (1990)

In 1990 the US State Department asked the Assistant Secretary of State for African Affairs, Herman Cohen, to propose plans in an attempt to end the Sudan conflict. Besides proposing a ceasefire Cohen's proposal included the establishment of demilitarized zones (Southern Kordofan and Southern Blue Nile) and an international peace keeping force in Juba. Moreover an interim government should be installed in Juba and a constitutional conference should be convened to discuss a lasting solution to the conflict.

The US Government also proposed to the Khartoum Government the following steps for finding a lasting peace:
1. The Sudan government should evacuate all its forces from Southern Sudan
2. A constitutional conference should be held
3. General free and fair elections should be conducted in order to restore democracy

The NCP regime, however, rejected the American proposals outright, and the start of the Gulf war and the 1992 Presidential elections in the USA diverted attention away from the Herman Cohen proposal.

The Abuja peace talks (1992-1993)

The US entry into the peace initiative in Sudan worried President Bashir as he saw the US involvement as a threat to his regime. To find a way out, at the Organization of African Unity (OAU) heads of state meeting in 1991 in Windhoek, Namibia, President Bashir asked the President of Nigeria, Ibrahim Babangida, the then chairman of the OAU, to mediate in the Sudan conflict using the rhetoric that "Africans are capable of resolving their problem".

President Babangida arranged peace talks both in 1992 and 1993, but both failed.

During the talks the SPLM was weakened due to the split between the Torit and Nasir factions, and the Bashir government tried to set the agenda. Any solution to the conflict had to accept, according to Bashir, Shari'a law as the basis for the legal system, Islam as the state religion and Arabic as the official language. These demands were unacceptable to the Southerners. The question of self-determination was also a contested issue that could not be resolved by the two parties in the conflict.

Work in pairs:
1. What could be the reason(s) why President Bashir and his NCP regime wanted to find another peace forum after the American intervention?
2. Why did NCP regime and Omar al Bashir select Nigeria in particular to take over the mediation?
3. What is your opinion of the slogan "Africans are capable of solving their problem"?

The Comprehensive Peace Agreement (CPA)

The Comprehensive Peace Agreement came as a result of involvement of regional and international bodies like the Inter Governmental Authority on Development (IGAD), formerly the Inter Governmental Authority on Drought and Desertification (IGADD). The member states of IGAD managed to bring the two parties to the negotiation table which ended in the peace agreement in 2005. It was in 1993 that the then IGADD established a Standing Committee on Peace to assist negotiations and end Sudan's civil war. This was the beginning of a long process that led to the signing of the CPA in 2005. Other key players to negotiating the CPA included the governments of Norway, Japan, Denmark, Italy, Holland and United States of America. These countries had supported the peace progress through diplomatic mechanisms, funding and also by exerting pressure on the two factions to end the bloody and unending war.

Fig. (1) IGAD (The Intergovernmental Authority on Development) in Eastern Africa was founded in 1996. Its precursor IGADD had been founded in 1986 in response to the draught disasters between 1974 and 1984. The mission of IGAD, however, is besides securing food and protecting the environment economic cooperation and promotion and maintenance of peace. Members of IGAD: Sudan, Somalia, Ethiopia, Eritrea, Djibouti, Kenya, Eritrea and Uganda.

The Secretariat for the IGAD Peace Process was 'to carry out continuous and sustained mediation efforts with a view to arriving at a peaceful resolution of the conflict'. On 20 July 2002 the Government of Sudan

(GoS) and Sudan People's Liberation Movement/Army (SPLM/A) signed the Machakos Protocol as a framework for the conduct of the negotiations. After two and a half years of negotiations the CPA was signed by both parties in the town of Naivasha.

Fig. (2)   Salva Kiir Mayardit (1951-)

Kiir is a Dinka from Bahr el Ghazal. He became the leader of SPLM/A in 2005 after the death of Dr. John Garang. Salva Kiir was the second Southern Sudanese to hold the position of 1st Vice President of the Republic of Sudan since independence – and he was the President of Southern Sudan and the leader of the SPLM/A after Dr. John Garang's death.

Salva Kiir started to fight for Southern Sudan in the 1960´s in the Anya Nya Movement and in 1972 he was incorporated into Sudanese Army. He is one of the founders of SPLM/A. Salva Kiir disagreed with John Garang about the handling of the issues of Nuba Mountains and Abyei and the two had serious conflicts in 2003-2004. He became the deputy leader of SPLM in 1992 and signed the Machacos protocol in 2002. Kiir is the first president of the newest nation in Africa, South Sudan. President Kiir was involved in a violent conflict in December 2013 and the beginning of 2014 with the former Vice President Riek Machar. The conflict was threatening the stability of the new country.

The official signing of the Comprehensive Peace Agreement (CPA) on 9th January, 2005 between the Government of the Republic of Sudan (GOS) and the SPLM/A marked a historical end of the armed conflict in Sudan. It brought to an end the 22 years of war which began on May 16 1983.

Dr John Garang, the leader of SPLM/A said on the occasion of signing the peace agreement: "With this peace agreement we have ended the longest war in Africa, with this peace agreement, the Sudan Peoples' Liberation Movement and the National Congress Party government have brought half a century of war to a dignified end, with this peace agreement, there will be no more bombs falling from the sky on innocent children and women."

Armed confrontation between the NCP and the SPLA stopped, and the ground was cleared for serious reconstruction efforts. Still the suspicions between the the North and the South continued after the signing of the CPA.

Summary: After several years of peace negotiations, the Comprehensive Peace Agreement (CPA) was signed in 2005, under the mediation of IGAD.

Pair work
1. Why do you think IGAD was successful in bringing together the two parties and make a peace agreement?

The signing of the Comprehensive Peace Agreement(CPA)

The Comprehensive Peace Agreement (CPA) was signed, in a formal ceremony, on January 9, 2005 after almost three years of negotiations. Key to the implementation of the CPA as outlined in the protocols below were issues such as the formation of the Government of National Unity (GoNU) and a Government of Southern Sudan (GoSS), the setting up of an integrated army, equitable sharing of oil revenues, and a referendum in six years to determine the issue of secession of the

South. The 'marginal' areas of Abyei, Nuba Mountains and Blue Nile were covered in a separate protocol (see 6 below).

A series of six protocols were signed between 2002 and 2004 under the mediation of IGAD, which described what had to be done.

The six protocols were

1. The Machacos Protocol signed in Machakos, Kenya, on 20 July 2002 where the main principles of governance, the transitional process and the structures of government as well as on the right to self-determination for the people of Southern Sudan, and on state and religion were outlined (see appendix 2)
2. The Protocol on security arrangements: Signed in Naivasha, Kenya, on 25 September 2003.

    The security arrangement included the end of hostilities between Sudan Armed Forces (SAF) and Sudan Peoples' Liberation Army (SPLA), and described the structure and functions of the armed forces during the pre-interim and interim periods. Three legally accepted armed forces were to be deployed in Sudan: Sudan Armed Forces (SAF) north of the January 1 1956 border line, Sudan Peoples' Liberation Army (SPLA) south of the January 1 1956 border line and the Joint Integrated Units (JIU) comprising both the SPLA and SAF. The parties (SPLM and GoS) agreed to establish the JIU with equal numbers from the SPLA and Sudan Armed Forces. It was stipulated that the joint integrated units should be deployed in major towns to keep the peace.

    The SPLA and the Sudan Armed Forces were to retain their troops in the South and North, respectively.

Fig. (3) Sudan before the Comprehensive Peace Agreement (*Cambridge University Press*)

3. The Protocol on wealth-sharing: Signed in Naivasha, Kenya, on January 7 2004.

   The protocol outlined in detail how both oil and non oil revenues in Sudan were to be equitably shared between the North and the

South, as well as the disputed areas of Southern Kordofan state, Blue Nile state, and Abyei. The Government of Southern Sudan (GoSS) and the central government were to split all oil and other revenues derived from the South evenly while states that produce oil also receive 2%. The issue of oil revenue was much more emphasised in the agreement than other sources of income.

The detailed wealth sharing agreement also provided for a new national currency and the creation of parallel central banks in the North and the South.

4. The Protocol on power-sharing: Signed in Naivasha, Kenya, on 26 May 2004.

    The parties agreed to run a decentralised system of governance with significant devolution of powers. The Government of National Unity (GoNU) were to be responsible for protecting and promoting the sovereignty of Sudan while the Government of Southern Sudan (GoSS) were to exercise governmental powers in the Southern region on a semi-autonomous basis. Moreover the various states were to run their own government affairs through local government provisions in consultation with the central government.

    States like Abyei and Nuba Mountains were to have their independent administrators and governors after the referendum.

5. The Protocol on the resolution of conflict in southern Kordofan/ Nuba Mountains and the Blue Nile States: Signed in Naivasha, Kenya, on 26 May 2004. This protocol stated that the three states were given the right to vote for either being united with the South or with the North.

6. The Protocol on the resolution of the conflict in Abyei: Signed in Naivasha, Kenya, on 26 May 2004. Abyei was one of the hotly contested areas during the negotiations because of her oil fields. The future of the Abyei (to belong to the South or the North) was to be decided through a referendum and voting was to run concurrently with the referendum in the South.

> **Questions**
> 1. What do you think was the most difficult protocol to agree upon?
> 2. Please give a short summary of the agreement.

The Implementation of the Protocols

The implementation modalities described in detail the implementation of the various protocols.

The implementation was to take place in two stages: 1) a 6 month pre-interim period, where the CPA was incorporated in the transitional constitution, and a six year interim period ending in a referendum to decide if the South will become independent and whether Abyei was to be incorporated into the South. The referenda were to take place on January 9, 2011.

The Implementation Challenges

After the signing of the CPA numerous challenges emerged. The untimely death of Dr John Garang on July 30, 2005 in a helicopter crash was a major setback since Dr. Garang had been the leader of SPLM/A since 1983 and the driving force behind the peace negotiations. The relationship between the NCP and the SPLM/A had always been tenuous, but became even more precarious when the NCP suspected that the new leader of SPLM/A, Salva Kiir, would be more committed to the New Sudan, a separate Southern Sudan, than his predecessor, Dr. John Garang. Other challenges:

- The NCP rejected the findings of a commission set up to determine the border of Abyei. The Abyei protocol has thus not yet been implemented since the border demarcation has not been finalized (October 2012). Sudan's Chief of Security, Mr. Salah Gosh made it clear on July 30 2010 that his government would not accept the ruling of the International Court of Justice on Abyei.

- The NCP rejected the demarcation of the north-south border, impacting on oil revenue sharing, national elections, and the referendum.
- The NCP delayed considerably to fund the national census which was central to the national elections during the interim period.
- The central government was not transparent about the oil revenue sharing.
- Both the Sudan People's Liberation Army and the Sudanese Armed Forces were slow to redeploy their forces, meaning that a big number of troops were located close to each other near the contested border areas.
- There were democratic deficiencies both in the North and the South regarding the transparency of the elections in April 2010.
- There was generally a lack of commitment to quickly and sensibly implement the CPA by the central government.. It was on this basis that SPLM withdrew her representatives in the national parliament in 2008. The SPLM accused the Northern government of not being serious in the implementation and using its majority composition in the parliament to pass bills that were not in the interest of Southern Sudanese. Two remarks by prominent NCP politicians in 2010 did not bode well for the referendum: On July 31 2010, the Minister of Finance, Mr. Awad Abu Jaaz said "We will never accept the secession of the South" whereas VP Taha reiterated his position on August 2, 2010 saying that if South is allowed to separate it would continue to split even more and more into minor tribal entities.
- There was inadequate institutional capacity for the GoSS officials to effectively run the government. This affected greatly service delivery for the citizens of Sudan.

- There was rampant and widespread corruption in the Government of Southern Sudan leaving many citizens doubting if this could be a viable and sustainable government
- There were frequent ethnic and tribal conflicts in the South which posed a great challenge to the implementation of the CPA. Some of these conflicts were fuelled by the Khartoum government to destabilize the Government of Southern Sudan.
- Favouritism and tribalism in the employment market left many competent young people across Southern Sudan without a job. It was considered an acceptable practice for a ministry to have three quarters of its employees recruited along tribal lines.
- There were no competent legal courts at different levels of government in the South, and this made it difficult to implement the Comprehensive Peace Agreement.

Fig. (4) Ali Utman Muhammed Taha (1940-) has been a member of Islamic Charter since secondary school, when he attended Khartoum al-Gadeema together with al-Bashir. He graduated from Law school at University of Khartoum and set up a private Law practice before he became a member of Sudan's parliament in the 1980's. He has been a Judge.

Taha was the opposition leader in the democratic period from 1986 to 1989 and probably planned the coup of 1989. He was Foreign Minister between 1995 and1998 and First Vice President between 1998 and 2005. He became the ideologist in the NCP regime when Turabi was excluded. Taha signed the CPA agreement with John Garang. He was also responsible for the Darfur policy 2003 -2004.

Question
1. In your opinion, what were the greatest challenges related to the implementation of the CPA?

Achievements of the Comprehensive Peace Agreement

- Despite the challenges referred to above the Comprehensive Peace Agreement since January 9 2005 had numerous achievements. The formation of the Government of Southern Sudan running its autonomous activities with its interim constitution, legislative assembly and executive functions.

- Security and peace returned to most parts of southern Sudan, though some groups of militias still caused problems and the activities of the Lord Resistance Army (LRA) continued in some parts of Equatoria.

- The introduction of the New Sudanese pound managed by both the Central Bank of Sudan and the Bank of Southern Sudan, including the establishment of other financial and commercial banks like Sudan Microfinance Institution (SUMI), Nile Commercial Bank, Buffalo Bank and Kenya Commercial Bank.

- All children of Southern Sudan were by 2010 supposed to have access to either formal or informal education, with a new Southern Sudan curriculum. Still education suffered from untrained teachers, poor or non-existing school buildings, overcrowded classes and lack of school materials.

- There were basic health care facilities to prevent common diseases in the South, although unevenly spread and too scarce in rural areas.
- Freedom of movement, press and association were practiced throughout the states of Southern Sudan even though some censorship incidents occurred.
- The return of refugees from neighbouring countries and IDPs.
- For the first time after the 22 years' civil war the GoSS managed to pay salaries to both army and civil servants, although the latter on an irregular basis, especially after the cessation in oil production in 2012.
- GoSS was getting some share from the wealth sharing based on the oil revenue income. According to the London based Global Witness figures put out by Khartoum government were lower than those put out by the main Chinese operator of Sudan's oil fields, China National Petroleum Corporation. Even though the Global Witness report was contested, the lack of trust resulted in the cessation of oil production due to serious disagreements between Sudan and the new nation South Sudan in 2012.
- Economic recovery and progress was taking place, but primarily in the urban areas.

Summary: The CPA is a series of six protocols which treat the right to self-determination, security, wealth-sharing, power-sharing, conflict in southern Kordofan, Nuba Mountains, Blue Nile States and Abyei. Despite several difficulties, much has been achieved since 2005.

Discuss in pairs
1. What do you think were the greatest achievements of the CPA?

The CPA was not comprehensive

While the CPA was termed comprehensive it was not comprehensive in the sense that it did not address the problems in Darfur or Eastern Sudan. Moreover, the opposition parties in the North (like the Umma Party) were not part of the peace process. Neither were the Southern opposition parties. The SPLM failed to approach its opponents in the South for a combined strategy and policy. This was exploited by Khartoum who used militias to violate the agreement.

Challenges in relation to the CPA included violations by the Sudan Armed Forces (SAF), the lack of agreement over Abyei (no protocol signed), key ministries in the Government of National Unity (GoNU) were filled by NCP people, weak Southern ministers in the GoNU, unequal wealth sharing, the sponsoring of militias by the NCP, and the fact that the CPA observers were not mandated to enforce the implementation of the CPA.

There was no doubt that international involvement helped to achieve the CPA. However, the focus on the North-South conflict diverted attention away from the other conflicts and civil wars in the country, especially during the first years. The arrest warrant which the International Criminal Court (ICC) issued for al-Bashir on 4 March 2009, seemed, however, to shift the focus to the Darfur conflict.

Within the GoNU, which was composed of representatives both from the NCP and the SPLM, the basic conflict lines were maintained. One politician from the South working in the North summed up the view held by Southern informants in and around Khartoum: "Even though there is a Unity government, we from the South have very little say in the government's decisions, especially when religious principles are invoked" (Breidlid, 2010).

It was a bad omen when the SPLM pulled out temporarily from the National Unity government in 2007, because they perceived that major parts of the CPA were not being implemented. Moreover, the fighting in Malakal in Southern Sudan in February 2009, between Sudan People's Liberation Army (SPLA) and the Gabriel Tang-led militia, which was supported by NCP, exposed the fragility of the CPA.

The stalemate in late 2007, the Malakal fightings in 2009, and the dispute over oil revenues signaled a process of "back to normality." Political and military incidents confirmed the fragility of the situation and clearly exposed the suspicions and anxieties held by both parties in the conflict. Agreement over the distribution of oil revenues in October 2012, one year after independence, seemed to ease the tension between Sudan and South Sudan somewhat, but difficult challenges such as border issues and Abyiei remained unresolved. There was a sense of cultural and religious superiority among the Northerners that deadlocked their perceptions of the conflict. Conversely, in the South and in the IDP camps in and around Khartoum, the conflict was understood as something inevitable, given the attitudes of the NCP and the Arabs in general.

> **Discuss in class**
> 1. Describe some of the problems after the signing of the Peace Agreement in 2005.

Preparation for the referendum 2011

According to the Machakos protocol the referendum that took place in 2011 gave equal weight to the options "unity" and "secession." According to official SPLM/SPLA policy unity based on secular principles had earlier been the preferred option. However, there was little doubt that the grassroots in the South were sceptical to a continued unity with the North, based on the war and previous arrangements. Some sceptics characterised the last years of the interim period as "antagonistic co-operation." Secessionists made a strong case against the union based on previous experiences and argued for an independent Southern Sudan.

People in the South were anxious that the referendum would not be conducted freely and fairly. If the referendum process had been interfered with or had been postponed the likelihood for a new civil war or a Unilateral Declaration of Independence (UDI) was imminent.

While unity did not appear to be a very attractive option among Southerners, secession ambitions were not without its challenges.

One was the weak governmental structure in Southern Sudan with a lack of human capacity and competence, rampant corruption, deficient service delivery and decentralization challenges. Moreover, according to one study "tribal conflict", increasing cases of cattle-raiding and the role of marginalized youth were some of the challenges.

A study found that increasing intra-South violence killed more than 2,500 people and displaced 350,000 in 2009. The unclear role of chiefs and traditional leaders had also increased governance problems. The challenge was to avoid the establishment of ethnic chiefdoms, where ethnicity was a means to access leading positions and resources.

According to another study the clearest indication of the escalating tensions in the post-election period was three separate uprisings in Jonglei and Unity States by dissident former members of Sudan Peoples' Liberation Movement/Army (SPLA) and the SPLM. The first weeks after the conclusion of the electoral process in April 2010 were full of tensions in Southern Sudan, with some serious incidents in different areas of the region. A former independent candidate to Jonglei state governorship (and former SPLA deputy chief of general staff), General George Athor Deng, left Bor with his troops and clashed with SPLA soldiers in what at the beginning was described as a mutiny. Another alleged rebellion among SPLA forces was registered in northern Bahr al-Ghazal. The two events might be connected. Even if they were not, they proved tensions inside Southern Sudan were deep and widespread and might become a threat as dangerous as North-South disagreements. Similar fears were raised by *Human Rights Watch* in a report documenting rights violations during the April elections in 2010. The report stated that there was growing instability in the states of Central Equatoria, Jonglei, Unity, and Western Bahr el Ghazal, which was worrying in the context of the referendum on self-determination.

Summary: The referendum would determine the future of Southern Sudan. Essentially, the referendum would help to confirm the unity of Sudan by voting to adopt the system of government established under the CPA, or to vote for separation. To Sudan, the referendum was important in many ways: it would give the people of Southern Sudan a free choice to decide their own political status and how they would be governed without external compulsion. The referendum would provide the most practical means and democratic opportunity for the people of Sudan to resolve many outstanding issues pertaining to governance, wealth sharing, boundaries, and popular consultation over the people of Nuba Mountains and the Blue Nile states.

Pair discussion
1. What were the major challenges in the South after 2005?
2. What were the arguments for unity and what were the arguments against?
3. What do you think is needed in order to maintain sustainable peace in Southern Sudan?

Group task
a) Groups of three: Visit your community and ask a prominent person in the community about the CPA (chief, priest, headmaster or other persons). Write down the answers and present in class.
b) Collect newspaper articles about CPA and it's implementation. Write a summary of different points of view concerning the challenges of implementation.
c) Make interviews with three adults in your community about the referendum, and why they voted for or against unity. Write down the arguments. In class you may have a class discussion, where one group supports the arguments for unity and another supports the arguments against unity.

Time table

1989: Peace talks sponsored by Carter
1990: The Herman Cohen Blueprint for Peace
1992-1993: The Abuja peace talks
1994: The IGAD peace mediation
2002: The signing of the Machacos protocol
2004: The signing of the six protocols
2005: The signing of the CPA
2007: The SPLM pulled out temporarily from the GoNU
2009: Fighting in Malakal

10

The Referendum, Independence and its Aftermath

The referendum in January 2011 in Southern Sudan

As a consequence of the Comprehensive Peace Agreement (CPA) a referendum was held in Southern Sudan from 9 to 15 January 2011. The voters from Southern Sudan were to decide whether Southern Sudan should remain part of Sudan or become independent. Also Southern Sudanese living in the North and in the diaspora voted.

While the politicians in Southern Sudan headed by Salva Kiir openly favoured secession and independence for Southern Sudan, they also insisted that it was important that the transition was peaceful, whatever the outcome.

Sudan's President Bashir said that Southern Sudan had the right to decide their own future since unity "could not be forced by force." That the voting in the referendum turned out to be very peaceful was credited to the North and Southern Sudanese leadership.

The results of the referendum were published on 7 February 2011. The people of Southern Sudan voted overwhelmingly for secession and independence. The official figures are shown below.

Referendum results		
Yes or no	Votes	Percentage
✓ Yes	3,792,518	98.83%
✗ No	44,888	1.17%
Valid votes	3,837,406	99.62%
Invalid or blank votes	14,588	0.38%
Total votes	**3,851,994**	**100.00%**

Fig. (1)

A similar referendum was to be held in Abyei on the issue of whether Abyei should belong to Southern Sudan or Northern Sudan, but it was postponed due to disagreements over borders and residency rights. Still the issue of Abyei has not been resolved. At the time this book went to press, the government in Khartoum had consistently prevented this referendum from taking place, forcing the Republic of South Sudan to refer the issue to the UN Security Council.

The independence of South Sudan

South Sudan became independent on July 9 2011. The 56th nation in Africa was called the Republic of South Sudan even though other possible names like the Nile Republic and Kush were proposed. Interestingly Sudan became the first state to recognise South Sudan.

The Independence Day was celebrated all over South Sudan.

In an article in the South Sudanese newspaper *Citizen* it was stated:

> South Sudan's freedom at last was welcome by tears of joy, pomp, wide cheer and honor that engulfed Juba and other States' capitals as the South attains its independence. After decades of vicious oppression, marginalization, loss of innocent lives and massive displacement. This important July 9th 2011, tens of thousands gathered in Juba to celebrate the birth of the world's newest nation, South Sudan. Citizens along with a number of foreign dignitaries watched as the flag of the world's 193rd country was raised in its new capital. South Sudan seceded from Sudan after decades of civil war that cost millions of lives.

At the Indpendence Day ceremony in Juba, a statue was raised of Dr John Garang- the longtime leader of the Sudan People's Liberation Movement- and South Sudan President Salva Kiir Mayardit stood side by side with Omar al-Bashir, his counterpart in the north and a longtime opponent of Southern independence... The magnitude that turned up to celebrate the Independence Day was amazing and surprising... I am hoping that the leadership of our new nation will focus on strengthening the capacity of local communities and structures including the promotion of food production in rural areas, education for all, health, peace and security, rural and urban development, equality and fair distribution of services and resources to the people of South Sudan. Long Live South Sudan- Freedom- Peace- Prosperity. Guest writer Gatwech Peter Kulang, *Citizen*, July 13 2011.

Fig. (2) A man waives the South Sudanese flag on Independence Day, July 9 2011, in Juba.

The Referendum, Independence and its Aftermath 343

Fig. (3) A woman celebrates independence in Juba on July 9 2011

Fig. (4) Sudanese take part in the celebrations in Juba on July 9 2011

Challenges after independence

Conflicts with Sudan

Despite South Sudan's independence major issues with Sudan remained unresolved. Among the issues with Sudan was the dispute over the borders and citizenship in the region of Abyei.

Another conflict that was unresolved at independence was the issue over the distribution of oil revenues. The disagreement resulted in the shutdown of South Sudan's oil production in January 2012, and in April 2012 the issue of oil also sparked a very dangerous military conflict when South Sudan invaded and captured Heglig, a disputed town which produces more than half of Sudan's oil.

In August 2012, however, South Sudan and Sudan reached an agreement in Addis Ababa over the distribution of the oil revenues, and the export of oil from South Sudan through Sudan. South Sudan stated that it will pay a very high price of $9.48 per barrel to use one of Sudan's pipelines.

Other issues being negotiated in Addis Ababa were the demarcation of the long, joint border and the issue of Abyei, but these were not resolved during the talks between Sudan's president Omar al-Bashir and President Salva Kiir of South Sudan in late September 2012. Still the issues were not resolved by the beginning of 2014.

Domestic challenges

Inside South Sudan there were major challenges for the new government. One important challenge was the work to establish a democratic government where people on the grassroots were to take part in the decision making process of the new nation.

Since the majority of the country's top leadership were members of the SPLM these SPLM leaders had difficulties shedding their military mentality and accepting participation in decision making from the citizens. Even though South Sudan has in principle established a decentralized government the reality on the ground was a very centralized leadership style in decision making.

The cessation in the oil production due to the conflict with Sudan caused major economic problems for South Sudan as the government was not able to pay salaries to the civil servants. Moreover the food prices in the markets rose to unprecedented heights causing big economic problems for the citizens of the country. According to some commentators, however, the lack of oil revenue might also have been a blessing in disguise in two important ways.

One, since corruption had reached unprecedented levels among ministers and government officials in Juba the cessation in oil revenues might curb the possibility of top officials putting large amounts of money from the nation's coffer into their own pockets. As is well known African countries dependent on oil have tremendous problems in administering their oil resources in a way that benefits the common people. Nigeria is a case in point which gets billion of dollars in oil exports, but the majority of the people still live in abject poverty.

Two, the lack of oil revenue might force the government to work more seriously on alternative ways of generating income for the government. It is common knowledge, for example that the potential of agricultural production in South Sudan is grossly under-utilised and underexploited. According to an article in the *East African* newspaper, about "80 per cent of the country's 644, 329 sq. km of land is considered arable and home to permanent rivers... The potential for irrigation is limitless, better than even Kenya and other east African countries. However, for it to succeed, it will need political will and huge investments" (*The East African*, 2011).

Fig. (5)   The first anniversary of South Sudan's independence. Celebrations in Juba.

Corruption in South Sudan

Salva Kiir, the president of South Sudan, has accused current and former senior officials of stealing at least $4bn in state funds.

In a letter to those he suspected of taking the money, he said in 2012: "We fought for freedom, justice and equality. Yet, once we got to power, we forgot what we fought for and began to enrich ourselves at the expense of our people …."

Kiir said the credibility of South Sudan was on the line, but he also promised an amnesty and confidentiality for any of the 75 suspected officials who returned the embezzled funds. To facilitate this, he said the government had set up a special bank account in Kenya where officials could deposit the money they took. There was however no follow-up of the anti-corruption campaign, and it was alleged that the campaign was purely cosmetic since no corrupt politicians were put on trial.

In order to exploit the agricultural potential to serve the interests of the people land distribution and ownership is a central issue. Quite recently, information has emerged that large tracts of fertile land have been acquired by foreign investors through leases with local communities or government institutions. A report released by the Norwegian People's Aid (NPA) (2011) found that during the last four years "foreign interests sought or acquired 2.64 million hectares (26,400 sq. km) in the agriculture, forestry and biofuel sectors alone— an area that is larger than the whole of Rwanda" (*The East African*, 2011).

The heavy foreign investments are, according to the NPA, mostly based on "centralized business models that take advantage of economies of scale to maximize returns to the investor..." (NPA, 2011, p. 4). Moreover, foreign companies can often use the political capital of their domestic allies "to facilitate the land acquisition and may not need to rely as heavily on social capital within the communities. This may avoid some of the *ex ante* costs of negotiations involving affected communities, but it makes for weaker agreements and less sustainable developments in the long term" (NPA, 2011, p. 4). The question is if this land acquisition is another example of the oppression of the elite in the name of national economic development (See also Breidlid, 2013).

In terms of education and health the challenges are enormous. South Sudan has the second lowest primary school enrollment in the world, 46%, and the second lowest secondary school enrollment, 4% (*The East African*, 2011). One problem with primary school enrollment is the low retention rate among girls who often quit school after grade 4 or 5 due to early marriages, pregnancies or too heavy home chores. Moreover, the infant mortality rate was 76 in 2011(children under one year old dying per 1,000 live births).

South Sudan in internal conflict

Given the fact that South Sudan is emerging from decades of conflict both the leaders of the new nation and their people are obviously facing a mammoth task in building the nation. The liberation movement- SPLM- has experienced great internal conflicts in recent years. This is mostly due to the fact that the SPLM represents a diversity of political opinions: there are Marxists, socialists, social liberals and market liberals among the leaders of the movement. During the liberation war there was no time and energy to engage in internal political debates, but as an independent nation there is a need to transform the liberation movement into a democratic political party. It has, however, been very difficult to agree on a coherent political programme due to different ideological opinions among the members of the party. Differences between leaders such as President Salva Kiir and Riek Machar and the now deposed General Secretary of the SPLM, Pagan Amum Okiech, have centered around questions relating to democratization vs centralization of powers in the party. Politicians in the SPLM critical to Salva Kiir have claimed that the SPLM has not been governed according to democratic principles whereas since 2012, the President and his allies have claimed that ministers and other high ranking politicians have not delivered.

In July 2013 President Salva Kiir thus dismissed his Vice-President Riek Machar and all the ministers. This incident did not appease the dissident members of the party who claimed that there was an increasing concentration of powers in the hands of the President. Riek Machar said that the dismissals were a step towards dictatorship and that he would challenge Salva Kiir for the Presidency. On 6 December 2013 the dissidents in the party held a press conference in Juba where the government's policy, internal conditions in the SPLM, corruption in high places and the President's style of leadership were criticized. The three leaders of the opposition were Riek Machar, Pagan Amum Okiech and Rebecca Garang, the widow of the late John Garang De Mabior.

On 14 December the National Liberation Council (NLC) was meeting in Juba, but the meeting ended abruptly when the opposition members left accusing President Salva Kiir of having rejected all suggestions of dialogue and reconciliation. Yet, as *Africa Confidential* states, Salva Kiir's "opponents included those very people who had failed to provide health and education because of corruption and incompetence" (*Africa Confidential*, 10 January 2014).

On 15 December 2013 conflict broke out with subsequent fighting between the forces of the Government of the Republic of South Sudan and forces loyal to former Vice-President Riek Machar. The opposition forces became known as the Sudan People's Liberation Movement/Army – SPLM/A (in opposition).

The reports around what happened in the wake of National Council Meeting are contradictory. The government declared from the beginning that Riek Machar had staged a coup attempt on 15 December, and for that reason many members of the opposition including Pagan Amum were arrested. This version of the event seemed to have many supporters in the capital of Juba. Many other observers and politicians claimed, however, that there was no coup. "They claim that when the long-standing disagreements within the SPLM became public, this triggered violence in Juba and an opportunistic mutiny by General Peter Gatdet Yaka in Jonglei. That in turn triggered further mutinies in the armed forces… On either interpretation, the fundamental issues remain the long power struggle between Salva and Riek and a bid to modernise the SPLM" (*Africa Confidential*, 10. January 10 2014).

Unfortunately the armed conflict which started in Juba spread to many other parts of South Sudan, to Upper Nile, Unity and Jonglei, and towns such as Bentiu, Malakal and Bor were almost completely destroyed due to the fighting between the rival groups. The conflict, which began as a power struggle between the President and the Vice-President, gradually developed into a conflict along ethnic lines. Salva Kiir belongs to the Dinka, Riek Machar to the Nuer, and Pagan Amum to the Shilluk (Chollo). As well as fighting, the resulting dire humanitarian consequences, included the killing of thousands of civilians. Ethnic groups and specific communities were targeted and there were mass displacements of populations and widespread violations of international humanitarian law and human rights. Estimates of killed South Sudanese range from 1,000 to 20,000 and more than 500,000 have been displaced due to what Episcopal Archbishop Daniel Deng Bul Yak , a leader of reconciliation campaigns, termed a 'meaningless conflict.'

> **Discuss in class**
> 1. Why do you think the people of South Sudan voted so overwhelmingly for independence?
> 2. Tell what you did on Independence Day on July 9 2011.
> 3. What are the advantages of being an independent nation?
> 4. What are the challenges and problems facing the new nation?
> 5. Discuss why corruption is such a big problem in South Sudan. How can it be eradicated?

The new national anthem of South Sudan:

Oh God!
We praise and glorify you
For your grace on South Sudan
Land of great abundance
Uphold us united in peace and harmony
Oh motherland!
We rise raising flag with the guiding star
And sing songs of freedom with joy
For justice, liberty and prosperity
Shall forevermore reign
Oh great patriots!
Let us stand up in silence and respect
Saluting our martyrs whose blood
Cemented our national foundation
We vow to protect our nation
Oh God, bless South Sudan!

Appendix 1
The Addis Ababa Agreement

The Addis Ababa Agreement spelled out the powers and limitation of regional autonomy for South Sudan. Article 11 outlined the powers while article 7 outlined the limitations.

Powers of the Regional Autonomy (Chapter V Article 11):

The People's Regional Assembly shall legislate for the preservation of public order, interim security, efficient administration and the development of the Southern Region in cultural, economic and social fields and in particular in the following:

(i) Promotion and utilization of Regional financial resources for the development and administration of the Southern Region.

(ii) Organization of the machinery for Regional and Local Administration.

(iii) Legislation on traditional law and custom within the framework of National Law.

(iv) Establishment, maintenance and administration of prisons and reformatory institutions.

(v) Establishment, maintenance and administration of Public Schools at all levels in accordance with National Plans for education and economic and social development.

(vi) Promotion of local languages and cultures.

(vii) Town and village planning and the construction of roads in accordance with National Plans and programmes

(viii) Promotion of trade; establishment of local industries and markets; issue of traders' licenses and formation of co-operation societies.

(ix) Establishment, maintenance and administration of public hospitals.

(x) Administration of environmental health services; maternity care; child welfare; supervision of markets; combat of epidemic diseases; training of medical assistants and rural midwives; establishment of health centres, dispensaries and dressing stations.

(xi) Promotion of animal health; control of epidemics and improvement of animal production and trade.

(xii) Promotion of tourism

(xiii) Establishment of zoological gardens, museums, organizations of trade and cultural exhibitions.

(xiv) Mining and quarrying without prejudice to the right of the Central Government in the event of the discovery of natural gas and minerals.

(xv) Recruitment for, organization and administration of Police and Prison services in accordance with the national policy and standards.

(xvi) Land use in accordance with national laws.

(xvii) Control and prevention of pests and plant diseases.

(xviii) Development, utilization, and protection of forests crops and pastures in accordance with national laws.

(xix) Promotion and encouragement of self-help programmes.

(xx) All other matters delegated by the President or the People's National Assembly for legislation.

Limitations of the regional Autonomy (Chapter IV Article 7):

Neither the People's Regional Assembly nor the High Executive Council shall legislate or exercise any powers on matters of national nature which are:

(i)   National Defence
(ii) External Affairs
(iii) Currency and Coinage
(iv) Air and Inter-Regional Transport
(v)   Communications and Telecommunications
(vi) Customs and Foreign Trade except for border trade and certain commodities, which the Regional Government may specify with the approval of the Central Government.
(vii) Nationality and Immigration (Emigration)
(viii) Planning for Economic and Social Development
(ix) Educational Planning
(x)   Public-Audit.

Appendix 2
The Machakos Protocol

July 20, 2002

WHEREAS the Government of the Republic of the Sudan and the Sudan People's Liberation Movement/Sudan People's Liberation Army (the Parties) having met in Machakos Kenya, from 18 June 2002 through 20 July 2002 under the auspices of the IGAD Peace Process; and WHEREAS the Parties have reiterated their commitment to a negotiated, peaceful, comprehensive resolution to the Sudan Conflict within the Unity of Sudan; and WHEREAS the Parties discussed at length and agreed on a broad framework which sets forth the principles of governance, the general procedures to be followed during the transitional process and the structures of government to be created under legal and constitutional arrangements to be established; and NOW RECORD THAT the Parties have agreed to negotiate and elaborate in greater detail the specific terms of the Framework, including aspects not covered in this phase of the negotiations, as part of the overall Peace Agreement; and FURTHER RECORD THAT within the above context, the Parties have reached specific agreement on the Right to Self-Determination for the people of South Sudan, State and Religion, as well as the Preamble, Principles, and the Transition Process from the Draft Framework, the initialed texts of which are annexed hereto, and all of which will be subsequently incorporated into the Final Agreement; and IT IS AGREED AND CONFIRMED THAT the Parties shall resume negotiations in August, 2002 with the aim of resolving outstanding issues and realizing comprehensive peace in the Sudan.

Dr. Ghazi Salahuddin Atabani
For: The Government of Sudan

Cdr. Salva Kiir Mayardit
For: The Sudan People's Liberation Movement/Army
Witnessed by:
Lt. Gen. Lazaro K. Sumbeiywo
Special Envoy
IGAD Sudan Peace Process and
On behalf of the IGAD Envoys

AGREED TEXT ON THE PREAMBLE, PRINCIPLES, AND THE TRANSITION PROCESS BETWEEN THE GOVERNMENT OF THE REPUBLIC OF THE SUDAN AND THE SUDAN PEOPLE'S LIBERATION MOVEMENT/SUDAN PEOPLE'S LIBERATION ARMY

WHEREAS the Government of the Republic of the Sudan and the Sudan People's Liberation Movement/Sudan People's Liberation Army (hereafter referred to as the Parties) having met in Machakos, Kenya, from 18 June 2002 through 20 July 2002; and WHEREAS the Parties are desirous of resolving the Sudan Conflict in a just and sustainable manner by addressing the root causes of the conflict and by establishing a framework for governance through which power and wealth shall be equitably shared and human rights guaranteed; and MINDFUL that the conflict in the Sudan is the longest running conflict in Africa, that it has caused horrendous loss of life and destroyed the infrastructure of the country, wasted economic resources, and has caused untold suffering, particularly with regard to the people of South Sudan; and SENSITIVE to historical injustices and inequalities in development between the different regions of the Sudan that need to be redressed; and RECOGNIZING that the present moment offers a window of opportunity to reach a just peace agreement to end the war; and CONVINCED that the rejuvenated IGAD peace process under the chairmanship of the Kenyan President, H.E. Daniel T. Arap Moi, provides the means to resolve the conflict and reach a just and sustainable peace; and COMMITTED to a negotiated, peaceful, comprehensive resolution to the conflict based on the Declaration of

Principles (DOP) for the benefit of all the people of the Sudan; NOW THEREFORE, the Parties hereto hereby agree as follows:

PART A

(Agreed Principles)

1.1 That the unity of the Sudan, based on the free will of its people democratic governance, accountability, equality, respect, and justice for all citizens of the Sudan is and shall be the priority of the parties and that it is possible to redress the grievances of the people of South Sudan and to meet their aspirations within such a framework.

1.2 That the people of South Sudan have the right to control and govern affairs in their region and participate equitably in the National Government.

1.3 That the people of South Sudan have the right to self-determination, inter alia, through a referendum to determine their future status.

1.4 That religion, customs, and traditions are a source of moral strength and inspiration for the Sudanese people.

1.5 That the people of the Sudan share a common heritage and aspirations and accordingly agree to work together to:

1.6 Establish a democratic system of governance taking account of the cultural, ethnic, racial, religious and linguistic diversity and gender equality of the people of the Sudan.

1.7 Find a comprehensive solution that addresses the economic and social deterioration of the Sudan and replaces war not just with peace, but also with social, political and economic justice which respects the fundamental human and political rights of all the Sudanese people.

1.8 Negotiate and implement a comprehensive cease-fire to end the suffering and killing of the Sudanese people.

1.9 Formulate a repatriation, resettlement, rehabilitation, reconstruction and development plan to address the needs of those areas affected by the war and redress the historical imbalances of development and resource allocation.

1.10 Design and implement the Peace Agreement so as to make the unity of the Sudan an attractive option especially to the people of South Sudan.

1.11 Undertake the challenge by finding a framework by which these common objectives can be best realized and expressed for the benefit of all the Sudanese.

PART B

(The Transition Process)

In order to end the conflict and to secure a peaceful and prosperous future for all the people of the Sudan and in order to collaborate in the task of governing the country, the Parties hereby agree to the implementation of the Peace Agreement in accordance with the sequence, time periods and process set out below.

2. There shall be a Pre-Interim Period, the duration of which shall be six (6) months.

2.1 During the Pre-Interim Period:
   a) The institutions and mechanisms provided for in the Peace Agreement shall be established;
   b) If not already in force, there shall be a cessation of hostilities with appropriate monitoring mechanisms established;
   c) Mechanisms to implement and monitor the Peace Agreement shall be created;
   d) Preparations shall be made for the implementation of a comprehensive cease-fire as soon as possible;
   e) International assistance shall be sought; and

f) A Constitutional Framework for the Peace Agreement and the institutions referred to in
2.1 (a) shall be established.
2.2 The Interim Period will commence at the end of the Pre-Interim Period and shall last for six years.
2.3 Throughout the Interim Period:
   a) The institutions and mechanisms established during the Pre-Interim Period shall be operating in accordance with the arrangements and principles set out in the Peace Agreement.
   b) If not already accomplished, the negotiated comprehensive cease-fire will be implemented and international monitoring mechanisms shall be established and operationalized.
2.4 An independent Assessment and Evaluation Commission shall be established during the Pre-Interim Period to monitor the implementation of the Peace Agreement and conduct a mid-term evaluation of the unity arrangements established under the Peace Agreement.
2.4.1 The composition of the Assessment and Evaluation Commission shall consist of equal representation from the GOS and the SPLM/A, and not more than two (2) representatives, respectively, from each of the following categories:
   * Member states of the IGAD Sub-Committee on Sudan (Djibouti, Eritrea, Ethiopia, Kenya, and Uganda);
   * Observer States (Italy, Norway, UK, and US); and
   * Any other countries or regional or international bodies to be agreed upon by the parties.
2.4.2 The Parties shall work with the Commission during the Interim Period with a view to improving the institutions and

arrangements created under the Agreement and making the unity of Sudan attractive to the people of South Sudan.

2.5 At the end of the six (6) year Interim Period there shall be an internationally monitored referendum, organized jointly by the GOS and the SPLM/A, for the people of South Sudan to: confirm the unity of the Sudan by voting to adopt the system of government established under the Peace Agreement; or to vote for secession.

2.6 The parties shall refrain from any form of unilateral revocation or abrogation of the Peace Agreement.

Part C

(Structures of Government)

To give effect to the agreements set out in Part A, the Parties, within a framework of a unified Sudan which recognizes the right to self-determination for the people of Southern Sudan, hereby agree that with respect to the division of powers and the structures and functions of the different organs of government, the political framework of governance in the Sudan shall be structured as follows:

3.1 Supreme Law

3.1.1 The National Constitution of the Sudan shall be the Supreme Law of the land. All laws must comply with the National Constitution. This constitution shall regulate the relations and allocate the powers and functions between the different levels of government as well as prescribe the wealth sharing arrangements between the same. The National Constitution shall guarantee freedom of belief, worship and religious practice in full to all Sudanese citizens.

3.1.2 A representative National Constitutional Review Commission shall be established during the Pre-Transition Period which shall have as its first task the drafting of a Legal and

3.1.3 The Framework mentioned above shall be adopted as shall be agreed upon by the Parties.

3.1.4 During the Interim Period an inclusive Constitutional Review Process shall be undertaken.

3.1.5 The Constitution shall not be amended or repealed except by way of special procedures and qualified majorities in order that the provisions of the Peace Agreement are protected.

3.2 National Government

3.2.1 There shall be a National Government which shall exercise such functions and pass such laws as must necessarily be exercised by a sovereign state at national level. The National Government in all its laws shall take into account the religious and cultural diversity of the Sudanese people.

3.2.2 Nationally enacted legislation having effect only in respect of the states outside Southern Sudan shall have as its source of legislation Sharia and the consensus of the people.

3.2.3 Nationally enacted legislation applicable to the southern States and/or the Southern Region shall have as its source of legislation popular consensus, the values and the customs of the people of Sudan including their traditions and religious beliefs, having regard to Sudan's diversity.

3.2.4 Where national legislation is currently in operation or is enacted and its source is religious or customary law, then a state or region, the majority of whose residents do not practice such religion or customs may:

(i) Either introduce legislation so as to allow or provide for institutions or practices in that region consistent with their religion or customs, or

(ii) Refer the law to the Council of States for it to approve by a two-thirds majority or initiate national legislation which will provide for such necessary alternative institutions as is appropriate.

[sections 4 and 5 are not yet available; indications are that the subjects of these sections are still under negotiation]

Agreed Text on State and Religion

Recognizing that Sudan is a multi-cultural, multi-racial, multi-ethnic, multi-religious, and multi-lingual country and confirming that religion shall not be used as a divisive factor, the Parties hereby agree as follows:

6.1 Religions, customs and beliefs are a source of moral strength and inspiration for the Sudanese people.

6.2 There shall be freedom of belief, worship and conscience for followers of all religions or beliefs or customs and no one shall be discriminated against on such grounds.

6.3 Eligibility for public office, including the presidency, public service and the enjoyment of all rights and duties shall be based on citizenship and not on religion, beliefs, or customs.

6.4 All personal and family matters including marriage, divorce, inheritance, succession, and affiliation may be governed by the personal laws (including Sharia or other religious laws, customs, or traditions) of those concerned.

6.5 The Parties agree to respect the following Rights:
  * To worship or assemble in connection with a religion or belief and to establish and maintain places for these purposes;
  * To establish and maintain appropriate charitable or humanitarian institutions;

- To make, acquire and use to an adequate extent the necessary articles and materials related to the rites or customs of a religion or belief;
- To write, issue and disseminate relevant publications in these areas;
- To teach religion or belief in places suitable for these purposes;
- To solicit and receive voluntary financial and other contributions from individuals and institutions;
- To train, appoint, elect or designate by succession appropriate leaders called for by the requirements and standards of any religion or belief;
- To observe days of rest and to celebrate holidays and ceremonies in accordance with the precepts of one's religious beliefs;
- To establish and maintain communications with individuals and communities in matters of religion and belief and at the national and international levels;
- For avoidance of doubt, no one shall be subject to discrimination by the National Government, state, institutions, group of persons or person on grounds of religion or other beliefs.

6.6   The Principles enumerated in Section 6.1 through 6.5 shall be reflected in the Constitution.

Agreed Text on the Right to Self-Determination for the People of South Sudan

1.3   That the people of South Sudan have the right to self-determination, inter alia, through a referendum to determine their future status.

2.4 An independent Assessment and Evaluation Commission shall be established during the Pre-Transition period to monitor the implementation of the Peace Agreement during the Interim Period. This Commission shall conduct a mid-term evaluation of the unity arrangements established under the Peace Agreement.

2.4.1 The composition of the Assessment and Evaluation Commission shall consist of equal representation from the GOS and the SPLM/A, and not more than two (2) representatives, respectively, from each of the following categories:

* Member states of the IGAD Sub-Committee on Sudan (Djibouti, Eritrea, Ethiopia, Kenya, and Uganda);
* Observer States (Italy, Norway, UK, and US); and
* Any other countries or regional or international bodies to be agreed upon by the parties.

2.4.2 The Parties shall work with the Commission during the Interim Period with a view to improving the institutions and arrangements created under the Agreement and making the unity of Sudan attractive to the people of South Sudan.

2.5 At the end of the six (6) year interim period there shall be an internationally monitored referendum, organized jointly by the GOS and the SPLM/A, for the people of South Sudan to: confirm the unity of the Sudan by voting to adopt the system of government established under the Peace Agreement; or to vote for secession.

2.6 The Parties shall refrain from any form of unilateral revocation or abrogation of the Peace Agreement.

Further reading

Adwok, P. 1997. *The Politics of Liberation in South Sudan*, Fountain Publishers: Kampala

Africa Confidential," The state cracks." Retrieved from http://www.africaconfidential.com/article/id/5172/The_state_cracks on 10 January 2014

Akol, L. 2000. *SPLM/A Inside an African Revolution*, Khartoum University Press: Khartoum

Al Amin, N. Magied, A, 2001. "A history of Sudanese women organizations and the strive for liberation and empowerment", *Ahfad Journal*. Volume 18, Number, 1, 2-23

Alier, A. 1990. *Southern Sudan, too many agreements dishonoured*, Ithaca Press: Exeter

Al-Shai, A. 1981. "A Noah's Ark: The Continuity of the Khatmiyya Order in Northern Sudan", *Bulletin British Society for Middle Eastern Studies*, Vol. 8, No. 1, 3-29

Allen, T. 1994. "Ethnicity and Tribalism on the Sudan-Uganda Border." In John Markakis (ed.), *Ethnicity & Conflict in the Horn of Africa*, Ohio University Press: Athens, Ohio

Anderson, B. 1983. *Imagined Communities on the Origin and the Spread of Nationalism*, Verso: New York

Beshir, M. 1968. *The southern Sudan*, Khartoum University Press: Khartoum

Beswick, S. 2004. *Sudan's Blood memory: The Legacy of War, Ethnicity, and Slavery in Early South Sudan*, Rochester Studies in African history and the Diaspora, University of Rochester Press: Rochester

Breidlid, A. 2005. "Education in Sudan: The privileging of an Islamic discourse." *Compare*, 35, 3, 247-263

Breidlid, A. 2005. "Sudanese migrants in the Khartoum area: fighting for educational space." *International Journal of Educational Development*, 25, 253-268

Breidlid, A. 2006. "Resistance and education – counter-hegemonic struggle in Southern Sudan." *Nordisk Pedagogik,* 26, 16-29

Breidlid, A. 2010. "Sudanese Images of the Other: Education and Conflict in Sudan." *Comparative Education Review,* 54, 4, 555-579

Breidlid, A. 2013. *Education, Indigenous Knowledges and Development. Contesting Knowledges for a Sustainable Future.* Routledge: New York

Cheater, A. 1999. *The Anthropology of Power. Empowerment and Disempowerment in Changing Structures,* Routledge: London and New York

Collins, R. 1983. *Shadows in the Grass: Britain in the Southern Sudan, 1918- 1956,* Yale University Press: New Haven

Collins, R. 2008. *A History of Modern Sudan,* Cambridge University Press: Cambridge

Daly, M. 1986. *Empire on the Nile: The Anglo-Egyptian Sudan, 1898- 1934,* Cambridge University Press: Cambridge.

Daly, M. 1991. *Imperial Sudan: The Anglo-Egyptian Condominium, 1934- 56,* Cambridge University Press: Cambridge.

Davidson, B. 1978. *Africa in Modern History: The Search for a New Society,* Allen Lane: London

Deng, W. 1963. *The Problem of Southern Sudan,* Oxford University Press: London

Deng, F. 1995. *War of Visions: Conflict of Identities in the Sudan,* The Brookings Institution: Washington

East African, The, 2011. Investors in scramble for South Suda's fertile land. Retrieved from http://www.theeastafrican.co.ke/news/Investors-in-scramble-for-South-Sudan-fertile-land/-/2558/1197978/-/vifqlb/-/index.html on October 19 2013

Ellis, S. 2002. "Writing Histories of Contemporary Africa", *The Journal of African History,* Vol. 43, No 1, 1-6

European-Sudanese Public Affairs Council. 2001. *SPLA Responsible for Sudan's Lost Boys,* released January 21, retrieved on October 11, 2010, http://www.twf.org/News/Y2001/0121-SudanBoys.html

Evans-Pritchard, E. 1934. "Social Character of Bride-Wealth, with Special Reference to the Azande", *Man,* Vol. 34 (Nov), 172-175

Evans-Pritchard, E. 1970. "Sexual inversion among the Azande", *American Anthropologist*, New series, Vol. 72, No 6, 1428–1434

Evans-Pritchard, E. 1971. *The Azande, History and Political Institutions*, Oxford University Press: Oxford

Ga'le, S. 2002. *Shaping a free Southern Sudan, memoirs of our struggle 1934-1985*, Loa, South Sudan: printed by Loa Catholic Mission Council.

Greenberg, J. 1963. *The Languages of Africa*, Indiana University Press: Bloomington

Hildebrandt, J. 1987. *History of the Church in Africa*, Africa Christian Press: Achimota

Holt, P.M. & Daly, M.W. 1988. *A history of Sudan*, Fourth Edition, Longman Group UK Limited: Essex

Holt, P.M. & Daly, M.W. 1961. *A history of Sudan*, Longman Group UK Limited: London

Huchinson, S. 1994. "On the Nuer Conquest," *Current Anthropology* 35:5, 643-651

Hødnebø, K. 1997. *From Cattle to Corn, Economic Trends in Northeast Africa*, University of Bergen: Bergen

Ibrahim, A. 2009. "Sudan Nationalism or Sudan Nationalisms?" *Sudanese Journal for Human Rights' Culture and Issues of Cultural diversity*, 11th Issue, November

IGAD Portal, retrieved 06.09.10 from http://igad.int/

Johnson, D. 1981. "The Future of Southern Sudan's Past ", *Africa Today* 28/2, 33-41

Johnson, D. 1982. " Evans-Pritchard, the Nuer, and Sudan Political Service," *African Affairs*, Vol. 81, No. 323, Apr. 231-246

Johnson, D. 2003. *The Root Causes of Sudan's Civil Wars*, Fountain Publishers: Kampala

Jok, J. 2001. *War and slavery in Sudan*, University of Pennsylvania Press: Philadelphia

Khalid, M. 1985. *Nimeiri and the revolution of dis-may*, Ed. Kegan Paul: London

Lagu, J. 2006. *SUDAN, Odyssey Through A State, From Ruin to Hope*, MOB Center for Sudanese Studies in Omdurman: Omdurman

Lees, F & Brooks, H. 1977. *The economic and political development of the Sudan*, The Macmillan Press Ltd: London and Basingstoke

Lesch, A. 1998. *Sudan-Contested National Identities*, Indiana University Press: Bloomington and Indianapolis

Madut-Arop, A. 2006. *Sudan's Painful Road to Peace*: Book Surge LLC: Oxford

Mann, K. 1997. *Egypt, Kush, Aksum: northeast Africa*, Dillon Press: New Jersey

Moore-Harell, A. 1999. "Economic and Political Aspects of the Slave Trade in Ethiopia and Sudan in the Second Half of the Nineteenth century", *The International Journal of African Historical Studies*, Vol. 32, No. 2/3: 407-421

Nikkel, M. 2001. *Dinka Christianity*, Paulines Publications: Nairobi

Nyaba, P. 2000. *The Politics of Liberation in South Sudan: An Insider's View*, 2nd Ed. Fountain Publishers: Kampala

Nyibong, D. 2005. *The Impact of Change Agents on Southern Sudan History, 1898 – 1973*, PhD Thesis, Khartoum

Perner, P. 1997. *The Anyuak-Living on Earth in the Sky Vol.2*. The Human Territory, Helbing & Lichtenhahn Verlag AG: Basel

Philipps, J. 1926. "Observations on Some Aspects of Religion among the Azande ("Niam-Niam") of Equatorial Africa", *The Journal of the Royal Anthropological Institute of Great Britain and Ireland*, Vol.56, 171-187

Rahim, M. 1968. *The Development of British Policy in the Southern Sudan, 1899-1947*. Khartoum University Press: Khartoum

Rahim, M. 1969. *Imperialism and Nationalism in Sudan: A Study in Constitutional and Political Development, 1899-1956*, Clarendon Press: Oxford

Salaam, A.H. &. de Waal, A.2001. *The Phoenix State: Civil Society and the Future of Sudan*, The Red Sea Press: Lawrenceville, D, J and Asmara

Sanderson, L. 1980. "Education in the Southern Sudan: The Impact of Government-Missionary-Southern Sudanese Relationships upon the

Development of Education during the Condominium Period, 1898-1956," *African Affairs* 79, No. 315, April, 157-70

Sanderson, L.P. and Sanderson, N. 1981. Education, Religion and Politics in Southern Sudan 1899-1964, Itahaca Press: London

Seligman, C. G. and B. Z. S. 1932. *Pagan Tribes of the Nilotic Sudan*, Routledge & Kegan Paul: London

Sharkey, H. 2003. *Living with colonialism*, University of California Press: Los Angeles

Shinnie, P.L. 1967. *Meroe, A Civilisation of Sudan*, Thames and Hudson, London

Spaulding, J. 1988. "The business of slavery in the central Anglo-Egyptian Sudan, 1910-1930", *African Economic History* XVII (1988), 23-44

Sudan government 1952. Proceedings of the First Legislative Assembly of Sudan 1948 – 1952, deposited at National Records Office, Khartoum.

Sudan government 1958. Proceedings of the First Sudanese Parliament 1954 – 1958, deposited at National Records Office, Khartoum

UNICEF with AET (African Educational Trust Fund), 2002, *School Baseline Assessment Report Southern Sudan*, Nairobi

Vantini, G. 1981. *Christianity in Sudan*, Publishers EMI: Bologna

Wai, D. (ed.). 1973. *The Southern Sudan: The Problem of National Integration*, London: Frank Cass

Wawa, Y. 2005. *Southern Sudanese Pursuits of Self-determination: Documents in Political History*, Fountain Publishers: Kampala

Willis, J. 2003. "Violence, authority, and the state in the Nuba Mountains of Condominium Sudan," *Historical Journal*, Vol. 46, Issue 1, 89-114

Woodward, P. 1980."The South in Sudanese Politics, 1946-1956," *Middle Eastern Studies* [London], 16, No. 3, October, 178- 92

Index

'Abd al-Latif Ali 154
Abboud, Ibrahim (Gen) 205, 206, 207, 208, 235
Abdal Latif 167
absolute monarch 24, 32
Abuja peace talks (1992-93) 323, 339
Abyei massacre, 1956 194
Abyei protocol (2004) 330
Addis Ababa Agreement (1972) 205, 233, 236, 241, 246, 248, 250, 253, 259, 263, 268, 273, 275, 280, 287, 351
African cultures 26, 32
African National Front (ANF) 244, 245, 246
African resistance 148
Afro-Asiatic 53, 56
Afro-Asiatic languages 56
Ahmed, Muhammed 123, 183
Akobo incident 256
Akol Lam 298, 299, 301, 304
Al- Azhari Ismail 164
Al Dhahab Sowar 289
Al-Hayfa Bakhita 223
Aliab Dinka 140
Alier Abel Kwai 243
Ali Mohammad 114, 121, 125
Al-Khalifa Al-Hassan 216
Al Khalifa Sir al-Hassan 216
Al-mahdi abdel Rahman Sayyid 164, 197, 198, 199

al-mirghani Ali sayyid 164, 197, 198
al Turabi Hassan Abdallah 228, 273, 274, 333
Aman Sidonia 187
Ambomu people 84
Amin Idi Dada Alemi 234, 260
Amun god 26, 31, 33
Anglo-Egyptian agreement 1956 178, 184, 196
Anglo-Egyptian Condominium rule 165
Anglo-Egyptian rule 6, 129, 138, 166
Anglo-Egyptian Sudan 134, 137, 365, 368
Anok, Kon 140, 141
Ansar religious sect 199
Ansar sect 164
anthropological sources 2
anti-Arab sentiment 309
Anya Nya military struggle 226
Anya Nya National Organization 232
Anya Nya (poison) 205, 213, 218, 226, 231, 232, 236, 238, 246, 250, 256, 259, 276, 279, 283, 291, 297, 302, 325
Anya Nya soldiers/fighters 231, 257, 259, 279
Anywaa (Anyuak) 4
Apedemak god 31
Arab armies 41

Arab cultural unity 236
Arabian Peninsula 118
Arabic culture 207, 208
Arabization (Southern Sudan) 205, 207, 208, 221
Arab merchants 41, 43
Arab-Muslim nationalism 294
archaeological sources 2
archives 5, 6
Arok Thon Arok 298, 302
artefact 3, 4, 27
Ashigga Party 164, 178, 183
Atem Akuot 280, 281, 282, 284, 285
Atem Chagai 280
Avungara leadership 84
Aweil Rice Scheme 270
Azande people 5, 6, 7, 10, 55, 57, 58, 63, 83, 84, 85, 86, 88, 90, 92, 93, 112, 113, 149, 366, 367
Azania Liberation Front 232
Babangida Ibrahim 323
Baggara slave raids 77
Bahr-el-Ghazal 79, 116, 155, 156, 280
Baker W Samuel (Sir) 117, 119, 129
Bantu ethnic groups 55
Bany Nyuon William 285, 302
baqt of 652 AD 42, 43
Bari people 63, 126
Bashir, Omar Hassan Ahmad 293
Berlin conference 1884-1885 131
Bilinyang royal house 108
Bilpam Camp 282
Blue Nile 20, 105, 115, 118, 270, 304, 305, 322, 327, 329, 334, 338

Bol Benjamin 258
Bor massacre 1991 299, 320
Bor mutiny 284
Bruce James 10, 47
Byzantine church 36
Carter, Jimmy 322
cattle nomads 46, 49
Central African Republic 55, 56, 84, 85, 89
Chari Nile 53
Child soldiers (Sudan) 286, 301
Christian Bible 22
Christian calendar 12
Christian migrants 312
Christian missionaries 108, 129, 146, 148, 155, 211
Christian monks 35
Christian Nubia 33, 36, 42, 44
Chuol William Abdallah 280
Church Missionary Society (CMS) 146, 156
Closed District Ordinance 129, 151, 154, 159, 161, 165, 168
Cohen, Herman 322, 323, 339
Communist Party 201, 236, 288
Compagnie Centrale Internationale (CCI) 286
Comprehensive Peace Agreement 2005 10, 283, 303, 305, 321, 324, 326, 328, 332, 333, 340
Condominium Agreement, 1899 136
Congo basin 17, 83
Coptic language(s) 23, 38
Coptic Patriarch 36
cross-ethnic relations 308
cultural hostility 45

Democratic Unionist Party (DUP) 228, 289
Deng, William 205, 209, 211, 217, 219, 220, 233
Didinga groups 304
Dinka domination 232, 261, 262, 267, 302
Dinka Migrations 65
Dinka people 79, 160
Dinka villages 268, 291
Diu Buth 171, 175, 176, 177, 182, 192, 202, 204, 226
Dunqas Amara 47
Eastern Nilotics 53, 54, 57, 59, 61, 64, 67
Economic diversity 160
Egyptian Coptic church 40
Egyptian culture 20, 26
Egyptian Gallaba 49
El Mahdi Sadiq 226
El Tayeb Omar 259
Equatoria Corps 192, 193
Ethiopian highlands 17, 58, 61, 92
ethnic affiliation 308, 310
ethnic integration 308
ethnic resistance 308
Fashoda 98, 131, 132, 136
Fashoda incident - 1898 131, 132, 136
federal state 177, 200, 203
Funj Chronicle 47, 50
Funj Kingdom 47, 49, 50, 51, 52
Funj kings 44, 52
Funj people 44
Funj sultan 51
Gaddafi, Muammar 290
Gai Tut Samuel 280, 282

Garang John (Dr) 251, 257, 280, 281, 282, 283, 284, 285, 292, 298, 301, 307, 310, 321, 325, 326, 330, 333, 342, 348
Garang Joseph 201, 238
Gatkuoth Peter 277
Gbudwe, King 85, 114
General George Athor Deng 337
Gladstone, William 130
Gondokoro 103, 108, 109, 110, 117
Gordon, Charles (Col.) 118
Government of Southern Sudan (GoSS) 326, 329
Graduates General Congress 1938 183
Great Lakes region 17, 90
Greek Bible 22
guerilla struggle 297
Gulf war 323
Hebrew Bible 22
Helm Knox, Alexander 193
hereditary chief(s) 59
hereditary powers 75
hereditary rule 61
Hicks, William 122
Homo sapiens 17
IGAD negotiations 305
Ikang, Queen of Tirangole 96, 97
Indirect rule 148
infidels 79, 287
Initiation ceremonies 71
inter-clan fighting 12
inter-ethnic relations 315
Inter Governmental Authority on Development (IGAD) 324
interlinked clans 80

intermarriage 5, 59, 96
internally displaced persons (IDPs) 313
International Court of Justice (ICJ) 330
International Criminal Court (ICC) 295, 335
International Monetary Fund (IMF) 273
International Non-Governmental Organizations (INGOs) 316
international trade 28, 49
Inter-village relationships 75
Intra-southern trade 95
Iron working 29
Irro Siricio 192
Islamic Baggara 79, 95, 105
Islamic Charter Front (ICF) 228
Islamic community 43
Islamic constitution 200, 230
Islamic law (Shari'a) 228
Islamic missionaries 48
Islamic state 203, 227, 251, 252, 293
Islamic teachers 44, 45, 47
Islamist military regime 321
Islamization of Southern Sudan 207
Isma'il Khedive 117, 119, 120
Jaden, Aggrey 205, 209, 217, 219, 220
Jebel Barkal 26
jihadiyya (slave-soldiers) 106
Jonglei Canal 286
Jonglei state 337
Juba conference 1947 170
Kakwa people 139
Khalil Abdalla 197, 206

Khartoumers 110, 111, 112, 116
Khartoum Peace Agreement 299
Khatmiyya order 164
Khatmiyya religious sect 198
Kheir Muhammad 73
Kiir, Salva Mayardit 280, 285, 325, 342, 355
kinship system 78
Kitchener, Lord 130, 132, 144
Koka Dam Declaration 289, 290, 320, 322
Kuanyin Kerubino 285, 298, 302
Kushite civilisation 33
Kush Kingdom 20, 23, 24, 27
Lado enclave 134, 135
Lagu Joseph 213, 214, 220, 232, 233, 234, 235, 241, 242, 249, 252, 253, 259, 260, 261, 267, 277
Lagu Yanga 242
Lagu Yanga Joseph (Gen) 242
Latif Abdal 167
Legislative Assembly ordinance 175
levirate marriage 81
Liberal Party 176, 181, 182, 184, 191, 200, 219, 222, 223
lineage alliances 78
Linguistic sources 5
Linguistic studies 63, 64
Lohure Saturnino 201, 202, 209
Loi or Bari speaking groups 92
Lords of East Africa see Eastern Nilotics 61
Lord's Resistance Army (LRA) 303
Luki Benjamin 202
Luo language 68
Machakos Protocol (2002) 325, 354

Machar Riek (Dr) xv, 298, 299, 301, 302, 325, 348, 349
Machiek, Ngor Francis 280
Mading Deng Francis 3, 5
Ma'di oral tradition 58
Madi people 59, 61
Ma'di tradition 59
Mahdi rule 126
Mahdist Revolution 119
Mahgoub, Mohammed Ahmed 229
Majier Martin 281
Malakal fightings (2009) 336
Malwal, Bona 260, 270, 271
Mamluks 44, 98, 99, 100
manifesto (SPLM) 281
Mansur Zubeir Rahma 107
Marchand, Jean-Baptiste (Maj) 132
marriage arrangements 272
Marxist Ethiopia 273
Mboli (Azande) 85
Mboro Clement 171, 172, 173, 218, 258, 260, 267
Mediterranean Sea 23
Meroë 24, 25, 27, 28, 29, 30, 32, 33, 34, 44, 50
Meroitic civilisation 28, 31
Meroitic Kingdom(s) 32
Milner, James 152
Missionary Societies Act, 1962 211, 241
moinjaang (people of people) 78
Mongala Agro Industry Scheme 270
Mundari militia 303
Muortat-mayen, Gordon 245
Murahalin militia 287, 291, 303
Murle militia 303
museums 3, 352

Muslim Arabs 36, 45
Muslim Brothers 273, 276, 290, 292
Naath (Human beings) 77
Nadgo tribe 173
Napata Capital 23, 24, 25, 26, 29, 33
Nasir Faction 299, 303
National Alliance for National Salvation (NANS) 288
National Congress Party (NCP) 294
national identity 1
National Islamic Front (NIF) 294
National Unionist Party (NUP) 181
Native administration 148, 151
Ngok Dinka 194
Niger Kordofanian 54
Niger Kordofanian language(s) 54
Nile traders 111, 120
Nile Valley 63, 132, 153
Nilo-Hamites 54, 58, 61, 62, 67
Nilo-Saharan language (s) 18
Nilo-Saharan people(s) 18, 20
Nilotic groups 61, 66, 67
Nilotic languages 54, 95
Nimeiri, Jaafar 235, 280
Nobatia kingdom 36
nomadic pastoralism 82
Northern liberal party 227
Nuba Mountains 51, 55, 105, 109, 143, 317, 325, 327, 329, 334, 338, 368
Nubian church 36, 38
Nubian civilisation 20, 23
Nubian culture 20, 27
Nubian slave raids 64
Nuer language 93

Nuer militia 303
Nuer people 77
Nuer settlement 166
Nzara Agro-Industrial Complex 270
Oduhu, Joseph 219, 220, 258
Olduvai Gorge 17
oral history 2, 79
Oral tradition 2, 68, 77
Organisation of African Unity (OAU) 211, 281
Oromo tribe 61, 63
orthodox Islam 136, 294
Ottoman Empire 98, 153, 165
paramount chief 73, 80, 85, 86
Pasha Emin 119, 123
People's Democratic Party (PDP) 197
pidgin Arabic 56, 188
Plains Nilotes 61
Popular Defence Force (PDF) 294
power-sharing 329, 334
provincial governors (Azande) 49, 51, 87
provincial sheikhs (Funj) 48
pyramid tomb 30
Qurqusawi Karamallah 123
Rajaf language conference 166
Rasheed Khalafalla 268
Rassass, Gismalla Abdalla (Gen) 262
Red Sea 28, 41, 42, 43, 49, 100, 105, 133, 206, 367
Religious diversity 159
religious powers 59
Revolution Command Council (RCC) 294
River Lake Nilotes 64, 67
River raiding 72

Robertson, James (Sir) 170
Roman Catholics 108, 156
Sahara region 17, 66
Salisbury, Lord 132
Sama Baya 175, 201
second civil war (Sudan) 210, 264, 276, 297
segmentary lineages 139
Sellasie, Haille 238
semi-nomadic groups 187
Semitic languages 56
separatist policy 167, 169
Shangalla archers 12
Shari'a laws 271
Sharland Leonard 160
Shilluk (Chollo) Kingdom 67
Shilluk (Chollo) people 73
Shilluk clans 68, 70
Shilluk religion 71
Shilluk trade 72
Shilluk tradition 71
slave raids 45, 64, 76, 77, 79, 105, 106, 107, 115, 127, 146
Sobat River 77
social behaviour 94
Socialist Republican Party 181
social order 61, 91
Southern identity 308, 311, 313, 314, 315
Southern Kordofan state 329
Southern Party 181, 182, 184, 196, 200, 203
Southern Regional Autonomy 263
Southern Sudan Liberation Movement (SSLM) 244
South Sudan 2, 8, 10, 15, 17, 20, 53, 56, 61, 68, 74, 76, 81, 84,

89, 90, 100, 129, 166, 211, 212, 299, 325, 334, 336, 342, 345, 347, 349, 354, 356, 359, 362, 363, 364, 366, 367
Spiritual healers 66
Stack, Lee (Sir) 144, 154
strategic educational master plan 317
Succession practices (Azande) 87
Sudan Administration Conference 1946 169
Sudan African Nationalist Union (SANU) 205
Sudan Armed Forces 205, 253, 286, 302, 327, 335
Sudan Christian Association (SCA) 209
Sudan Defence Forces (SDF) 233
Sudanese culture 214, 294
Sudanese Muslims 114
Sudanese Peace Initiative 292, 293, 294
Sudanic kingdoms 115
Sudanic languages 54
Sudanic peoples 56, 57, 67, 89
Sudanic zone 90
Sudan National Union (SANU) 211
Sudan People's Liberation Movement /Army (SPLM/A) 275
Sudan's Women Union 272
Tabaqat-biographies 44, 47
Taha, Ali Utman Muhammed 332
Temple of Apedemek 31
Tombura, Joseph James 263
Toposa militia 53, 54, 61, 66, 185, 303, 304

Torit faction 301, 303, 304
Torit mutiny, 1955 191, 193, 197, 210
trade routes 25, 41, 49, 51
traditional African religion 48
traditional ceremonies 59, 94
traditional rainmakers 111
Transitional Military Council (TMC) 289
tribal militias 283, 287, 288
tribal sheikhs (Funj) 52
Turkiyya regime 122, 127
Turko-Egyptian government 107, 114, 115, 121, 122, 127
Turko-Egyptian rule 102, 121, 122, 125, 128, 130, 138, 149, 162
Umma Party 164, 176, 178, 179, 181, 197, 199, 203, 226, 227, 233, 288, 290, 335
Unilateral Declaration of Independence (UDI) 336
United Nations High Commission for Refugees (UNHCR) 254
United Presbyterian Mission (UPM) 146, 156
Unity State (South Sudan) 77
Upper Nile Province 77, 142, 157, 175
Upper Nile region 17, 46, 283, 301
Urabi revolution 125, 126
Verona Fathers (Comboni Fathers) 156
Visual sources 6
Wahhabis (Sunni Islamic sect) 99
White Flag League 153
White Nile 49, 67, 68, 69, 72, 98, 102, 103, 104, 107, 108, 109,

111, 114, 115, 120, 121, 122, 127, 133, 151, 152, 268
White Nile trade 110, 114
White Nile traders 111, 120
Wingate Reginald (Sir) 144
word-borrowing 5
World War II 22, 161, 167, 207, 227
Yakanye resistance 138, 139
Yei River region 109, 111
Yondu clan 139
Zande Scheme 184, 187, 191
zaribas (trading stations) 112, 113, 116, 127, 161

www.ingramcontent.com/pod-product-compliance
Lightning Source LLC
Chambersburg PA
CBHW070806300426
44111CB00014B/2437